T0381107

The Islamic Inversion

Exposing the Contrary and Ironic Aspects of Islamic Theology.

ROBERT SIEVERS

WESTBOW
PRESS®
A DIVISION OF THOMAS NELSON
& ZONDERVAN

WestBow Press books may be ordered through booksellers or by contacting:

WestBow Press
A Division of Thomas Nelson & Zondervan
1663 Liberty Drive
Bloomington, IN 47403
www.westbowpress.com
1 (866) 928-1240

Unless otherwise noted, scripture quotations taken from the New American Standard Bible® (NASB), Copyright © 1960, 1962, 1963, 1968, 1971, 1972, 1973, 1975, 1977, 1995 by The Lockman Foundation Used by permission. www.Lockman.org

Scripture quotations marked (NLT) are taken from the Holy Bible, New Living Translation, copyright ©1996, 2004, 2015 by Tyndale House Foundation. Used by permission of Tyndale House Publishers, Inc., Carol Stream, Illinois 60188. All rights reserved.

All quotes from the Qur'an are taken from the translation by Yusuf Ali. The Yusuf Ali English text is based on the 1934 book, *The Holy Qur-an, Text, Translation and Commentary*, (published in Lahore, Cairo and Riyadh).

All quotes from the Hadith compiled by Bukhari (full name **Abu Abdullah Muhammad bin Ismail bin Ibrahim bin al-Mughira al-Ja'fai**) are taken from http://www.sahih-bukhari.com/. Quotes from Sahih Muslim are taken from https://sunnah.com/muslim/.

ISBN: 978-1-9736-3009-8 (sc)
ISBN: 978-1-9736-3010-4 (hc)
ISBN: 978-1-9736-3008-1 (e)

Library of Congress Control Number: 2018906538

Print information available on the last page.

WestBow Press rev. date: 6/18/2018

Acknowledgements

Before I was saved at the age of 33, I worked in the field of software quality assurance. God used this time in my life to teach me how any conscientious and hardworking effort would still be laced with errors and oversights. When preparing a work with such theological overtones, a well-meaning effort is not good enough. As Dr. Richard Gross from Gordon College has said, "Christian shoddy is still shoddy." I have endeavored to take what God has shown me over the years and present it in the most coherent, precise, and error-free manner as possible. This couldn't have been done on my own.

First and foremost, I would like to thank my wife, whose keen theological mind and careful editing made this work possible. Your commitment to excellence and high standards is what allowed such complex topics to be discussed with clarity. May God richly reward you for all your work behind the scenes.

I would like to thank many editors. Thanks to Aaron Hanford, whose blunt honesty was a necessity in the early stages. Thanks to Jamie Taylor and Jeff Bulmahn for countless fixes. I want to thank Joel Richardson for showing me the courage to write the truth, even though it invites trouble. Also, I must extend a special thank you to David Krehbiel for his unique encouragement. Finally, this work is significantly better documented thanks to the thorough work of Fred Newport.

Additionally, this book could not have been completed

without faithful prayer partners. These included Corey Steffen, Timothy Mark Smith, Dan and Katy McCue, Aron Fey, and Sujay Kodamala. I would also be remiss without a special thank you to Jason Schiffo for his timely advice and continual efforts to assist others.

Most importantly I want to thank my Lord and Savior Jesus Christ. Why you chose to save me after all the times I mocked and verbally assailed you during my early years defies explanation except for your tremendous love for sinners. Your love for me can never be repaid. I commit this work to You that you may use it to advance your kingdom in whatever way You see fit.

Introduction

If you have a Muslim friend, then you have likely tried to share the good news of Christ. After doing so, was there a spirit of confusion, discouragement, and bewilderment from hitting a brick wall head on? If so, you have just encountered the obstinate and entrenched attitude that pervades Muslim thought. The level of confusion that springs forth from religious dialogue with Muslims seems to be substantial and ever present. This perplexity often leads to a fruitless debate rather than a meaningful witness. This book is not designed to train Christians to debate Muslims; it is rather a guide to help Christians with established friendships with Muslims engage in religious discussions that slice through the confusion and point back to Christ. Without grasping the techniques typically employed by Muslims, the Christian may find himself dazed and baffled trying to understand why normal evangelistic methods do not seem to produce results. This book will identify, expose, and disassemble the systematic patterns of Islamic thought, which I have labeled "The Islamic Inversion."

The Islamic thought pattern, when followed to its logical conclusion, always undermines Islam as a religion and points back to the reality of Christ. Recognizing this pattern will allow Christians to easily identify the difference between Muslims who are seeking truth and Muslims who have no interest in open-minded dialogue. It will also enable the Christian to have meaningful dialogue with Muslims without finding himself shocked, stunned, and blindsided. Cleverly hidden anti-logic that repeatedly employs the same recognizable diabolical and sinister flaws will become readily apparent.

Christians need to be well equipped in both attitude and wisdom to share the gospel with Muslims. There must be a correct heart attitude toward Muslims and their culture, firm understanding of Christian doctrine, understanding of why Islam is structured the way it is, awareness of typical Muslim assaults on the truths of Christ, and strategies for how to turn such assaults into productive discussions. As such, this book is divided into those five parts.

We will first prepare our hearts by examining the reasons why it so difficult for Muslims to accept Christ. These reasons are both practical and spiritual. We must understand the pragmatic and cultural reasons why Muslims are reticent to receive the good news of Jesus Christ. Everyone who accepts the truth of the cross at one time counted the cost. For Muslims, that cost is often much higher than we in the West would imagine. Also, there are very real spiritual roadblocks in place. Many of these have been constructed within Islam itself as a type of firewall to prevent the truth of Jesus from shining though. Understanding these obstacles is essential if we are to be loving and effective witnesses.

We must then prepare our minds by ensuring that we have a sound knowledge of the pronouncements of Christ and the nature of God. Obviously there is not room for a theology book within the confines of this work. However, it is important to fully understand the deity of Christ and the nature of the Trinity in order to effectively counter the usual misinformed arguments posed by Muslims. These chapters assume the inerrancy of Scripture. The issue of the reliability of the Bible itself will also be dealt with in later chapters, but only from the perspective of Muslim assaults, not from a systematically apologetic approach.

With our hearts and minds ready, we then investigate the

typical strategies used by Muslims to undermine Christ and how to recognize them. The strategies used against Jesus and His message that have been employed by men throughout the ages are quite similar to those of today. Most are variations on a few simple themes. We will specifically see how Islam uses these same few strategies to push its own agenda at the expense of Christ's wisdom, His promises, and indeed Christ Himself.

The majority of this book then deals with the claims of Islam and how those claims are exactly opposite from those of Jesus Christ. These chapters will catalog the most common Muslim apologetics and demonstrate how to identify the patterns of reversal in order to respond in truth and love without getting detoured. The book will delve into the typical places of retreat for Muslims, and how to dismantle these from a broad-based approach without getting bogged down into meaningless and fruitless arguments over details.

Finally, we will move past identification of the antithetical arguments of Islam into how to hook those arguments back to Christ. Almost always, the typical Islamic assaults on Christ inadvertently expose the truth of His teachings, death, crucifixion, and indwelling Spirit. It is not easy to spot these hooks until first getting comfortable with recognizing "The Islamic Inversion." At that point, a Christian can let the Muslims discuss Islam and point them to Christ without being confrontational.

The skeptic may ask why a work such as this focuses on differences between Islam and Christian doctrine rather than on similarities. Shouldn't we be stressing commonalities rather than areas of disagreement? Many people seek to build bridges between Muslims and Christians, and I applaud those efforts. Such bridges between Christians and Muslims are necessary. Some people invariably go too far by compromising on core values. It is inherently evident that a bridge cannot be built until a firm understanding exists of what two locations are to be connected. A bridge between point A and point B cannot be built until the two ends to be joined are clearly located and established. It is in this spirit that "The Islamic Inversion" is written.

In conclusion, the best way to understand what this book is about is to understand what it is not about. It is not a primer on Islam. It is not a book about politics. Nor is it not a book dissecting the cause for terror within the Muslim community. It is not a comparison of Jesus and Muhammad, neither is it a comparison of the Bible and the Qur'an. It is not an apologetic work designed to help Christians win a debate with a Muslim. The book is rather a guide to help diagnose Islamic arguments, understand their systemic pattern of reversal, know how to disassemble them, and subsequently lead the discussion back to Christ in a constructive way.

Contents

Section 5: Applying the Islamic Inversion

Section 1

Preparing Our Hearts to Reach Muslims

If someone says, "I love God," and hates his brother, he is a liar; for the one who does not love his brother whom he has seen, cannot love God whom he has not seen. And this commandment we have from Him, that the one who loves God should love his brother also.

1 JOHN 4:20-21

Chapter 1

Recognizing Cultural Roadblocks

In this first chapter, many questions will be asked, but few will be answered. We must first construct a context to place answers. After reading the first two chapters, there may be some feelings of sadness rather than enlightenment. That is to be expected. We should all grieve for Muslims who currently live in the darkness that is a life without Christ. So if a feeling of discouragement sweeps in, do not be alarmed. Remember that this is the compassion of Christ manifesting itself within us. We all should feel compassion for our Muslim friends who truly want to serve God, yet do not know how. This love comes from God. (1 John 4:7)

A Loving Relationship Is Paramount

In all discussions, it is the assumption that a friendship of some kind or another with a Muslim has already been established. This relationship is of primary importance and thus comes as the first section of this book. If a relationship does not yet exist, having a debate will inevitably be fruitless. Almost everyone will give more credence to someone with whom they already have a connection. Very few people will heed the advice of a total stranger. This is true to a greater degree in Islam. As Edward Haskins notes in *A*

1

Muslim's Heart, "…it takes time for a friendship to develop to the point at which it can bear the intensity of the gospel."[1]

This reality is one many people must learn for themselves, wasting significant time and energy doing so. Many Christians think that if they can just present the truth of the Scripture, then Muslims will be swayed by logical arguments. Logical arguments are appropriate in the context of friendships, but they typically do not result in decisions for Christ in the context of a debate between mere acquaintances.

This point needs to be stressed. So many of us with a heart for our Muslim friends, coworkers, and family members go through a phase where we believe that presenting the evidence for Christ in a logical order will produce results. Almost every Christian, when confronted by Islam for the first time, feels that the Muslim just needs to see the evidence for the resurrection, the reliability and perspicuity of Scripture, or the evidence of fulfilled prophecy. The Christian believes that after seeing the facts, the Muslim will immediately recognize the Truth. However, most Muslims never choose Islam, so choosing to leave it never enters their minds. Islam is such an ingrained part of their lives that the thought of leaving it is as foreign as the idea of cutting off a limb. One analogy would be if I were to logically convince a man that his given name could be replaced with a better one. However, doing so would mean complete separation and alienation from family, perhaps the loss of employment, and possible death threats. Would this man want to change his name even if convinced that it was really in his best interest?

This truth cannot be stressed enough. If anyone reads this book with the intent to evangelize online or from a distance, expect few results. Seeds may be planted, but few souls typically will be won, even with the exposition techniques that will be presented. Ultimately, Muslims are won with love and not logic. Reading this book will help with the latter, and it therefore assumes the former. If love is not present, logic will have little effect. As it says in 1 Corinthians 13:1:

¹ If I speak with the tongues of men and of angels,
but do not have love, I have become a noisy gong
or a clanging cymbal.

This realization was made by one of the most effective modern day agents for social change, Dr. Martin Luther King, when he said, "Love is the only force capable of transforming an enemy into friend."²

Ergun Caner, the author of several insightful Christian books relating to Islam, tells of his conversion from Islam to Christianity. It was not clever arguments that won him to Christ. It was the persistence of a high school classmate who loved him enough to continually invite him to church. The church body then loved him to the cross in the same way Jesus did for us.³

Keeping such an attitude requires perseverance. It is difficult enough when the person encountered is unreceptive, let alone overtly hostile. Yet love is the attitude that must be maintained. Something that has helped me to keep such an attitude is to remember the difference between Islam and Muslims. "Islam is an assault on the gospel of Christ – A Muslim is a soul for whom Christ died."⁴

Avoiding Profitless Debates

Let's get underway by recognizing the typical styles of fruitless debates Christians have with Muslims. Encountering the Islamic argumentation style can be frustrating at first. After a time, an observant and clever person will realize that what makes the discussions so difficult is that often there are aspects of theology or reasoning that are turned completely inside out. In the heat of the moment, it is often impossible to articulate or even be aware of where the conversation got derailed. It is critical to recognize a clear pattern of distortions, spot them for what they are, and transform misunderstandings, half-truths, and misdirection into profitable dialogue. Before reading this book, you may have experienced a gut feeling that something in a conversation has been spiritually turned around, but you were unable to discern exactly how. After reading this book, the patterns of Islamic argumentation will be exposed. Once aware of the common methods Muslims use to twist an argument, responding becomes much easier.

To recognize how most conversations get stuck, let us first examine the primary Muslim assaults, of which there are four. These fall into the categories of steadfast adherence to the Qur'an even in the face of errors, attacks on Jesus' deity, the omission of Biblical context, and using an "ends justify the means" mindset in argumentation. It is imperative to understand and identify these four tactics. By doing so, the discussion can move past irrelevant debate and head for the reality of Jesus Christ. Often, Muslims are simply regurgitating arguments they have been trained to repeat, not those that are significant to them personally. By employing the techniques laid out in this book, Muslims who will genuinely consider the truth of Jesus Christ can be distinguished from those who are only interested in arguing for the sake of arguing.

To begin with, the Muslim looks on any non-Muslim as a *kafir*, which means an unbeliever of Islam. As such, the Muslim enters any conversation assuming that the kafir is full of ignorance. After all, any Muslim will tell you that any person of intelligence whatsoever would be Muslim. So before learning any specific topics that tend to get discussed, first view the various directions that ineffective conversations tend to take. Once we examine these Muslim approaches, it will be easier to identify them, and therefore we will be less likely to get sidetracked and mired in debate.

The Qur'an is the premier place of retreat for Muslims. As they believe it is the direct revelation from Allah, the book has unique significance for them. So it should not be surprising that they will fall back on the Qur'an during any discussion, just as any Christian would tend to fall back on the Bible. Since many people are not acquainted with how to establish or corroborate holy books' claims of authorship, conversations such as the following often arise. The Muslim states that a verse of the Qur'an or the Qur'an in its entirety is the word of Allah. The Christian asks why and is told because the Qur'an says it is the word of Allah and therefore it is perfect. Of course, this is circular reasoning. Pointing that out doesn't get anywhere though, and it just convinces the Muslim that you are too blind to see the truth.

It is easy to understand why a Muslim would take this approach. Many Christians do the same. They know the Bible to be true, and consequently "the Bible says so" is a good enough reason for them. It is a reasonable statement when speaking with other Christians, but nonetheless, it is a logical fallacy. That is not a criticism as much as it is a reality. It is a reality that must be dealt with when speaking with a Muslim. Many conversations wander through all kinds of territory when ultimately it was the issue of how to determine what is God's Word and what is not God's Word that was at the core of the discussion.

While this book will examine Biblical authority from a somewhat unique viewpoint later, a larger point to ponder is even knowing how to determine whether any past written account is true. How does anyone know that Williams Shakespeare wrote *Romeo and Juliet*? How does anyone really know George Washington was the first president of the United States? Can any past event be proven beyond a shadow of a doubt, or must we rely on other corroborating evidence by looking for confirmation with other contemporary sources? Even if everyone agrees, how certain can we be, given that nobody alive today can personally testify to it? Past events always come under bizarre attack, as we see today by those who deny the moon landing or the Holocaust. Words such as "proof" and "truth" can be bandied about while the two people talking may not even be able to agree on how to define them. We must ask the question that Pilate asked Jesus; "What is truth?" (John 18:38) How do you know it when you see it?

A second major assault on the gospel is the variety of Islamic verbal attacks on the nature and person of Jesus. These do deserve serious answers. However, Muslims often use these as a tactic to deflect serious inquiry about Islam. Imagine that you pose a legitimate question about an aspect of Islam. The question asked is immaterial; the pattern of response is what is noteworthy. As a Christian, you ask about something related to Islam that holds a contradiction or at the minimum seems a bit odd. The Muslim informs you that this is an inappropriate criticism of Islam and then begins to relate why Jesus is not the Son of God, and thus why you are an idolater for worshiping a man. You politely suggest taking up that question next and then try to get back to the original point at hand. However, you are informed that Christianity has just been proven false, so the original comment about Islam is now off the table. You have now reached an impasse.

The first time I encountered this line of conversation, I was stunned. I asked myself if what just happened really did just happen. Did I get bulldozed while simultaneously having my original question evaded? Typically, when such conversations take place, the list of verses used to invalidate the Trinity or deity of Jesus is relatively short and routinely misapplied. While this book will deal with these common Islamic objections individually in later chapters, remember that pursuing that tangent is exactly what must be carefully and temporarily avoided. It may seem odd not to immediately rush to defend the gospel, especially when Jesus Himself is under attack. Of course, it is necessary to defend tenets of faith, particularly those related to Jesus' true identity. The issue though, is the best method and timing to do so.

It is true that the Muslim gave an opportunity to discuss a specific part of Christianity, and that is great, but use caution. The person with whom this dialogue occurs may not even truly want to know about the particular verse introduced. More likely, the response is simply how he or she has been trained to respond. Answering the criticism posed can and often does lead to opportunities. However, often answering the Muslim's objection requires a great deal of research only to find out it was not even a personally relevant one anyway. Rather, after performing painstaking documentation to provide an answer, the Christian may find out the denigration was not even genuine. Rather, it was nothing more than an Islamic talking point used as a mechanism to deflect attention away from the original question about Islam. Before the Christian engages on a particular point, use discernment to ascertain whether the Muslims' countercharge is one he actually wants answered. Does the Muslim truly want to know the answer because he is seeking or is he merely attempting to divert the issue? Ultimately, the original question about Islam is still lingering and needs to be addressed.

Make sure the Muslim friend knows his rebuttal questions will not be ignored. Discussing the nature of Jesus' relationship to God is obviously of critical doctrinal importance. Yet engaging those concerns voiced by the Muslim should be a second conversation. The original question is still on the table. Find out whether the Muslim wants to discuss the point given, and address the second issue after the current one is finished. As the book progresses, effective methods of handling the assaults on Jesus' deity will be shown. Yet these are not presented in order to debate; they are presented with a view to foster meaningful interaction with Muslims who are seeking.

Another style of argument that often leads to dead-ends is encountered when Muslims take Scripture out of context. Typically when this is done, the argument falls into the category of a straw man argument. In a straw man argument, the opponent first misrepresents his adversary's position. Having done so, he can easily refute the manufactured substandard position. Muslims will quote a Bible verse, letting the Christian know its interpretation, and then proceed to tear down the straw man that the Muslim has set up. Of course, the interpretation given by the Muslim was far from accepted doctrine, but in the Muslim's mind, he has "proven" Christianity wrong. It is easy to make the Bible say whatever someone wants by quoting Scripture in isolation. A typical conversation finds a Muslim bringing up a Biblical contradiction. The Christian responds with context explaining the deeper meaning of verses that exist in tension and balance within the whole counsel of Scripture. The Muslim rejects the answer, states that the contradictions stands, and tells you that you are too blind to see the truth.

What is so hard about experiencing this self-confirmation style of debate is that the outcome is pre-determined. In the Muslim mind, the debate was over before it ever began. Bringing any facts to the table regarding contextual issues is irrelevant. Muslims have been told that the Bible has contradictions and this fits comfortably into their worldview. The Christian feels that if they can clarify the particulars of any given straw man argument, then progress with the Muslim can be made. However, debating the specific argument given by providing context is akin to trying to level a skyscraper by tearing out the furniture. The structure will remain standing. The entire thought process itself must be confronted, not just the individual argument. Getting the Muslim to read entire chapters of Scripture is not easy, but only by progressing to this as the initial means of analyzing individual passages will stop the onslaught of misapplied Biblical verses.

As an illustration of a Muslim's training in setting up this straw man style of debate, examine 2 Timothy 2:8:

⁸ Remember Jesus Christ, risen from the dead, descendant of David, according to my gospel,

I have had Muslims tell me that this verse is proof that the apostle Paul is a liar. If it is not immediately evident, don't feel bad. It takes quite a feat of mental gymnastics to read it the wrong way. The argument proceeds that Paul claims it is "his gospel," not the gospel of Jesus. Therefore, the Muslim explains that this verse proves that Paul corrupted the gospel, because he changed it from that of Jesus to his own gospel, confirming the Muslim view of Biblical corruption. Of course, if you misrepresent the meaning of the verse, you can fallaciously think you have proven anything.

Anyone with a clear understanding of the Bible knows that the word gospel means good news and furthermore knows that Paul is pointing back to Christ with this statement. Reading the verse preceding or following 2 Timothy 2:8 illustrates the point. More to the point, all of Paul's writings agree with those of the other Biblical authors. This point will be given an entire section later, but for now it is enough to note that we know there is no discrepancy to Paul's version of the gospel when compared to that presented by any other Biblical author.

The example goes to show that regardless of the absurdity of the accusation, and regardless of how easy it is to refute, the typical response is that the Christian, otherwise known as the kafir, is just too blind to see the truth. The omission of context allows the Muslim to comfortably confirm his worldview and circumvents him from engaging in serious discourse.

Finally, the last style of fruitless dialog comes out of the fact that Islam is often a pragmatic religion. Rules for ritual washing before prayer can be averted if on a journey. Prescribed fasting can be skipped for certain ailments and for women who are pregnant or nursing. Jihad is not mandated if a person is not healthy enough for combat. This kind of pragmatism often breeds an attitude that the ends can justify the means. This comes out often in conversation in subtle ways. The Muslim presents an argument from some renowned scholar to prove the validity of Islam. You find a logical contradiction or fallacy within the argument. However, since the advancement of Islam is the primary goal for the Muslim in the conversation, the argument's deficiencies are immediately rejected. Perhaps a new argument is put forth or there is an exception discussed as to why the error of the argument is not applicable.

In any event, the result is that the Muslim had the end in

mind, to prove Islam true. How he got there may not be important to him. Once again, the follower of Jesus Christ finds himself in an awkward position. Of course, the Christian must stand firm in what is true. Unfortunately, refuting whatever foolishness is thrown out will rarely do anything in and of itself. The Muslim probably will respond out of training, not out of thought.

The Muslim's goal is to prove Islam true and Christianity false by any means possible. To combat this, logical progression through the arguments seems useful, but it rarely is. A direct head-on assault on logical fallacy is not how most people come to know Christ. Therefore, it is important to set expectations accurately. Continuing to pursue reasoning from a purely apologetic approach may convince the Muslim that the person from whom he obtained the information may have made a mistake, but nothing more. He will still approach theological discussions with the end in mind of showing Islam to be true at all costs. So in the bigger picture, nothing has changed. His faith is not shaken. In his mind, perhaps he will consider listening to different Islamic scholars, but even that would be a stretch.

So how can we escape these ridiculous and time wasting arguments in order to present the gospel in a manner where it can be heard? In this book, we will discuss how to take the Muslim's argument and flip it back on Islam. When Muslims see how their own logic undermines their own religion, they are often much quicker to recognize where their thought patterns went awry. When the ends justify the means mentality leads them to undermine Islam itself, the overarching approach to debate can be dismantled, and genuine conversations can begin. In this way, the Christian can set the stage for helping the Muslim reach the point where he can legitimately question what he has been told.

It is easy to get frustrated when bombarded with this type of erroneous thought. I have seen many Christians start off with the best of intentions and wind up getting overwhelmed, hurt, and hardened. There is the temptation to begin lashing out. In some cases, Christians give in to this temptation. This only serves to reinforce the Muslim viewpoint that the Spirit-led life is only a shallow claim without substance. It is much harder to persuade someone of the fruit of the Spirit after exhibiting fruits of the flesh, such as outbursts of anger. (Galatians 5:20)

In all such discussions, it is paramount to remember the difference between Islam and Muslims. Do not forget, as earlier quoted, that Islam is an assault on the gospel of Christ – a Muslim is a soul for whom Christ died. Try not to forget that the individual is truly lost. Making this distinction will help when experiencing inevitable feelings of frustration and aggravation.

How To Avoid Being Branded Mischief-Maker

In all of this, there are two more things to remember about the Muslim perspective. First, Muslims have been told their entire lives that the kafir, or unbeliever, is there to "make mischief in the land" and deceive them with flowery discourse (Qur'an 2:11-12, 8:73). So anything a Christian might say, regardless of how convincing or obvious it is, will be immediately discounted. Not only that, but when asking a Muslim insightful questions that expose sin and the need for Jesus Christ or some other difficult questions for which the Muslim does not have an answer, he will walk away assured that if only his imam were there the kafir would have been soundly defeated. Perhaps he will even be motivated to learn more about Islam as a result¾perhaps not.

The Qur'an even gets so specific as to tell Muslims not to take as friends those who do not respect Islam. From Qur'an 5:57:

> O ye who believe! take not for friends and protectors
> those who take your religion for a mockery or sport,-
> whether among those who received the Scripture before
> you, or among those who reject Faith; but fear ye Allah,
> if ye have faith (indeed).

11

Muslims are instructed only to be friends with those who respect Islam. Therefore, becoming friends with a Muslim may be contingent upon respecting Islam as a legitimate religious choice. This confirmation bias results in the Muslim having an implicit assumption that Islam has validity from the kafir's viewpoint. To many Muslims, this validity reinforces their own belief structure. In other words, in their view, the unbelieving friend chose unbelief but admits Islam is an honorable religion. If the Muslim discovers that the kafir does not respect Islam, the rules of Islam mandate the friendship must cease. Of course, the definition of what constitutes respecting Islam varies. Even though the Christian does not believe Islam is an acceptable path to God, the Muslim may well assume that he does. When pressed, if Islam is in any way debased, the friendship will likely end then and there. Thus the Muslim is safe from experiencing any potential conflicting ideologies that would expose his fraudulent system of belief.

In fact, Muslims are explicitly told to avoid conversation with anyone who criticizes Islam. Qur'an 6:68a says:

> When thou seest men engaged in vain discourse about
> Our signs, turn away from them unless they turn to a
> different theme.

Nevertheless, many Muslims truly want to serve God. Remember that Islam is a religion based on rules. One rule is that they are required to share their faith (Qur'an 3:104, 16:125). Since Muslims are rewarded for obeying the rules (Qur'an 24:55), some may engage in religious debate just to score points with Allah. Some Muslims are very fervent about this, and it takes a while to sift through their standard litany of assaults until finally reaching something meaningful and relevant to their life.

So don't be surprised when initiating discussions if they tend to get sidetracked. Getting to real issues of the heart requires overcoming several obstacles. First, the Muslim must forget a lifetime of learning that non-Muslims are just there to serve as the agents of Satan trying to get them to disbelieve. Once past that obstacle, it may be that the Muslim does not really care about your questions anyway, but is just trying to win you over to Islam via the Qur'an's mandate to evangelize. Therefore, don't expect to see immediate results. Also, navigating through all these spiritual landmines carries the risk of losing your relationship with the Muslim if he discovers that you do not consider Islam to be a wonderful religion.

Luckily, friendship is not something that begins at a distinct moment. Friendships develop over time. If you think about a current friend, it is difficult to pinpoint the exact time and place when that person changed from being an acquaintance to a friend. This allows us Christians to minister to our Muslim neighbors. The friendship forms before either party would cognitively acknowledge its inception. It is not as if a Muslim will stop and say, "If this non-Muslim acts in such and such a manner, he will become my friend, so I should stop interacting". Once the friendship has developed, the Spirit can more easily work through you.

Once a strong friendship is established, it can begin to bear the weight of the heavy questions that will lead to the truth of the gospel. Yet this only brings us to the next obstacle to be overcome.

Asking Difficult Questions

When insightful and relevant spiritual questions begin to arise, the Christian may start to wonder: "Why isn't a Muslim's faith shaken?" Of course, a Christian is certain as to why he believes, because of his personal relationship with Christ. Yet it must be pondered as to what the Muslim has that is similar. To find the answer, we must again peer into Islamic culture.

First, doubting is a sin in Islam (Qur'an 22:11, 49:15). The Muslims are taught to treat any doubt as temptation and immediately dismiss it as irrelevant. Second, most Muslims never chose Islam; they were born into it. It is part of who they are. It would be analogous to a person attempting to persuade someone to change his gender or racial makeup. Most people would never even consider it, so the thought never really crosses their minds. Thirdly, the Qur'an itself warns Muslims against pondering difficult questions in 5:101:

> O ye who believe! Ask not questions about things which, if made plain to you, may cause you trouble. But if ye ask about things when the Qur'an is being revealed, they will be made plain to you, Allah will forgive those: for Allah is Oft-forgiving, Most Forbearing.

The Qur'an instructs Muslims not to ask questions that may cause them trouble. In fact, the next verse tells Muslims that past generations went astray because they asked too many such difficult questions (Qur'an 5:102). The Islamic culture mandates avoiding difficult religious questions. Understanding such cultural norms can allow us as Christians to be very strategic in how we engage Muslims in dialogue. A frontal assault of nettlesome problems within Islam may only arouse defense mechanisms. This does not mean we cannot ask hard questions. Rather, we want to be precise and purposeful when we help Muslims themselves break down the barriers Islam has forced upon them. Those barriers were put in place as a means to disguise the truth, so getting to the truth will require their removal.

The Problem of Nationalism

Another aspect of Islam that is difficult for Westerners to understand is that of nationalism. Specifically, it is not immediately evident that Islam has a very nationalistic nature. Islam is not just a religion; it is also a culture and a way of life. This truth is expressed in many ways at various times, but it is hard to understand it until seeing it in action. To that end, consider the following example as an illustration.

The May 9, 2005 issue of Newsweek reported that soldiers stationed at Guantanamo Bay had flushed a Qur'an down the toilet as an interrogation tactic. (This article was soon retracted as false.) Since the Qur'an is considered sacred, when this article was originally published it outraged Muslims worldwide. Various protests ensued resulting in fifteen deaths. Muslims the world over showed their disfavor by burning American flags.

What is immediately obvious is the "eye for eye, tooth for tooth" mentality here. "You debase our Qur'an, we will debase your flag" is the Muslim call to arms. Yet, look at this scenario a little closer. Just what is being equated? They did not burn Bibles or Torahs; they burned the American flag! This is because in the Muslim mind the Qur'an represents more than the religion, it is part of their national identity. They are Muslims in the same way we are Canadians, Americans, or Australians. To a Muslim, insulting the Qur'an is not just about insulting their religion; it is an insult to their identity and nationalism. Assaulting a Muslim belief is analogous to someone assaulting our national heritage.

Talking with a Muslim about leaving Islam is similar to asking someone from Britain to become Irish or vice versa. Again, this is not something most people would want to do. Remember that Islam is not just a religion, but also a nationality.

Dealing with Discouragement

Many of us have friends and relatives who do not know Christ. Most likely, we have attempted to share God's good news with them to no avail. Of course, we are saddened by their choice not to accept God's free gift of redemption. This is a natural feeling because we have a heart for the lost. We have compassion, and our souls are deeply troubled at the thought of anyone spending an eternity without God. It is awesome to experience the joy of knowing God, and as such sharing it with others seems natural, logical, and normal. Learning that sharing such joy with so many Muslims is next to impossible may cause sadness. God Himself grieves when people reject Him, so feeling any other way ourselves should cause us concern. (Ezekiel 18:32)

As caring Christians, we are seeking to reach Muslims with the salvation offered by Jesus. True caring Christians, of course, cannot accept the Qur'an as authentic. Muslims, however, cannot be friends with someone who does not accept the Qur'an as authentic. Therefore, Muslims do not become friends with faithful and caring Christians. We have reached a seeming contradiction. Thankfully, there is an answer. As previously noted, if you consider your friends, try and remember at exactly what instant they changed from acquaintances to friends. This cannot be done, as friendships sneak up on you. They grow out of the normal flow of life events, and as such, Muslims wind up becoming friends with kafirs without realizing it. This is why it is important not to storm the gates of Islam before a friendship has formed. Doing so will prevent its formation. Yet once a friendship has been established, you can start to share the love of God with them in productive ways.

Sadness may creep into your burgeoning friendship due to love for the lost. This is natural since we should all grieve for those who are trapped within darkness. Islam is a religion without eternal security and without the tools for overcoming life's spiritual dilemmas. As such, many Muslims are inwardly discouraged about both their earthly and eternal prospects. This type of hopelessness tends to pervade life circumstances and thought patterns. Discouragement and hopelessness settle in because it is not easy from a human perspective to alter your thought process to one of hope and encouragement. Just thinking "I will not be discouraged" doesn't work. For example, if I say "Do NOT think of a watermelon," what goes through your mind?

Of course, the thought of a watermelon materialized even though I said not to think of one. In that same way, trying not to think of the discouraging situation only backfires. We need to replace the thought with something more powerful (Philippians 4:8).

Again, working around discouragement all day long brings even more discouragement, as it tends to create a negative feedback loop on itself. Muslims work for the favor of Allah, yet they do not know their ultimate destiny. What could be more discouraging than trying to win Allah's favor without having a clue whether your ultimate destination is paradise or hell? So, when the unsuspecting Christian enters such an environment and surrounds himself with it, it is inevitable that such discouragement will tend to rub off, or even soak in via osmosis. Next, throw in the fact that there may be upcoming spiritual battles, and the stage is perfectly set for some emotionally trying times.

Experiencing trials and discouragements is not anything new. There are many great passages given to us to help us gain perspective. One such passage details the circumstances under which we are to be servants of God. 2 Corinthians 6:4-10 speaks to this in great detail, and concludes this way:

> [10] as sorrowful yet always rejoicing, as poor yet making many rich, as having nothing yet possessing all things.

We are regarded as deceivers though we bring the truth of the gospel (2 Corinthians 6:8). We are held in evil report and yet must persevere. We are sorrowful for others as we rejoice in our own relationship with God. We come to the table with nothing, yet He that works within us shows Himself strong through our weakness, storing His great treasure in our inadequate earthen vessels (2 Corinthians 3:4-6).

With Jesus, there is always hope. Throughout this book we will discuss ways of focusing on that only hope, Jesus Christ.

ROBERT SIEVERS

Examples of Islamic arguments will be given, and a pattern of spiritual reversal will be identified. With that, a mechanism will be shown to flip the discouragement upside-down and point it back to Christ. Inevitably, the Muslim's argument can be inverted to channel the discouragement back at Islam itself, or it can highlight for the Muslim his need to accept the reality of Jesus' incarnation, crucifixion, and resurrection. So we will see how to direct the Muslim argument to lead back to Christ, replacing discouragement with hope. We will learn how to keep our eyes on Him, not get sidetracked, and unravel the maze the enemy has laid before the follower of Christ.

Chapter 2

How Muslims View Christianity

The myriad of cultural roadblocks we saw in the last chapter presents a steep incline to navigate. Unfortunately, that is only half of the story. Not only do cultural issues make it difficult to reach Muslims, but Islam itself has built in firewalls that present spiritual roadblocks as well. These obstacles should come as no surprise. The Bible itself tells us about these and warns us not to take such obstacles personally. It encourages us to persevere nonetheless (Hebrews 12:3).

In this chapter, we will be examining in more detail exactly how Muslims view Christians and Christianity. Since Muslims have a different view of the Bible, Jesus, the cross, and prophets in general, we must understand their perspective in order to avoid endless arguments that miss the mark.

Wearing Muslim Shoes

The core of Christianity is the death, resurrection, and atoning sacrifice of Jesus the Messiah. Before we leap headlong into a theological treatise of the nature of Jesus Christ, it will pay to take a step back out of our assumptions. Just for a moment, pretend that Christ was neither crucified nor resurrected. This is what the Muslim believes. Paul wrote about what this would mean, if true, to the Corinthians in 1 Corinthians 15:14-19. Follow this argument closely, because it will shed light on how the Muslim thinks.

> [14]and if Christ has not been raised, then our preaching is vain, your faith also is vain. [15]Moreover we are even found to be false witnesses of God, because we testified against God that He raised Christ, whom He did not raise, if in fact the dead are not raised. [16]For if the dead are not raised, not even Christ has been raised; [17]and if Christ has not been raised, your faith is worthless; you are still in your sins. [18]Then those also who have fallen asleep in Christ have perished. [19]If we have hoped in Christ in this life only, we are of all men most to be pitied.

Paul says here that if Christ has not risen, Christians have a worthless faith, are bearing false witness against God, and are of all people most miserable. This statement squarely hits the mark. We base our entire hope on the death, resurrection, and atoning sacrifice of Christ. If those were proven false, Christianity as a religion would be worthless. Yet even more wretched would be Christians peddling this worthless charade to those around them by proclaiming that Christ is the true hope of mankind. Christians would be the premier charlatans of history for placing their faith in what turned out to be only a common man, and worse yet, persuading others to participate in such meaninglessness.

This should not be surprising. The Bible makes mention of how, without Christ, the whole idea of the cross is outrageous, even foolishness. It also needs to be admitted how outrageous the proposition of Jesus is to some people. Why would anyone trade his or her own son for the life of an ungodly person? Yet God, through His Son Jesus Christ, gave up His own life in order to become sin for anyone who would agree to accept His gift (2 Corinthians 5:21). It is the most outlandish and one-sided deal ever struck! It is outrageous that God would show such love. Without the true knowledge of the cross, it is impossible to understand. 1 Corinthians 1:18 sums it up.

> **¹⁸ For the word of the cross is foolishness to those who are perishing, but to us who are being saved it is the power of God.**

Since Muslims believe Christ to be neither crucified nor resurrected, they view Christians, of all people, as most to be pitied. As Jesus' death and resurrection have no spiritual meaning to Muslims, the heart of God's mercy and love has been removed from their view, and thus Christians are seen in a totally different light.

Jesus Through the Muhammad Filter

Anyone who has studied Islam a bit knows that Muslims consider Jesus a prophet. Many good books discuss this topic in more detail, so we will take a slightly different approach. Typically, Christian-Muslim dialogue will focus on the Trinity, whether Jesus is God, whether the New Testament has been altered, and so on. These are usually unfruitful discussions. Of course, such doctrines are important and even central to the good news of Jesus Christ. However, before having such conversations, we should understand the Muslim view of Jesus. This allows us to avoid being both offended and offensive as we help them get ready to hear this good news. Then we can get at the core of who we are as individuals and how God can reach each one of us.

Muslims claim that they respect and honor Jesus. As an example, the Council on American-Islamic Relations (CAIR) declares that "...Muslims love and revere Jesus as one of God's greatest messengers to mankind..."[5] Yet after some discussions with Muslims about who Jesus is, such statements generate a feeling that Jesus is not truly respected within Islam. The Muslim will emphatically state that he or she respects Jesus even more than Christians do. Yet this claim of respect comes across as empty, without substance, and perhaps even token language. It is difficult to articulate exactly why the Muslim's view of Jesus seems so flawed.

It is critical to understand from what vantage point Muslims view Jesus. Specifically, Muslims draw all information about Jesus from the Qur'an. In other words, Muslims respect Jesus, but only in the way Muhammad instructs them to. An analogy would be that a person is a big fan of a certain novelist because a friend told him of this good writer. Maybe this friend subsequently even shared information regarding one of his stories. This original person has not actually read the author but is satisfied to be a fan because he trusts his friend. Later he meets a fellow enthusiast of this author, and the two begin talking.

"I am a big fan of so-and-so," the friend says.

"Oh, so am I." might be the response.

"Which of his books have you read?"

"Well, none, but I heard he is really good."

Look at how ridiculous this would be! If someone claims to be a fan, certainly he should investigate the original writings at least marginally. This kind of ridiculous situation is exactly what Muslims do with respect to Jesus. Few have actually read any of His words, but they say they revere and respect Him because Muhammad gave this as an instruction. Muslims respect Jesus only because Muhammad tells them to. It is true that Muslims are to respect all the prophets (Qur'an 2:136). Yet this lumps Jesus into the same category as others with the status of prophets in Islam, such as Lot and Solomon. Muslims only respect Jesus in that He is a prophet to them, and so as such they are required to respect Him, but nothing more. Muslims have held this view from the inception of the religion until today. Many notable Christians throughout the ages have noticed this attitude that Muslims have toward Jesus. For example, Martin Luther described the Muslim's view of Jesus in light of Muhammad in these terms:

> They pay the most honorable testimony to Jesus Christ, saying that he was a prophet of pre-eminent sanctity, born of the Virgin Mary, and an envoy from God, but that Mohammed succeeded him...[6]

In the same vein, Muslims believe there was an *Injeel*, or a book given to those of Jesus' time, regarding the true nature and teachings of Jesus. They believe that this Injeel was later corrupted by human hands. Yet Muhammad spent no time searching for this original Injeel, which Muslims believe is the uncorrupted gospel. Therefore, the Muslims of today do not search for it either. What they know about Jesus is entirely filtered through Muhammad. A Muslim will claim all prophets are equal because the Qur'an says so (Qur'an 2:136). In reality, some prophets are more equal than others. Muslims acknowledge the equality of prophets because Muhammad tells the Muslim to consider them equal, and as the greatest and last prophet, Muhammad must be obeyed.

As we get more into these types of distortions, stop and examine the irony involved. Muslims venerate Jesus, but not because of His accomplishments, nor because of who He claimed to be. Rather, they honor Him because the Qur'an instructs them to honor Him as an equal to Muhammad, their last and greatest prophet.

Christianity and Incest

A major point of division between Muslims and Christians is how each views historical Biblical figures and their actions. Muslims interpret historical sections of the Bible much differently

than Christians. A Muslim's view of Biblical accounts is based
through the lens of Islam in which they are raised. The following
illustration will help us understand the filter by which Muslims
view the history of the Bible.

Consider the Biblical account of Lot. A major question to
ponder is what manner of man Lot was. On the one hand, we know
Lot was a righteous man (2 Peter 2:7-8). Lot was spared from the
destruction of Sodom. He also provided safety to strangers. On
the other hand, he offered to give up his daughters, chose to reside
in Sodom, and even hesitated before leaving town. It is plain that
righteous Lot had some serious character flaws, and it is after this
checkered past that the account picks up in Gen 19:30-36:

> ³⁰Lot went up from Zoar, and stayed in the
> mountains, and his two daughters with him; for he
> was afraid to stay in Zoar; and he stayed in a cave,
> he and his two daughters. ³¹Then the firstborn said
> to the younger, "Our father is old, and there is not
> a man on earth to come in to us after the manner
> of the earth. ³²"Come, let us make our father drink
> wine, and let us lie with him that we may preserve
> our family through our father." ³³So they made
> their father drink wine that night, and the firstborn
> went in and lay with her father; and he did not
> know when she lay down or when she arose. ³⁴On
> the following day, the firstborn said to the younger,
> "Behold, I lay last night with my father; let us make
> him drink wine tonight also; then you go in and lie
> with him, that we may preserve our family through
> our father." ³⁵So they made their father drink wine
> that night also, and the younger arose and lay with
> him; and he did not know when she lay down or
> when she arose. ³⁶Thus both the daughters of Lot
> were with child by their father.

After citing these verses, Muslims are then quick to pose potentially embarrassing questions. The Qur'an teaches them that Lot is a prophet (Qur'an 6:86). The Qur'an also teaches them that prophets are a higher caliber of people (Qur'an 3:161). So the Muslim starts raising questions such as "How is it that your Bible advocates incest?" or "Would you read this to your children?" or "How is it you Christians can ascribe such behavior to a prophet?" Since Muslims believe Lot is a prophet, and since they believe that prophets cannot sin in such a way, the only logical alternative left for them is to believe that the Scriptures are corrupt.

There are many ways to approach this response, but keep in mind the Muslim's qualms as we first examine the facts. It also helps to examine the passage in light of the truthfulness of the rest of Scripture. Remember, many Muslims will just say that the Scriptures are corrupted, and this is one of those stories they use in order to suggest that the Bible cannot be true. They may say this because they believe God would not tell such a dishonorable story or because Lot would never have to endure such an ignominious event. Either way, the suggestion that this story has been changed over the years is indefensible. As usual, looking at the passages just before or just after the cited verses will typically clear the confusion. The Muslim stance is that this account of Lot is false. While such historical accounts do not lend themselves to purely mathematical logical analysis, the very next verse sheds some light on the facts:

> **37The firstborn bore a son, and called his name Moab; he is the father of the Moabites to this day. 38As for the younger, she also bore a son, and called his name Ben-ammi; he is the father of the sons of Ammon to this day.**

This next verse indicates both Moabites and Ammonites existed. This has been confirmed through archeological and historical record. It shouldn't be surprising that the Biblical account is corroborated by external evidence. It is true that using the Bible to prove the Bible does not furnish logical proof. What it does do, however, is illustrate a consistent story line that points us toward truth given its historical accuracy. However, we have found ourselves laboring over the history of people groups of 4000 years ago, and that is not profitable. Our goal is to get the focus back on the redemptive work of Jesus Christ, not debate archeology and genealogy. Arguing the veracity of the Scriptural account has its place, but here it only serves as a detour, and typically won't go anywhere.

A second major misunderstanding is that an egregious assumption is made regarding application. Many Muslims will ask a Christian if he or she agrees with the passage. To them, agreement with the truthfulness of the story equates to agreement with the approval of incest. Of course, we know that the behavior is reprehensible, but the veracity of Scripture is untouched. The accuracy of the reporting of an event has absolutely nothing to do with the morality or righteousness of the actions reported. The Bible interprets itself by stating why such stories are present. While this particular verse refers to the 40 years of wandering in the wilderness, the application of it throughout Scripture is sound. 1 Corinthians 10:6:

> **[6] Now these things happened as examples for us, so that we would not crave evil things as they also craved.**

Again, from 1 Corinthians 10:11:

> **[11] Now these things happened to them as an example, and they were written for our instruction, upon whom the ends of the ages have come.**

So clearly there is a difference between descriptive passages and prescriptive passages. Descriptive passages recount a story without stating an opinion on the ethics or morality of the actions involved, whereas a prescriptive passage commands us to follow the example given. It is obvious that the accounts of Lot are given as a descriptive passage only, and no Christian in the world would assign it a prescriptive context. Still, attempting to discuss this point with a Muslim friend may leave you disenchanted with the lack of results.

To understand the Muslim's mental process fully, remember that Muslims look to Muhammad for everything with respect to life application. So, from an early age, they are trained to listen to their prophet and attempt to imitate everything he does. This breeds a mentality of taking for granted that a prophet's actions are always to be imitated. It is no wonder that a Muslim cannot differentiate between commands and sins! They have been trained all of their lives to examine the stories of prophets, and subsequently try to integrate that behavior into their daily experience. A Muslim's upbringing teaches that accepting the story of Lot as true equates to the approval of incest. Thus they soundly reject the story as a fabrication. Frankly, their logic is consistent if it is assumed that Lot is a prophet and that the actions of prophets are always to be emulated. Rather than calling Muslims misguided for not accepting Scripture, we must help them understand the error of their assumptions.

Ultimately, this points back to a lack of understanding of the sin nature, prophet or not, and consequently the need for sin to be forgiven. If sin is not acknowledged, a Savior is not required. This is the root of the problem, but it takes a while to get there. Meanwhile, the journey to the core of the matter tends to wander through all kinds of rocky territory laden with snares and traps. Many Christians get caught in a debate with a Muslim and easily win, but the Muslim is no closer to Christ.

Many Christians might consider this a moot conversation since Lot is not a prophet. However, such a view misses the point. This exact conversation could happen with reference to Moses' killing of the Egyptian (Exodus 2:12) or David's commission of adultery with Bathsheba and subsequent murder of Uriah the Hittite (1 Samuel 11). Usually such a conversation will involve Lot since Muslims are more aware of Lot's indiscretions than these others. The point is that referencing Biblical accounts such as that of Lot can result in argument over whether Lot is or is not a prophet. Thus the conversation bypasses the larger issue of how Muslims view all Scripture as prescriptive rather than recognizing that sometimes it is descriptive only.

Let's return to the story of Lot and the subsequent discussion of it as an example. Unless we understand the Islamic mindset of coupling a prophet's actions and required application, winning the argument will not help Muslims understand what this passage is talking about. I include all of this in order to help shed light on the possible avenues to take when confronted with such attacks. Talk about whether prophets are sinless, which can lead back to Christ. Talk about whether all actions of prophets are worthy of following, and discuss several examples. This too can point back to Jesus' perfect example. Again, try not to get mired in the details of these Muslim arguments unless it is for personal study and growth.

Making Spiritual Appraisals without the Spirit

If there is any word pertaining to Christian doctrine that Muslims know, it is "Trinity." Muslims are confident that they know what the Trinity is, even though prominent Christian theologians have wrestled with and probed the concept for centuries. So it is only logical that many present-day Christians do not have an accurate understanding of what the Tri-Unity of God does and does not entail. Nevertheless, in any discussion, Muslims will be quick to reference the issue of the triune nature of God and attempt to explain what it means. Muslims are confident that we Christians worship three gods, no matter how many times they are informed of the contrary. As if it has not been said enough, debating the point is typically fruitless, but maintaining composure requires knowledge well grounded in what the Bible says about the nature of God. So before wandering into a hopeless escapade trying to convince a Muslim friend that Christians believe God is one, it is essential to understand their point of view.

In Islam, the gravest sin that can be committed is *shirk*, which means "ascribing partners to Allah." Muslims truly believe that this is what Christians are doing. Of course, we know that we worship one God and one God only, since the Trinity is "three in one." To the Muslim, admitting the existence of the Trinity is committing shirk, the cardinal sin of Islam. Therefore, any mention of the Holy Spirit, Jesus as God, or the Trinity in general causes the Muslim's fiercest defense mechanism to be raised. So hold fast to monotheism, and focus on how God describes Himself. Again, I cannot emphasize enough that this understanding of the intricacies of God's three-in-one nature is to help provide wisdom, not to pound Muslim friends over the head with these truths. In rare cases, they might be ready for this, but that would be the exception, not the rule.

It is also important to retain compassion as we remember that Muslims, like anyone else who has not accepted Christ, cannot know what the Spirit is. It is not surprising that those who do not believe struggle with the concept of the Trinity. This concept is one that our fleshly brains cannot process because it is a spiritual concept. Therefore, it must be spiritually appraised. Without the Spirit, there is not a place in the brain to assimilate this kind of information. Scripture speaks clearly to this in 1 Corinthians 2:14:

> **14 But a natural man does not accept the things of the Spirit of God, for they are foolishness to him; and he cannot understand them, because they are spiritually appraised.**

Accepting the truth of the Triune nature of God without the indwelling of the Spirit is impossible. As humans we feel we can use strictly logical methods to present the case, and it will be accepted through logical means. Getting past this misconception is imperative. It must be admitted that all of the arguments put forward do not offer conclusive proof about the nature of God. However, each of them independently, and all of them cumulatively, do point to the true nature of God.

It is important for us to know these truths anyway, even though it is not the place to start a discussion. Therefore, we must first make certain that our own theology is solid before we begin to delve into the correct way to bring Muslims to these truths.

Section 2

Preparing Our Minds to Reach Muslims

but sanctify Christ as Lord in your hearts, always being ready to make a defense to everyone who asks you to give an account for the hope that is in you, yet with gentleness and reverence;

1 PETER 3:15

Chapter 3

The Root of All Insight: Jesus Is Lord

Throughout out interactions with others, and of course throughout life itself, the central issue is the question of who Jesus Christ claimed to be, and the veracity of those claims. It is easy to get distracted from this central truth, and the further that the conversation drifts from the reality of His divine incarnation, the less effective any evangelistic efforts will be. As with anyone who is not a follower of Christ, Muslims do not understand the concept of Jesus as the Son of God. The whole concept of the Trinity is foreign to them. However, view this in perspective; many Christians do not adequately understand the Trinity and the Sonship of Christ either. Therefore, a Christian must have an attitude of compassion with regard to such difficult concepts. So let us begin our look at some theology relating to Jesus Christ with Muslim arguments in mind.

Is Jesus God or the Son of God?

Muslims will quote from various Scriptures in an attempt to prove that Jesus is not God. Of course, since the New Testament is full of evidence to the contrary, you might wonder how this is done. Typically, it is done by taking Scripture out of context. We will deal with this topic more fully later in the book. For now, take a look at a direct assault on Jesus. Muslims will often assail the phrase "Son of God." For example, one Muslim I talked to argued this way:

> You Christians say that Jesus Christ is God, then you say that Jesus Christ is the Son of God. You do this to create confusion, but even your own Scriptures tell you that God is not the author of confusion. Why can't you see the truth?

Just what is the difference between being God and the Son of God? This question can be quite disarming without full use of the sword of the Spirit, which is the Word of God (Ephesians 6:17). As always, God has provided us with understanding right from His Word. In this case, it comes from a profound and often overlooked verse, John 5:18:

> **18 For this reason therefore the Jews were seeking all the more to kill Him, because He not only was breaking the Sabbath, but also was calling God His own Father, making Himself equal with God.**

This verse brings up a subtle truth that passes by most Christians. Why does calling God "His own" Father translate into making Himself equal with God? When Jesus said this, it provoked the Jews into a furious desire to take His life as a blasphemer. In other words, something about Jesus' statement here sets off the Jewish blasphemy detector to its maximum level. Remember that the Jews had plenty of practice looking for heretics, so it was not a struggle for them to recognize one. What was it about Jesus' statement that so enraged them?

Part of the answer lies in the nuances of the original language. The word translated as "own" in the original Greek is *idios*, which carries the meaning "uniquely one's own." It is a common word, used over 100 times in the New Testament, so its meaning is quite clear (John 1:11, Romans 8:32, 1 Corinthians 3:8, 1 Corinthians 4:12). What Jesus says here is "God is my Father in a special way that does not apply to others, but my own unique Father." By doing so, He claimed the same nature as God. To be clear, parents pass down characteristics to their offspring. In America, we have an expression, "The apple does not fall far from the tree." This concept is well understood, as seen in the analogous well-known Arabic proverb "The son of a duck is a floater."

So we know that a son inherits characteristics from his father, but just what characteristics would a perfect God share with His own offspring? What would God's Son have in common with God other than God's own perfect character? Could it be anything less than the very nature of God? Could a perfect God do an imperfect job of transmitting his characteristics to His unique Son? Such a son must be an eternal and perfect representation of His Father, as God would not haphazardly nor incompletely transfer his nature and qualities to His offspring. When Jesus says that God is "His own" Father, He is not merely implying, but explicitly asserting that God's nature was His own. The Jews were quite aware of the meaning, which doesn't come through in full force when translated into English.

Of course, in one sense of the word, everyone who is led by the Spirit of God is a son of God (Romans 8:14). Yet it must be remembered that this inheritance is an inheritance stemming from adoption, not from a direct transfer of God's substance (Romans 8:15, Galatians 4:5). That adoption comes about through the Spirit, while Jesus is the unique, only-begotten, Son of God. Not only that, but throughout John chapter 5 Jesus goes on to emphasize exactly who He is. Robertson's Word Picture of the New Testament elaborates on this point. In it, he states:

> Besides, if the Jews misunderstood Jesus on this point,
> it was open and easy for him to deny it and to clear up

the misapprehension. This is precisely what he does not do. On the contrary Jesus gives a powerful apologetic in defense of his claim to equality with the Father.[7]

Note that the interpretation of John 5:18 by the Jews of Jesus' time speaks volumes. They knew the statement was blasphemous for a human to say. Even more to the point, Jesus does not correct them. This verse illustrates the importance of having a firm understanding of Jesus' words and their meanings prior to talking to Muslims. Of course, such statements should be examined within the framework of the Spirit's leading. The better our understanding of what Jesus said, the less likely our misspeaking will set off landmines while walking through such perilously delicate theological territory.

Now that we know just who Jesus claims to be, the next avenue to pursue is how often He makes these claims.

The Obscure Verses about Christ

While it is true that you cannot assume what any individual Muslim believes, there are some common threads. One such thread is that most Muslims do not believe they need to read the Bible to know who Jesus claimed to be. Some Muslims will say the Scriptures were corrupted, and others will say Christians take obscure verses out of context. No matter which error is made, the conclusion is that Jesus was a prophet, that He was nothing more than a servant. As an example, here is a comment made by arguably the greatest Islamic apologist of all time, Sheikh al-Islaam ibn Taymiyyah in the 13th century. His views are still popular among Muslims today. Shaikh Taymiyyah argues that they (the Christians) misrepresent verses from the Qur'an the same way Christians misrepresent verses from the Bible. He believes that they (the Christians) seize upon obscure verses from Scripture to assert the Trinity while ignoring countless verses that deny it.

> This procedure which they follow with the Qur'an is similar to what they follow in the earlier books and the teaching of the prophets in the Torah, Gospel, Psalms and other books. In those books there are so many clear passages on the Oneness (*tawhid*) of Allah and the servanthood of Christ that they can only be counted with difficulty. In them there are a few phrases that contain ambiguity, they seize upon the few, hidden, complex ambiguities of the earlier books, and omit the many clear, definite, unambiguous passages.[8]

It is nice that he recognizes that the Bible speaks of the oneness of God. Christians completely agree on oneness, but the Sheikh rejects the verses that tell about the triune kind of oneness. Trying to take a walk through the Bible without seeing a reference to Jesus as the Son of God is impossible. To illustrate this fact, I have listed roughly 50 verses showing what the Bible says regarding Jesus being God or the Son of God. I left out countless other references to that effect because frankly, the list is too large to be given completely and still hope to maintain the reader's attention. Anybody who wants to have serious discussions with Muslims should be aware of these and other passages. I strongly suggest lingering here before moving on. Take some time and look up many of these verses to get a good feel for where to find the relevant passages, and what they say.

Who is Jesus?

Who said it	Verses
God	Matthew 3:17, Matthew 17:5
Isaiah	Isaiah 9:6 (the human aspect is born, the God aspect is a gift)
David	Psalm 2:7

Who said it	Verses
John the Baptist	John 1:29-34, John 3:34-36
Martha	John 11:27
Nathaniel (disciple)	John 1:47-49
Thomas (disciple)	John 20:28-29
Peter (disciple)	Matthew 16:13-17, Acts 2:36
Jude	Jude 1:4
John (disciple)	John 1:1-3,14, 1 John 1:1-3, 1 John 1:7, 1 John 2:22-23, 1 John 3:23, 1 John 4:9-10
Paul	Colossians 1:13-15, Colossians 2:9, Titus 2:13
Various	Matthew 14:31-33 (Note Jesus accepts worship, to which God alone is due), John 5:18, Hebrews 1:1-2, Hebrews 1:8, Luke 8:39
Angels	Luke 1:32-35
Demons	Matthew 8:29, Luke 4:34
The Jews	Matthew 27:43
Jesus Himself	John 4:25-26, John 8:58, John 9:35-37, John 10:30, John 10:37-38, John 14:9, Matthew 26:63-65, Luke 22:70 Mark 2:5-11 (note verse 7), Matthew 22:42-46, John 12:27-28 (Jesus calls to his Father, and his Father answers), Revelation 1:8, Revelation 1:17-18, Revelation 2:8, Revelation 2:18, John 17:5

In addition to the direct statements listed above, there are many other paired statements that make claims about Jesus Christ. These must be read together in order to recognize and identify correctly who Jesus is. Again, this list is not meant to be exhaustive, but I have listed several of them here to reveal more fully the reality of Jesus' identity. Do not rush past these without lingering and meditating on these passages in their context.

Psalm 23:1 "The LORD is my shepherd, I shall not want."	John 10:11 "I am the good shepherd; the good shepherd lays down His life for the sheep."
Isaiah 45:23 "I have sworn by Myself, The word has gone forth from My mouth in righteousness And will not turn back, That to Me every knee will bow, every tongue will swear allegiance."	Philippians 2:10-11 "so that at the name of Jesus EVERY KNEE WILL BOW, of those who are in heaven and on earth and under the earth, and that every tongue will confess that Jesus Christ is Lord, to the glory of God the Father."
Isaiah 44:6 "Thus says the LORD, the King of Israel and his Redeemer, the LORD of hosts: 'I am the first and I am the last, And there is no God besides Me.'"	Rev 1:17 "When I saw Him, I fell at His feet like a dead man And He placed His right hand on me, saying, 'Do not be afraid; I am the first and the last'"
Isaiah 48:12 "Listen to Me, O Jacob, even Israel whom I called; I am He, I am the first, I am also the last."	Rev 1:8 "'I am the Alpha and the Omega,' says the Lord God, 'who is and who was and who is to come, the Almighty.'"
Isaiah 43:11 "I, even I, am the LORD, And there is no savior besides Me."	Luke 2:11 "for today in the city of David there has been born for you a Savior, who is Christ the Lord."

Ultimately, John summed it up as follows in his Gospel in 20:30-31:

> [30] Therefore many other signs Jesus also performed in the presence of the disciples, which are not

> written in this book; [31]but these have been written
> so that you may believe that Jesus is the Christ, the
> Son of God; and that believing you may have life
> in His name.

The bottom line is that the Bible consistently and frequently points to Jesus as God's Son, while never referring to Jesus as a servant only. In fact, the Bible explicitly denotes this distinction in Hebrews 3:5-6:

> [5] Now Moses was faithful in all His house as a
> servant, for a testimony of those things which were
> to be spoken later; [6] but Christ was faithful as a
> Son over His house--

What the Bible says is clear, consistent, and unambiguous: Jesus is the Son of God.

Does Proving a Positive Prove a Negative?

The Bible asserts in a number of places that Jesus is both fully man and fully God (John 1:14, Romans 1:3-4, Colossians 2:9). Such a dual nature poses some intriguing dilemmas to be sure. While we know who Jesus is by the promise of His Spirit within us, we may not be able to explain exactly how it is that a man could be God, or how it is that God could be a man. Jesus is unique in history, and this uniqueness poses some interesting hypothetical questions. For example, how would one God with multiple aspects communicate with His other aspects? Particularly, how do the Father and Son interact when the Son is manifested in human form? Would He worship Himself or pray to Himself? How would this transpire? These are tricky questions indeed, but ones that may be asked.

Many Muslims will inquire about these hypothetical

questions in order to set a snare for the Christian but are generally unwilling to discuss them themselves. This is because for a Muslim even daring to imagine such a thing is too close to shirk, ascribing partners to God, which is the one unforgivable sin in Islam. Yet that will not stop them for barraging you with nettlesome questions about the dual nature of Christ. As we get further in the book, we will learn techniques to engage Muslims on these subjects in a productive way. For right now, the following information is provided as background material only, and not as fodder for debate.

A Muslim may tell you that since Jesus prays to God the Father, this proves that He cannot also be God. The assertion is that Jesus is merely a human and thus prays to God just as we do. Rather than speculate, what can we learn from examining one of Jesus' prayers with these questions in mind? Perhaps the best place to start is John 17. Just hours before His betrayal, we are given an extended account of Jesus' last plea for Himself, His disciples, and the world. It is true that Jesus prays to God the Father. When we read His prayer, though, we find that Jesus prays in ways that only God can. For example, in John 17:2 Jesus acknowledges that He has been given authority over all flesh. In John 17:5 He prays that He will be glorified together with God the Father. In John 17:11 Jesus mentions that He and God the Father are one. There are many other times throughout this prayer that Jesus implies equality with God. If Jesus were human only, these statements would be blasphemous. The point is that while Jesus has a human nature, which results in Him praying to God, He also has a God nature which results in Him praying in ways that only God is allowed to pray.

The larger point is that asserting Jesus' humanity in no way negates His divinity. Since this issue often arises, we must continue to analyze this from a more general perspective. A typical tactic used by Muslims is to focus on passages of the Bible that speak to the human aspect of Christ. Of course, we know Christ to be both fully human and fully God. Since Muslims do not understand this fusion of God and man, they often refer to various passages referring to the humanity of Christ in an attempt to disprove His deity. Muslims focus on Jesus' humanity; he was born (Matthew 1:25), he grew up (Luke 2:52), he experienced basic human needs such as hunger (Matthew 4:2), and felt emotion (John 11:35). The problem is that all this does is prove Christ was human, but it does not prove He was human *only*.

Of course, proving that Christ was human does just that, proves He was human. Such a proof says nothing about whether or not He was God. As has been stated, we know Jesus Christ is both human and God. The Muslim will go to great lengths to show that Jesus was human. By doing so, the conclusion is that He therefore cannot be God. However, such a conclusion is drawn from to an error in logic. If an object has two characteristics, proving the existence of one of them does not disprove the existence of the other. So we see proving the humanity of Jesus does not disprove His deity. To put it yet another way, being both human and God is not mutually exclusive. There is an old saying "you cannot have it both ways," but that saying has no relevance here. God can have it both ways and does have it both ways. If God wants to become human, certainly He has the power to do so.

This may seem odd and silly, but it is quite important. Many gospel tracts have led people down the "Romans Road," but the focus on Jesus' humanity can help lead people down the "Hebrews Road." If Jesus were not human, He could not have been tempted as we are (Hebrews 4:15). If Jesus had not been tempted as we are, how could He have overcome temptation to lead a sinless life? (Hebrews 7:26) If He had not overcome temptation to lead a sinless life, how could He have been the perfect sacrifice (Hebrews 9:14)? If He was not the perfect sacrifice, how could He have paid for our sins (Hebrews 10:11-12)? So being a human, simultaneously being God, of course, is a spiritual requirement for the whole redeeming work of Jesus Christ. The fact is so obvious we seldom explicitly say it. However, if a Muslim argues that Jesus was human, do not disagree. When the point is brought up, it is a mechanism by which to lead a Muslim to the rest of the story of Christ. In a strange way, the Muslim is ironically paving his own way for understanding the Hebrews road.

So when the topic of the humanity of Jesus comes up, remember these three points, and let the Holy Spirit guide you.

- Asking questions about the implications of Jesus being human are legitimate.
- Proving Jesus was human does not disprove His deity.
- Jesus was human as well as God in order to accomplish His redeeming work.

The Word of God speaks to this last point in Hebrews 2:14. For this verse, the New Living Translation is quoted:

> **14. Because God's children are human beings – made of flesh and blood – Jesus also became flesh and blood by being born in human form. For only as a human being could he die, and only by dying could he break the power of the Devil, who had the power of death.**

The following verses add even more clarity to this point. It was only being both human and God that allowed Jesus to form the redemptive bridge over the chasm of sin. Only by being human could Jesus tackle the specter of sin and conquer it, thus allowing Himself to be able to pay the price for us, a price that only the God-man could pay. In other words, not just any human could accomplish this; in fact, no mere human could, but only one who is both human and divine. The author of the book of Hebrews goes on to sum this up in chapter 2, verses 17-18:

> [17] Therefore, He had to be made like His brethren in all things, so that He might become a merciful and faithful high priest in things pertaining to God, to make propitiation for the sins of the people. [18] For since He Himself was tempted in that which He has suffered, He is able to come to the aid of those who are tempted.

It is hard to comprehend how Jesus could be both all man and all God at the same time. Sometimes an object has two seemingly different constituent parts at once. While no direct analogy to the God-man exists, consider light as an example. Over the past four centuries, physicists have tried to grasp whether light was a particle or a wave. Then, with the advent of quantum mechanics, we find it is simultaneously both a particle and a wave. Sometimes light behaves like a particle, and sometimes light acts as a wave. While physicists can mathematically describe this wave-particle duality, they do not entirely understand it. Light somehow has both wave and particle aspects rolled up together as its nature. Similarly, we can only describe how the "Light of the world" is both man and God simultaneously. Sometimes He acts like God, and sometimes He behaves like a sinless man. He has both natures wrapped up together in His earthly existence.

When confronted with the issue of Jesus being both man and God, a verse often quoted by Muslims is Numbers 23:19.

> [19] God is not a man, that He should lie, Nor a son of man, that He should repent; Has He said, and will He not do it? Or has He spoken, and will He not make it good?

The logic is the same. Of course, God is not merely a man. God is a Triune being of Father, Son, and Spirit. Even though God the Son exhibited characteristics of both God and man, God is qualitatively so much more than man. Jesus Christ the man possesses the fullness of God but simultaneously only represents one aspect of the Trinity. So don't get flustered. Use this as an opportunity to talk about the true God, the God who created the world, the God who spoke to Abraham, Isaac, and Jacob, the God who sent His own Son to die for us, and the God who speaks to us now through His Holy Spirit. No man or prophet could ever accomplish this otherwise impossible task. However, a being that is wholly God and wholly man does have such power and is the only way to bridge the gap between God and man. It is true that God is not a man; but rather God temporarily walked the earth as a man.

We find Jesus as the merger of both man and God throughout Scripture. For example, examine these two nearly adjacent verses, Matthew 1:16 and Matthew 1:18.

> [16] Jacob was the father of Joseph the husband of Mary, by whom Jesus was born, who is called the Messiah.

> [18] Now the birth of Jesus Christ was as follows: when His mother Mary had been betrothed to Joseph, before they came together she was found to be with child by the Holy Spirit.

In verse 16, Jesus is identified as the son of Mary. In verse 18, Jesus is identified as the Son of God by the Holy Spirit. Muslims will see these two passages as contradictory because their belief system tells them someone cannot be both God and man. Therefore, Muslims will quote Scriptures such as these as proof of Biblical contradiction. In their minds, they genuinely do see these passages as inconsistent, because they start with the assumption that the reality of the incarnation is impossible. Therefore, they read passages such as these and they conclude that there is a contradiction. In reality, it is precisely such dual passages that correspondingly point to the dual nature of Jesus Christ. Perhaps no such passage is more evident than that of Isaiah 9:6.

> **⁶ For a child will be born to us, a son will be given to us;**
> **And the government will rest on His shoulders;**
> **And His name will be called Wonderful Counselor, Mighty God,**
> **Eternal Father, Prince of Peace.**

Notice that the child is born, but the son is given. The human aspect is a child and is born, but the God aspect is given as a gift by God Himself. Jesus is both man and God, and this fact is one of the central issues of Christianity. Therefore, we would expect God to inform us of this two-fold nature of Christ in a clear and repeated fashion. Throughout the Bible, reason insists that we find various passages indicating both Jesus' humanity and His deity. If we saw confirmation of only one and not the other, we would have reason to be suspicious. If only one of His natures were shown, the dual nature of His existence would be in question. Ironically, by pointing out this seeming contradiction, the Muslim actually solidifies the position of who Jesus Christ claimed to be. The Biblical citations the Muslims give in an attempt to disprove the deity of Jesus can serve as a launching pad to understanding the truth of His dual nature.

This is the first example what I term an Islamic *inversion*. This book will continue to return to this theme, as it is the pattern of Islamic thought that is being exposed. An inversion is the twisting of a truth inside out and proclaiming it a lie, or contorting and disguising a lie just enough to call it the truth. It is similar to when a person looks into a circus mirror and sees an image that resembles himself, but the reflection is a disfiguration of reality. Citing passages regarding Jesus' humanity and passages about His deity and declaring them contradictory is an example of this. Such a tactic starts with a flawed assumption. If the flawed assumption is that Jesus cannot be both man and God, then proving He is man denies He is God. In the Muslim mind, he has just proven to himself the very assumption he began with. If Jesus is both man and God, the very verses quoted to discredit the gospel only serve to reinforce it. It is ironic yet encouraging that in the very attempt to undermine Christianity, the Muslim unknowingly proclaims the redeeming work of Christ.

This inability to accept an all-man all-God being is so prevalent that we must linger for a bit. Since this is such a stumbling block, this same argument appears in diverse forms. Often Muslims rebel at the more mundane aspects of human life being experienced by God. For example, one Muslim I spoke to voiced this all too common sentiment:

> It seems the Muslim ALL Powerful God is just too much to bear. A Christian needs someone to be just as pitiful as they are so he or she can relate. You Christians seem to like to see your god bleed, beg, urinate, defecate, and to be found lacking in power and knowledge.

Here again, the Muslims have it totally inverted. In order to see this more clearly, turn toward the perspective of Christ, not the Christian. It is not about what we want God to be so that we can relate to Him. It is about what God chose to be so that He could relate to us. He chose to constrain Himself to human form so as to provide an avenue of salvation for us. What we want is irrelevant. Notice how subtle these misapplications are. When we divorce Jesus' humanity from His divinity, His humanity gets contorted completely out of shape. Jesus endured suffering to reach us, not so that we could reach Him.

This particular angle of assaulting the biological aspects of

Jesus' humanity is employed quite frequently, so let's continue looking into the more lowbrow aspects of Jesus' daily life. As a rule, Muslims are quick to point out the dishonor of God enduring normal human bodily functions. When you think of it, being a bit disgusted is an understandable reaction. As a Christian, we do not like to ponder such matters. I have never heard a sermon on whether Jesus wet the bed as a child or what Mary thought as she changed His soiled clothes as a baby. I doubt I ever will. Such sophomoric topics are not the point. The point is to consider what Jesus did for us, and it should humble us. Yes, these ignominious aspects of Jesus' life are repugnant, yet they point back to what Christ did for us during His incarnation. It is these undesirable aspects of humanity that only add to helping us understand the sacrifice He made for us. He left the glories of heaven to come to a smelly, dusty, and sweaty world. He chose hunger, discomfort, pain, and ultimately the cross.

Another way to think of this is that Jesus had absolute power, but never used it for His own gain. That is the definition of meekness, and that is our lesson. To lead a sinless life, Jesus never chose to use His divine power for His own comfort or gain at any opportunity, including those profound times when he calmed the storm and those not-so-profound times when He may have been suffering from the common cold. Again, if Jesus were human only, discussing bodily functions is both disgusting and irrelevant. However, that God Himself endured our lives from beginning to end without ever intervening on His own behalf is the story of genuine beauty. It is the story of divine love that humbles us and causes us to love Him all the more.

So what is our response when Muslims like to pounce on the fact that Jesus was human? There is certainly no reason to argue the point. Jesus was indeed human. The important point though is that this is only half the story. Jesus was both God and man. Talking about His humanity while simultaneously stripping Him of His divinity will lead to all sorts of erroneous conclusions.

However, contemplating His humanity in light of His divinity points to the gospel in all sorts of ways. So when Muslims want to talk about Jesus' humanity, instead of pushing back, consider how to redirect the conversation to the truth of what it means for God to take human form.

The humanity of Jesus is one major angle of misunderstanding and attack by Muslims. The second is the Trinity. Thus, we move on to our second area of theological discourse required for successfully engaging Muslims, the Trinity.

Chapter 4

The Tri-Unity of God

Muslims are quick to point out that the Trinity was not officially adopted as a Christian doctrine until the fourth century. It is true that the church officially voted at the Council of Nicaea to clarify doctrinal positions. However, the Muslim view reverses cause and effect. The Council of Nicaea did not cause the Trinity to be standard Christian doctrine; the standard and well-accepted doctrine of the Trinity resulted in the effect of the Council codifying it in order to avoid later confusion.

Nevertheless, understanding the Triune nature of God is not something that can be appraised without the Spirit. Even with the Spirit, comprehending the divine nature of God is not easy, as Christians have wrestled with the implications for 2,000 years. Nonetheless, while our Muslim friends will likely not be able to digest these truths, we must be clear on them when the time is right. Therefore, we will look at Scripture relating to God's three-in-one nature. Again, this is not to present an ironclad proof, which is impossible, but rather so that we can be confident in what we know to be true. In this way, we can share accurately with Muslims when the Holy Spirit is at work.

The Life of Christ

Muslims are quick to point out that the word Trinity is not mentioned in Scripture. It is true that the term was coined later after the Biblical record was finished. This word came into existence because the Triune nature of God is constantly mentioned throughout Scripture. The term was created to give a name to what the Scripture described. To see this fully, we will quickly glance at a few points in the life of Christ, His conception, His baptism, and the Great Commission.

Here is a verse quoted often relating to the conception of Christ from Luke 1:35.

> [35] The angel answered and said to her, "The <u>Holy Spirit</u> will come upon you, and the power of the <u>Most High</u> will overshadow you; and for that reason the holy Child shall be called the <u>Son of God</u>."

This verse referencing the birth of Christ has all three aspects of God coming into play simultaneously. Both the Holy Spirit and the power of the Most High, the Father, are mentioned at this critical juncture in human history. All three aspects of God are acknowledged at this time in history when the human manifestation of God the Son is being conceived.

All three aspects come into play again at His baptism when Jesus starts His ministry. From Matthew 3:16-17:

> [16] After being baptized, Jesus came up immediately from the water; and behold, the heavens were opened, and he saw the Spirit of God descending as a dove and lighting on Him, [17] and behold, a voice out of the heavens said, "This is My beloved Son, in whom I am well-pleased."

Here again, we see God the Father declaring His Tri-Unity as Jesus' ministry is endorsed. All three aspects of God are operating simultaneously. Here is yet another well-known verse recounting Jesus' words just before His ascension. From Matthew 28:19:

> [19] Go therefore and make disciples of all the nations, baptizing them in the name of the <u>Father</u> and the <u>Son</u> and the <u>Holy Spirit</u>,

This verse is such an obvious reference to the Trinity, and we have read it dozens if not hundreds of times. Nevertheless, most people may have missed something ever so subtle and yet so profound. Three names are mentioned, Father, Son, and Holy Spirit, yet we are supposed to baptize in the name of these three! We are not to baptize in the names of these three, but we are instructed to baptize in the name, singular number, of these three. Technically, this sentence is grammatically incorrect if it were not for the fact that Father, Son, and Holy Spirit are indeed one, and therefore we are to baptize in that one name.

The typical Muslim response to this will be to claim that Matthew 28:19 is a deviation from normal Scripture, and then wander off to some Scripture like Acts 2:38, insisting that in that verse baptism should only be performed in the name of Jesus. However, such an analysis overlooks the obvious to the extent that it is embarrassing. Look at the verse itself, Acts 2:38:

> [38] Peter said to them, "Repent, and each of you be baptized in the name of <u>Jesus Christ</u> for the forgiveness of your sins; and you will receive the gift of the <u>Holy Spirit</u>. [39]For the promise is for you and your children and for all who are far off, as many as the <u>Lord our God</u> will call to Himself."

Here in Acts 2:38-39 we see the call for baptism in the name of Jesus, who has the right to forgive sins, a right that only God has. Next, the gift of the Holy Spirit will be given as a promise to those whom God the Father has called. Again, we see the triune nature of God unfolded in these verses, even though some Muslims would attempt to use it as a refutation. Operationally, all three aspects of the Trinity are in action here. It is uncanny how frequently the verses Muslims use to refute the Triune nature of God only reinforce that view when examined carefully. Since God has purposefully created Scripture with these myriad verses of corroboration, the opportunity to discuss Scripture in more detail often presents itself. Watch for these opportunities. God has created His word in such a way that the assaults by Muslims backfire when scrutinized.

This brings us to our next section; how does each New Testament author view the three-fold nature of God.

Testimony of New Testament Authors

One attack Muslims constantly hurl at Christians is that Paul fabricated the Trinity in his writings. They do so because it is what they are taught. Many Muslims will be quick to point out that the word Trinity never appears in the New Testament, thus proving its non-existence. Such errant logic would deny the existence of cellular phones and airplanes as well, since they are not explicitly mentioned in the New Testament either.* However, responding in such a manner is both rude and ineffectual.

Therefore, to better understand how to reply to such unsubstantial assaults, we can investigate whether all New Testament authors are in agreement. The question is whether Paul preached a gospel different than that of the other authors. We

---

* The Arabic word "tawhid," which means the oneness of Allah, doesn't appear in the Qur'an either. However, Muslims don't have difficulty digesting this fact. Nevertheless, arguing down this road should not be done lightly, nor with intent to debate, as it tends only to foment hard feelings.

should expect to see agreement between all gospel narratives and epistles. What do Peter, John, James, Jude, the author of Hebrews, Matthew, Luke, and Mark have to say regarding the Trinity when compared to the writings of Paul? Starting with Peter, notice what he has to say about the nature of God. From the beginning of the first of his letters, Peter makes the nature of God clear. He greets those who are chosen by God, while informing them of the process by which they were chosen. From 1 Peter 1:2:

> [2] **according to the foreknowledge of God the Father, by the sanctifying work of the Spirit, to obey Jesus Christ and be sprinkled with His blood: May grace and peace be yours in the fullest measure.**

We are chosen according to the foreknowledge of God the Father. At the same time, it is the Spirit that does the sanctification, which only God can do. The verse also makes reference to the shed blood of Jesus, which was required for forgiveness of sins, which only God can do. This three pronged process points directly to the Trinity. Peter's view of Jesus was not a view fabricated out of hearsay, but rather it came from extended and direct contact with Jesus. Here is how Peter describes his doctrine from 2 Peter 1:16.

> [16] **For we did not follow cleverly devised tales when we made known to you the power and coming of our Lord Jesus Christ, but we were eyewitnesses of His majesty.**

There is no debate about what Peter thought or why he thought it. He believed in one God: Father, Son, and Spirit. He was a direct eyewitness, and as such, his statements come from personal observation and interaction.

The next author we will examine authored one of the Gospels

as well as several epistles. John was in Jesus' inner circle, so it is paramount that his view of Jesus aligns with the other disciples. John tells us that God's commandment to us is that we believe in the name of Jesus Christ, the Son of God. Yet how do we know if we have believed? We know this by the testimony of the Spirit that lives within us. John gives us yet another picture of the threefold nature of God working in unison. From 1 John 3:23-24:

> 23 This is His commandment, that we believe in the name of His Son Jesus Christ, and love one another, just as He commanded us. 24 The one who keeps His commandments abides in Him, and He in him. We know by this that He abides in us, by the Spirit whom He has given us.

As one of the inner circle, John's theological analysis would be quite suspect had it not lined up with every other New Testament author. It is crucial that all New Testament authors be in agreement, and we see this to be the case for John and Peter. John believed in one God; Father, Son, and Spirit. Of course, the references by John are many, so space requires that we move on to our next New Testament author.

James was the most practical of the New Testament authors. The entire book of James is about doing the Word and not just hearing the Word. Yet even he starts his book with a clear opening as to exactly who Jesus is. From James 1:1:

> 1 James, a bond-servant of God and of the Lord Jesus Christ, To the twelve tribes who are dispersed abroad: Greetings.

James makes it plain right from the beginning whom he serves, God and the Lord Jesus Christ. He later references the Spirit which now lives within us (James 4:5). James also makes it clear that these are not separate gods in 2:19 when he says "God is One." While James' reference to the Trinity is more implied than explicit when compared to other authors, it is more due to the nature of James' topic than from anything else. Yet within this short and pragmatic epistle, James states that God is one, but he also mentions how he serves both God and the Lord Jesus Christ, and he knows this by the Spirit. Additionally, nothing in the book of James gives any indication that his opinion of the three-fold nature of God in any way differs from that of the other New Testament authors. In other words, James offers no counterexample of God's nature that contradicts His triune nature.

Even Jude, the least prolific author of the New Testament, makes sure to reference the Trinity. Jude only had one chapter to write, but he made sure to explain the triune nature of God in his short epistle. While reading this verse, remember that only God is worthy of prayer, and only God can ultimately show the divine mercy of eternal life. Yet Jude tells us to pray in the Spirit and to look to the mercy of Jesus Christ for eternal life. Jude 20-21:

> [20]But you, beloved, building yourselves up on your most holy faith, praying in the Holy Spirit, [21]keep yourselves in the love of God, waiting anxiously for the mercy of our Lord Jesus Christ to eternal life.

This brings us to the author of Hebrews. Here references to the Trinity are not as succinct as others are in the New Testament. While they are more spread out, they are also more frequent. Specifically, the author of Hebrews spends the entire first chapter asserting the deity of Christ. One such excerpt describing Jesus as the Son of God is found in Hebrews 1:2:

> [3]And He is the radiance of His glory and the exact representation of His nature, and upholds all things by the word of His power When He had

57

> made purification of sins, He sat down at the right
> hand of the Majesty on high,

The expression "exact representation of His nature" is tough to misinterpret. Any attribute of God is also present in the Son (John 5:18). After spending much time elaborating on this passage, the author of Hebrews makes it clear that the Spirit is also an eternal being, without beginning or end. From Hebrews 9:14:

> [14] how much more will the blood of Christ, who through the eternal Spirit offered Himself without blemish to God, cleanse your conscience from dead works to serve the living God?

So we see Jesus is given the exact representation of God, and the Spirit is also cited as having the attribute of eternality, which only God has.

Since every epistle writer makes sure to mention the Trinity, we would expect and demand that the Gospel writers agree. Earlier in the chapter, we already mentioned passages from the life of Christ, and therefore there will be some overlap here. We have seen where Luke puts forth the idea of the Trinity (Luke 1:35 and Acts 2:38-39). We have also already examined two clear cases where Matthew describes the Trinity (Matthew 3:16-17 and 28:19). This only leaves Mark, the author of the shortest Gospel.

To make sure he gets his point across, Mark starts his account this way, chapter one, verse one.

> [1]The beginning of the gospel of Jesus Christ, the
> Son of God.

This leaves no room for doubt as to Mark's view of Jesus. Even still, Mark offers this interesting theological question posed by Jesus Himself. From Mark 12:35-36:

> ³⁵ And Jesus began to say, as He taught in the temple, "How is it that the scribes say that the Christ is the son of David?
>
> ³⁶ "David himself said in the Holy Spirit,
> THE LORD SAID TO MY LORD,
> "SIT AT MY RIGHT HAND,
> UNTIL I PUT YOUR ENEMIES BENEATH
> YOUR FEET."

Here we see David was speaking in the Holy Spirit, confirming the role of the eternal Spirit as the means of Biblical authorship. Additionally, we see David referencing the foreshadowed Messiah, his Lord, and that this Messiah would sit at the right hand of God. Just to be clear, Jesus interprets His own words in case there is any confusion about what He meant. Mark 12:37:

> ³⁷ "David himself calls Him 'Lord'; so in what sense is He his son?"

Jesus confirms that He, the Messiah, existed before David.

Finally, we come full circle and arrive back at Paul. Muslims make a hobby of lambasting Paul for changing the gospel. Therefore, we need to ask if Paul changed the gospel, or if he said all the same things as the other gospel and epistle writers said. So let's verify that Paul's assessment of the nature of God is in harmony with other New Testament authors. From Ephesians 2:18:

> ¹⁸ for through Him we both have our access in one Spirit to the Father.

And from Romans 8:9-10:

> [9] However, you are not in the flesh but in the Spirit,
> if indeed the Spirit of God dwells in you. But if
> anyone does not have the Spirit of Christ, he does
> not belong to Him. [10] If Christ is in you, though the
> body is dead because of sin, yet the spirit is alive
> because of righteousness.

This passage merits dissection. First, Paul introduces the concept of the Spirit of God. Then he notes that the Spirit of God dwells in us. He refers to the Spirit of Christ as if it were the same as the Spirit of God, making Christ equal to God. He declares that if we do not have the Spirit, we do not belong to Christ, whose Spirit should be in us. Finally, he says that it is Christ Himself that should be in us, equating Christ with the Spirit.

It should not be surprising to us that Paul falls into line with the rest of the New Testament authors regarding the nature of God, His Oneness, and how that Oneness manifests itself in three different ways. Had Paul neglected to describe God's nature in this way, we would have cause to be concerned. The irony is that Muslims insist Paul's language is a deviation from other Biblical authors, yet the reality is that it lines up perfectly. Had Paul not discussed the Trinity, we would be surprised, because every other New Testament author does. Such an absence would have caused us to wonder why Paul was giving a different account of God's nature. As it is, we stand confident from the full agreement by all New Testament authors.

The careful reader of the Bible will also take note of many references to the Trinity that are not initially obvious. Here is a prime example from 1 Thessalonians 5:23:

> [23] Now may the God of peace Himself sanctify you
> entirely; and may your spirit and soul and body be
> preserved complete, without blame at the coming
> of our Lord Jesus Christ.

Here we see that humans are beings with a triune nature. We have body, spirit, and soul, yet we are only one being. God also tells us that He created man in His image. What exactly does that mean when considered in light of the previously cited passages? If man has a triune nature and is created in the image of God, according to His likeness, (Genesis 1:26) what would our conclusion be? Be on the alert, because the references to the three in one nature of God are pervasive.

Time and time again Muslims will claim that the Bible denies this triune nature of God, or they will argue that only Paul asserts its existence. Oddly enough, if a Muslim would truthfully consider Scripture, the consistent and recurrent message is unmistakable. The Trinity is laid out at the critical times in the life of Jesus the Christ. Every New Testament author references and corroborates the triune nature of God. Perhaps more surprisingly, even the Old Testament foreshadows the triune nature of God.

The Trinity in the Old Testament

Even though the Trinity was more fully revealed in the New Testament, the Old Testament strongly hinted at God's true nature. To see this point more clearly, look at the doctrine of the Trinity as taught in the Old Testament. A full rendition of such teaching is beyond the scope of this book. However, we will take a brief look so that the concept is not completely foreign. The Trinity is revealed both in the way God refers to Himself, as well as within the Hebrew language itself.

Various Old Testament passages make reference to God's Son. For example, examine the following two passages. First, Proverbs 30:4:

> [4] Who has ascended into heaven and descended?
> Who has gathered the wind in His fists?
> Who has wrapped the waters in His garment?

> Who has established all the ends of the earth?
> What is His name or His son's name?
> Surely you know!

This next passage from Psalm 2 is pieced together for the sake of brevity. The entire Psalm is one that is easy and useful to memorize. Psalm 2:7,11-12:

> [7] "I will surely tell of the decree of the LORD:
> He said to Me, 'You are My Son,
> Today I have begotten You.
> [11] Worship the LORD with reverence
> And rejoice with trembling.
> [12] Do homage to the Son, that He not
> become angry, and you perish in the way,

Other passages such as Isaiah 48:16 reveal the surprising type of oneness that God possesses.

> [16] "Come near to Me, listen to this:
> From the first I have not spoken in secret,
> From the time it took place, I was there
> And now the Lord GOD has sent Me, and His Spirit."

Notice here that God is doing the speaking, yet the Lord GOD has sent both God and His Spirit. It is unmistakable. Scripture also makes many references to the Spirit of God, and the effect He has on men. Without going too far in depth, these passages are frequent throughout the Old Testament. A partial list is Numbers 11:17, Numbers 24:2, Judges 3:10, Judges 6:34, Judges 11:29, Judges 14:6, 1 Samuel 10:6, 1 Samuel 16:13, and 2 Samuel 23:2.

If all this were not enough, even the language itself makes some claims about God's makeup. When God refers to Himself,

He often does so in the plural (Genesis 1:26, 3:22, 11:7, Isaiah 6:8). One might argue the use of the plural pronoun is akin to the royal "we," but a close inspection of the verses shows the folly of such thinking. For example, Gen 3:22 uses the language "one of Us," which goes far beyond such historical-grammatical usage. Yet it does not stop there.

As we have discussed, Muslims are quick to point out that God refers to Himself as being one being. Indeed He is. Nevertheless, the issue is what kind of oneness. As a matter of fact, the Hebrew language itself gives us some clues as to the type of oneness that God possesses. The language of the Old Testament speaks to God's true nature within the context of oneness. To understand, we must take a short Hebrew lesson.

In Hebrew, multiple words translate to the English word one. The first is transliterated *echad*, which can mean the number one, the word each, or a unified one. It is this usage we will examine closely. The second is *yachiyd*, which means a solitary one, or a unique one. Again, I must emphasize this type of material does not win over Muslims, but it is provided for better understanding of who God is.

Bear in mind that often, echad does mean one in number, just as we would say one rock, one banana, or one flower. Yet, sometimes its meaning is not so numerically isolated. In the following Scripture, the translation of the Hebrews word echad is italicized for emphasis.

Genesis 2:24:

> 24 For this cause a man shall leave his father and his mother, and shall cleave to his wife; and they shall become *one* flesh.

Genesis 11:6:

> [6] And the Lord said, "Behold, they are *one* people, and they all have the *same* language. And this is what they began to do, and now nothing which they purpose to do will be impossible for them."

Exodus 24:3:

> [3] Then Moses came and recounted to the people all the words of the Lord and all the ordinances; and all the people answered with *one* voice, and said, "All the words which the Lord has spoken we will do!"

Ezekiel 11:19:

> [19] "And I shall give them *one* heart, and shall put a new spirit within them. And I shall take the heart of stone out of their flesh and give them a heart of flesh,"

Surely even the most literal Bible interpreters do not believe that in Exodus 24:3, the term "one voice" means that a million people all answered, but only one pair of vocal cords were vibrating. Nor would a literalist say that only one frequency, amplitude, and tone of voice were heard. Clearly here the word one refers to a unity of purpose of speech. There was a multiplicity within unity. All of the people's reaction was fused so that they spoke in a coherent and united fashion.

Other passages that illustrate this usage are Genesis 34:16 and Exodus 26:6. Now it is this same word, echad that is used in the most critical passage discussing God, and one often quoted by Muslims.

From Deuteronomy 6:4:

> [4] **Hear, O Israel! The LORD is our God, the LORD is *one*!**

Just what kind of oneness is being attributed to God in this passage? Does it suggest that God is one in the way Muslims believe, an absolute oneness that denies His ability to exist within His own creation? Alternatively, does the verse suggest that God's oneness allows for multiplicity within unity, that He operates in a unified way with multiple aspects? God could have easily chosen a more precise word, yachiyd, to signify absolute oneness, but He does not. Rather, He chooses echad, a word that can signify oneness of purpose and execution. It is clear that God specifically leaves the door open in this verse to later reveal Himself as a type of unified one.

At this point, we have a better grasp on how God describes Himself. Still, while many Muslims are not legitimately looking to understand God's triune nature, a seriously seeking Muslim may ask for a description of the Trinity. Just how would someone go about explaining the Trinity in common language?

Geometric Analogy

There are various analogies of the Trinity. Some of them are better than others. One is comparing the Trinity to H_2O, which can exist as ice, water, and steam. Another is to look at a man who may be a father, an employer, and a husband. He is still only one person even though he has three roles. Another common analogy is the sun, which gives off both heat and light. While these analogies are simple and contain some truth, Dr. Nathan Wood presents an amazing analogy in his work, *Secrets of the Universe*. He refers to the analogy as geometric, since it is an analogy that is particularly accurate and compelling, as a geometric similarity would be. Dr. Wood begins with the premise than any master architect will reflect his personality in his creations. Therefore, we would expect God, the master architect, to do the same. We would expect to see fingerprints of a triune nature in the universe itself. We must examine the universe and its construction to see what it might reveal about its architect. Drawing on Dr. Wood's work, Dr. D. James Kennedy expounded on the analogy:

> Universe comes from the Latin words, Uni and verteri--
> To turn into one! That all things with their manifold
> differences turn and form one single Universe. And we
> will find, if we examine this Universe, that it consists
> as any scientist will tell you, of space, time and matter.
> Those three, no more. Furthermore, it is not possible
> in this Universe which we know, to have any two of
> those without the other. This Universe always exists of
> space, time, and matter. This Universe cannot exist as
> we know it in any other way, but with all three of them.
> Take away any one of them and you have no Universe.[9]

Notice that space is not one-third of the universe, but rather it permeates all of it. Neither is time one-third of the universe. It is intrinsic to all of it. So too matter is the whole universe. This one universe is made up of all three, yet each one is the whole. Space and matter have no meaning outside of time, and neither would matter or time have any meaning without space to exist in. Space and time could not make a universe without matter to fill it. In other words, without space, where would we put it? Without matter, what would we put in it? Without time, when would we put it? All three comprise the universe and are requirements of it, and fill the whole universe, yet all three make up the one and only one universe that we live in.

Dr. Wood goes on to note that this Triune nature of the universe is then reflected in each part. Matter can be solid, liquid, or gas. Space has three dimensions, yet a volume cannot exist without height, width, and depth. Without any of the three, only a 2-dimensional surface of zero volume would remain. Time has past, present, and future. In essence, the universe consists of a trinity of trinities.

This is an outstanding analogy of the Trinity. He is all one God. Yet God has three aspects. The nature of God is to exist in all three aspects at once, yet each aspect is the whole. Removing one aspect changes who God is unmistakably and permanently. Neither is any aspect one-third of God, but each part is whole.

I hope this analogy more clearly illustrates the nature of the triune God. Without a firm understanding of His nature, engaging in conversation with someone who will attack this very nature puts you in a perilous position. Of course, we do not need a seminary level understanding of God's nature for the Holy Spirit to move and work through us at any time. Nevertheless, we should love the Lord our God with all our heart, with all our soul, and with all our *mind*. We should be as well-informed as reasonably possible in order to be ready to stand firm in our belief that God is one. We know that understanding the Trinity will be an obstacle for many Muslims. So in the rare case that a Muslim honestly wants to understand the Trinity, the Christian should know how to explain it.

It seems an inordinate amount of time has been spent in preparation. Yet there is still more. We next move into understanding why Islam has such an inverted pattern of spiritual appraisals and the overarching principles for recognizing it.

Section 3

Preparing Our Strength for the Islamic Inversion

Put on the full armor of God, so that you will be able to stand firm against the schemes of the devil. For our struggle is not against flesh and blood, but against the rulers, against the powers, against the world forces of this darkness, against the spiritual forces of wickedness in the heavenly places.

EPHESIANS 6:11-12

Chapter 5

What Is the Islamic Inversion?

Islamic arguments vary from the utterly ridiculous to quite cunning. Through it all, one item remains the same: Islamic thought is typically an inversion of Christian thought. An inversion is a distinct spiritual truth that has somehow been turned on its head. It is a pattern of thought that expresses an entirely backward method of looking at God or living one's life. An inversion can be uncovered by examining Jesus from the wrong perspective, by applying an improper cultural filter, or by comparing principles from the Qur'an to those from the Bible.

It is difficult to grasp this concept of the Islamic Inversion that has been alluded to. As with any abstract concept, it is much easier to understand the abstract by looking at concrete examples. For instance, nobody can define the word four without using other numbers. The only real way to understand "fourness" is to extend your stretched-out hand without the thumb, view a square, or drop enough quarters on the floor to make one dollar. At such a point, a person can understand what four is, even though it was never actually defined. In the same way, the best way to define the Islamic inversion is to give some examples and view the pattern. But first, the question comes into play as to why these inversions exist in the first place.

71

Why Inversions Exist

Here we come to the meat of understanding the concept of an inversion. Before launching into countless examples of these, it bears noting why they exist. Why does Islam contain so many tenets that at first glance look real enough, but upon close inspection show up as fraudulent copies of the Truth that God has given us?

To better understand why inversions are so pervasive within Islam, consider the art of counterfeiting. If we were criminals and wanted to start our own counterfeiting business, how would we proceed? What we would not do is take paper and crayon and let a young child draw $100 bills for us. When we started passing them, they would instantly be seen as fake. Everybody easily recognizes Monopoly[a] money for what it is. To come up with a good counterfeit bill, we must accomplish several goals. We must make the money look and feel as if it were the real thing. It must have proper coloring, weight, feel, and texture. We must disguise and obfuscate the lie by making it appear true. The bill must adhere to the parameters of official issue currency. This is required to conceal the subtle but crucial flaws, which expose the fake for what it is.

I know of a bank teller who once took a counterfeit bill. She did so because at first glance the bill looked real enough. It was only later, when she examined it in more detail, that the flaws became apparent. Similarly, many people accept counterfeit religion because it looks legitimate at first glance. To pass a counterfeit, it must look more than plausible on the surface. Of course, under scrutiny, the lie will be exposed. However, if a lie can be masked well enough, it can pass for some time before being revealed.

It is exactly this scenario that presents itself when we deal with Islam. Any counterfeit religion must look genuine on the surface to gain adherents. If it were not so, it would instantly and easily be recognized as fraudulent. It must be able to pass for truth under nominal scrutiny. Thus, we find ourselves with Islam, the counterfeit religion. Its members portray the virtuous points of Islam to bolster their case. Indeed, many tenets of Islam are honorable. Muslims pray, have a system for distributing money to the poor, and follow a code with mostly reasonable duties. At first glance, it appears that its members worship God. Without the initial plausibility of seeming correct, it would never be an effective method of leading people astray. Those with a shallow understanding of Islamic teaching easily pass it along even though it is counterfeit.

This concept was put succinctly by a character in a science fiction story, Star Trek. In one of the episodes, a main character, Captain John Luc Picard, had exposed a traitor who originally seemed to have everyone's best interests at heart. Later, after the malicious intent of the antagonist was revealed, he said, "Villains who twirl their mustaches are easy to spot. Those who clothe themselves in good deeds are well camouflaged." Evil masquerading as good is not a new or original idea. God warns us about this in 2 Corinthians 11:14:

> [14] No wonder, for even Satan disguises himself as an angel of light.

To understand what this means, consider Satan's strategy in the Garden of Eden. We find ourselves in Genesis 3, where Satan is trying to trick Eve into taking a bite of the forbidden fruit. Examine Satan's words carefully here from Genesis 3:5:

> [5] "For God knows that in the day you eat from it your eyes will be opened, and you will be like God, knowing good and evil."

Is this statement true or false? Consider carefully. This statement, uttered by Satan and used to deceive man into the fall, is absolutely true! God knew that if they ate that fruit, their eyes would be opened, and indeed they were (Genesis 3:7). They were also like God, in that now they had knowledge of good and evil. The statement above is 100 percent correct. So why did Satan uttering truth cause the fall of man?

Satan left out some vital information. What he neglected to mention were the immediate and long-term consequences. In verse 4 Satan lies in that he tells Eve that she "surely will not die." That lie was encapsulated within a larger and more tantalizing truth. Satan hid the terrible truth of undesirable results behind a statement that at first glance looked quite reasonable, because on the surface it was.

Satan asks "Indeed, has God said" (Genesis 3:1) and thus undermines the authenticity of God's Word. Likewise, many discussions with Muslims revolve around what God has said. Christians quote from the Bible while Muslims quote from the Qur'an. Eventually, we must determine what God has spoken, and what is a deceptive attempt to sabotage God's communication to mankind.

As we move ahead to reveal how Islam inverts the reality of the gospel, remember that this should not surprise us. Any cleverly counterfeited religion will require effort to expose.

Recognizing Satan's Tactics

Now that we are on the lookout for counterfeit religion, it is time to more closely examine how the master counterfeiter himself operates. We have a record of a conversation between him and Jesus, and pastors have given numerous sermons reflecting on this temptation of Jesus by Satan while in the wilderness. There are many profound truths to learn from this passage. They include how to use Scripture to fend off the enemy, how Jesus was tempted and what significance that temptation has, and how each temptation falls into common categories of temptation we all face. However, focus instead on an aspect of this dialogue often overlooked -- Satan's tactics. Just how did Satan attempt to twist things to suit his own purposes?

In brief, the three tactics he uses are attacks on Jesus' deity, the omission of context, and ends justifying the means. These methods of attack sound very familiar as we recall the general assaults on the gospel by Muslim apologists. To elaborate on these three tactics, look at Matthew 4, where the first question posed by Satan offers an interesting dilemma. Matthew 4:3:

> **³ And the tempter came and said to Him, "If You are the Son of God, command that these stones become bread."**

The Greek word *ei*, translated as "if," can also be translated as "since," but doing so doesn't change the cleverness of this tactic. Satan does not just suggest that Jesus turns the stones into bread. Asking such a straightforward question does not achieve his goal; it is not nearly malicious enough. Rather, he puts a dependent clause in front of the statement in order to offer a catch-22. Satan knows that if Jesus turns the stones into bread, He commits a sin by attending to His own physical needs rather than obeying the will of God. When Jesus does not turn the stones to bread, the implication is that the initial "if" or "since" clause must be false. Satan twists the circumstances to conceal Jesus' true nature.

In other words, by framing the question in this way, Satan allows the unsuspecting reader to assume that Jesus is not the Son of God. The faulty reasoning proceeds that if Jesus were the Son of God, then He would immediately demonstrate His power, proving once and for all who He is. The correct choice by Jesus of not acting leaves the unsuspecting reader mistakenly wondering why Jesus did not just exercise His power to prove His identity. The flawed argument hinges on not realizing that Satan already knows who Jesus is. Satan is not wondering whether or not Jesus is the Son of God. Satan is not providing this test to once and for all prove it to himself, as he already knows Jesus' identity. Therefore, the uneducated reader inappropriately views Jesus' decision as a denial of deity rather than a confirmation of His sinless nature. In this way, Satan supplies an outlet of doubt for those who seek it.

It is equally important to notice what Satan does not say as it is to notice what he does say. Why doesn't Satan say, "If you are the Messiah, turn these stones to bread"? Why doesn't Satan say, "If you can perform miracles, turn these stones to bread"? Why doesn't Satan say, "If you are born of a virgin, turn these stones to bread"? Satan could have attacked Jesus on any of these points, and chose not to. Satan's strategy is not to disprove that Jesus was the Messiah, that He could perform miracles, or that He was born of a virgin. Satan's ultimate goal is to cast doubt on His identity as the Son of God. Satan squarely directed his assaults on hiding the deity of Jesus, and that should instruct us as to what is of prime importance.

Satan's tactics continue. Matthew 4:5-6:

> **5 Then the devil took Him into the holy city and had Him stand on the pinnacle of the temple, 6 and said to Him, "If You are the Son of God, throw Yourself down; for it is written, 'HE WILL COMMAND HIS ANGELS CONCERNING YOU'; and 'ON their HANDS THEY WILL BEAR YOU UP, SO THAT YOU WILL NOT STRIKE YOUR FOOT AGAINST A STONE.'"**

In this passage, the devil quotes Scripture, but in a way that omits some important information. Just as before, he does not simply suggest that Jesus jump. Rather, Satan embeds his suggestion into another "if" clause as well as quoting a piece of Scripture from Psalm 91 out of context. However, he specifically leaves out the conditions under which the quoted statement is true. Satan ignores the context of the promise in order to drastically misrepresent God's Word. To see the deception, examine Psalm 91:1-2:

> [1] He who dwells in the shelter of the Most High
> Will abide in the shadow of the Almighty.
> [2] I will say to the LORD, "My refuge and my fortress,
> My God, in whom I trust!"

God gives His protection to those who dwell in the shelter of the Lord and who acknowledge that it is God whom they trust. God tells us that He protects those who trust in Him. Now, were it God telling Jesus to jump, we would expect Jesus to trust Him, and therefore His response would be quite different. However, it was not God who was giving the order. It was Satan making the suggestion! Who would ever recommend taking orders from Satan? Jesus' refusal to jump illustrates His lack of trust in Satan's suggestion, not a lack of trust in God's ability to protect Him. We cannot act recklessly and expect God to protect us, but should He Himself call us to a task, we can obey a seemingly dangerous command and put our faith and trust in Him. By inappropriately and inadequately quoting Scripture, Satan again cleverly masks the reality of Jesus' righteousness. He makes it appear that Jesus does not trust God. In reality, it is *because* Jesus trusts God (Psalm 91:2) that He does not jump, as it was not God giving Him the order.

This section is deep, so a review is warranted. This whole dialogue of Matthew 4:1-11 illustrates Satan's tactics of disguising Jesus' identity, quoting Scripture out of context, and taking shortcuts rather than obeying God. First, Satan inserts an extraneous "if" statement when inquiring about Jesus' identity in order to confuse the issue. Next, Satan offers the same misleading conditional "if" clause while simultaneously and strategically quoting a subsection of Scripture in order to make it appear as if Jesus does not trust God. In reality, it is just the opposite. It is precisely Jesus' trust in God that compels Him not to follow Satan's instruction. This tactic is one of Satan's favorites, and we still see it today. He uses those "if" clauses to attempt to undermine God's promises to us. Satan says to us, "If you are truly a child of God, why isn't He blessing you in this particular way?" or "If you are truly a child of God, why have you sinned in this way." Satan's pattern of attack has not changed, and we need to be alert to it.

So far, we have seen Satan's first two verbal assaults were an attack on Jesus' deity and then a straw man argument created by omission of context. Observant readers may already have figured out what category his third attacks come in. Finally, since the semantic trickery does not seem to work, Satan tries an appeal to the logic of expediency, tempting Jesus to let the ends justify the means. Matthew 4:8-9:

> **8 Again, the devil took Him to a very high mountain and showed Him all the kingdoms of the world and their glory; 9 and he said to Him, "All these things I will give You, if You fall down and worship me."**

Many people look at this temptation as foolhardy. After all, doesn't Jesus know He is going to gain it all anyway in the end? Such a statement misses the subtlety and power of this last attack. In this final temptation, just what exactly is Satan offering? Jesus came to die as a ransom for many, to reconcile the world to Himself. Yet Satan clearly has been allowed rule of this world temporarily until the Second Advent of Jesus. So why doesn't Jesus just take control back in that moment, since Satan was offering to relinquish control? Why should Jesus go through all the agony of torture, death, and resurrection? Why doesn't

Jesus simply accomplish in a moment what will otherwise take Him through agony and suffering? Why allow so many billions to suffer needlessly throughout the ages when Satan was offering a quicker and seemingly more efficient way to achieve Jesus' goal of wresting control back from Satan?

Examine this from a parent's point of view. How often has a child gone down the wrong path? The parent faces a choice. One choice is the hard way. It will result in allowing a child to make a mistake and likely suffer the consequences, yet learn an invaluable lesson. The easy way is for the parent to fix the problem for the child before it gets too bad. The immediate path of least resistance is to rescue them in the moment. Don't we often incorrectly choose out of convenience? We tell ourselves it is out of love, that we do not want our children to ever suffer. So we swoop in and save them, preventing them from discovering what went wrong. Yet rescuing them preempts the process of growth. We think we choose out of love, and yet, in reality, we choose out of selfishness. We choose to make our lives easier because cleaning up a small mess now is easier than cleaning up a big mess later, even though doing so precludes our child from learning how to deal with difficult situations.

Jesus is love, and so this temptation targets this vulnerability. How could Jesus let His children suffer through countless epochs of temptations and consequences when instead He was given the opportunity to nip it right then? The answer is because God's way is not the easy way. God required a sacrifice. Trying to fix the problem by taking back control from Satan does not fix the underlying problem of sin. Had Jesus given in to this temptation, He could not have been the redeemer, and ultimately He knows that only God's way will allow us to be children of God.

Moreover, it is never right to disobey God in order to avoid the process of growth, even if that growth requires some pain. Clearly, choosing disobedience to God never justifies the ends, no matter how valid we think our intentions. Taking shortcuts to achieve the noblest goal is never worth the price if it means breaking the first commandment. Disguising sin within a veil of twisted love is the most diabolical temptation in existence. Does it surprise us that Satan tried this most sinister tactic?

In fact, it is this final temptation that results in Jesus commanding Satan to leave. Consider that Jesus could have told Satan to leave at any time, yet He endures the temptations to a point. Something about this last assault made Jesus say that enough is enough. Perhaps we as humans needed to see the variety of temptations that could be thrown at us. Perhaps this last temptation was the most sinister and inverted logic Jesus would tolerate.

To recap, first Satan obfuscates the truth by placing true statements within other catch phrases to confuse the issue of who Jesus is. An entire sequence may seem true at first glance, but some examination reveals a subtle flaw. Second, Satan attempts to discredit God by quoting Scripture out of context. He takes a true statement when under the umbrella of God's promises, and stands it on its own outside of God. Again, this is an attempt to undermine God's credibility, as such statements look true at first glance, but a closer inspection exposes their misuse. Finally, Satan tempts people to achieve what seems to be worthwhile ends through means that initially seem righteous. He tempts us to choose disobedience over patience.

If we find a religion created by Satan, we would expect to see these same three tactics of attacks pervasive throughout its teachings. We should expect to see a religion that systematically questions God's word by replacing it with little catch phrases within its talking points to confuse the issue regarding the identity of Jesus as God. We should see a religion which teaches its followers to quote the Bible out of context, leaving out critical sections in order to advance its own goals. Finally, we expect to see a religion that believes that any means necessary to reach an end are considered acceptable. Islam has all of these items in abundance. Continuing to prepare ourselves to penetrate the confusion requires a closer investigation of where Islamic doctrine agrees and disagrees with Christian doctrine.

Majoring on the Minors

Since we have spoken about the art of counterfeiting, let's take a look at one of the most telling Islamic Inversions. To see this clearly, we will examine salvation. What does the Bible teach us regarding what God requires from us in order to be saved? How does this compare to what the Qur'an teaches regarding these same doctrines? We will expect to see many similarities as we compare Christianity and Islam, but if Islam is counterfeit, we will also see some clear signs that expose it for what it is. As we begin to examine the doctrine of salvation from center to periphery, a striking pattern emerges.

There are many points of Christian faith, but only certain core elements are a requirement for salvation. There are many Christians with areas of bad doctrine who are saved and will find themselves with Jesus in eternity because they accepted His free gift of salvation. As a gauge to what Muslims believe about Jesus, we will ask tough questions about what tenets of faith are essential for salvation. Then, these essential points of doctrine will be compared to how Islam views them. To get the thrust of this, we need to distinguish between what is just flawed doctrine, and what is non-negotiable. Doing this is not easy, so consider an example.

Must a Christian believe in the virgin birth to be saved? On first inspection, we might be inclined to answer in the affirmative. After all, in one sense the Christian must believe in the virgin birth, because without the virgin birth, Christ would have original sin and therefore not be able to be a sinless sacrifice. However, back up a bit. What if someone had never been taught the doctrine of original sin? What if all a person knew was that Christ died for his or her sins, was crucified, resurrected, and that if the gift of salvation were accepted, Christ would send His Holy Spirit? If we met such a person, our first inclination might be to more accurately inform him or her of sound doctrine, but would we confidently say such a person is not saved? Wouldn't such an understanding and acceptance of Christ be enough for God to establish a relationship with that person? Nowhere in Scripture does it say that one must believe Jesus was born of a virgin to be saved.

As another example, consider young children who want to accept Jesus. They do not even know what a virgin is yet. Would we dare to suggest that they cannot be saved without first understanding the physical intricacies of the sexual relationship? Would we demand they must first attend sex education class in order to have a full understanding of what a virgin is? Obviously, we would want them to learn proper doctrine eventually as they approached adulthood, but we must admit it is not a requirement for salvation.

Similarly, consider whether believing that Jesus is the Messiah (Greek, the Christ) is a requirement for salvation. Some people would argue that understanding that Jesus is the Messiah, the anointed One of God, would be such a necessary condition. As prophet, priest, and king, He was uniquely ordained, qualified, and designated as the One to bring deliverance to His people. As such, restoration and redemption with God can only come through Jesus' salvific work as the Messiah. However, Christians and Muslims have a major terminology gap when using this title. From a Muslim point of view, the term Messiah does not come with all this underlying meaning. In Islam, Messiah is nothing more than a title. Does believing that Jesus is the Messiah carry any weight if a person doesn't know what that title entails? Calling Jesus Messiah is completely different than believing that He is uniquely equipped to once and for all deliver His people from sin.

Looking at it from the opposite side of the salvation line, perhaps someone believes Jesus is the Messiah but denies the crucifixion. Would such an understanding, with nothing else, meet God's criteria for salvation? The Bible passages cited below clearly say it does not. So knowing Jesus is the Messiah is not enough; a fuller understanding and acceptance is required.

With this in mind, consider what is required for salvation and compare it to the Islamic view of Jesus. In John 3:18 Jesus tells us that we must believe in His name, the only begotten Son of God. We must confess Jesus (Matthew 10:32), and we must truly believe He died and rose again (Romans 10:9-10, 1 Corinthians 15:2-4). We also must come to Him in order to receive this life (John 5:40, John 10:9, Acts 2:21).

With the stage now fully set, it is time to list the Islamic view of doctrines related to Jesus. Some articles of faith they confirm, and some they deny. When we examine which doctrines the Muslims grant and which they dispute, what we find is an exact reverse barometer when viewed in the light of salvation. In other words, if we need it for salvation, Muslims dispute it. If it is not needed for salvation, Muslims grant it.

Concept	Salvation requirement?	Do Muslims Agree with Christians?	Reference
Virgin birth	No	Yes	Qur'an 3:47, 3:59, 19:20
Jesus performs miracles	No	Yes	Qur'an 2:253, 3:49
Jesus led a sinless life	No	Yes	Qur'an 19:19
Jesus was the Messiah	No	Yes	Qur'an 3:45, 5:75
Second coming of Christ	No	Yes	Qur'an 43:57-61
Incarnation	Yes	No	Qur'an 4:171, 19:88-89
Crucifixion	Yes	No	Qur'an 4:157
Resurrection	Yes	No	Qur'an 4:157

This pattern is nothing short of shocking. Literally, Muslims discount everything required for salvation as a fabrication. Similarly, Muslims are content to agree regarding everything not required for salvation. These exact reversals shout in no uncertain terms where Islam stands when viewed in the light of Christ. The Muslim view of Jesus is a clever facsimile designed to distort the core message of salvation that Jesus brought.

To understand the diabolic nature of Islamic doctrine relating to the work of Christ, consider the alternative approaches. A very ineffective technique would be to deny the existence of Jesus as a historical figure. Such a bold lie would be easily thwarted. Similarly, it would be difficult to deny that He performed miracles or had a profound impact upon humanity. Such a bold-faced lie would be easily recognized. Instead, Islam employs a truly effective strategy of undermining Christ by preventing people from understanding His work of atonement. The position of Islam effectively leads people away from Christ by feigning respect and acknowledging Jesus and his miracles, yet denying the power of His atoning death and resurrection. Islam fully admits everything about Christ that is not tied to salvation and harshly denies anything that is required for salvation. Islam leaves all the secondary matters of Christian faith intact while ripping the core out of Jesus' message. In other words, the best counterfeit is one that looks and feels real enough but is not genuine legal tender.

Islam has a filtering mechanism through which to view Jesus in order to weed out those aspects of His teachings that lead to salvation. Muslims acknowledge what He did to a degree but deny his deity. They acknowledge that He brought the Word of God, but claim that the Qur'an contains all that is preserved of His teachings. They acknowledge His special birth but not His death. Muslims acknowledge His miracles but aren't familiar with those that point to His true identity. The inversion is astonishing. To know what a Muslim thinks of Jesus, just consider how critical it is to eternal destiny. If it is critical, the Muslim rejects it; if it is not critical, the Muslim accepts it. It is the cleverest counterfeit devisable.

Given that we now have a better understanding of how Islam counterfeits Jesus' message, it is time to examine how God equips us to unravel these falsehoods.

Chapter 6

Some Final Preparations

The Scripture reference for Section III of this book comes from Ephesians Chapter 6. It is fitting, then, that we finish our preparation by looking at prayer and the sword of the Spirit. Engaging a Muslim without prayer and the Word would be akin to leaving on a long voyage without supplies, to handling explosives without training, or, dare I say, to a warrior going into battle without armor.

Of course, we all know the power of God's Word. Yet curiously it shines all the more when dealing with attacks from Muslims. God's Word tends to be sprinkled with profound wisdom in the very places Muslims try quoting to discredit it. This peculiar and frequent placement of insight in nearby verses leaps out in many different ways. For example, consider God's advice on dealing with recalcitrant hearers of His Word.

When to Say When

Often during conversations, the Christian may find himself unable to share the gospel effectively. He may wonder whether he has faithfully done all that is possible. Of course, our Lord gave admonition about what to do when the message is not received well. From Mark 6:11:

> [11] Any place that does not receive you or listen to you, as you go out from there, shake the dust off the soles of your feet for a testimony against them.

Again, regarding the Pharisees in Matthew 15:14:

> [14] Let them alone; they are blind guides of the blind. And if a blind man guides a blind man, both will fall into a pit.

Many evangelical Christians have been praying for the 10/40 window for some time. The 10/40 window is that region of the globe between 10° and 40° latitude. It stretches from North Africa to Indonesia and is predominately Muslim. Indeed it has opened up slightly. Still, there are more stories about missionaries who are there, often even anonymously, and not making much headway. As a result, many Christians in the West question if it is a waste of time, whether the results warrant the effort. On a more personal level, many Christians similarly wonder if their time should be spent elsewhere rather than evangelizing Muslim friends and neighbors. Besides, some argue, Jesus provides plenty of admonition regarding avoiding those who refuse to listen. Within the Sermon on the Mount, Jesus gives us this warning from Matthew 7:6:

> [6] Do not give what is holy to dogs, and do not throw your pearls before swine, or they will trample them under their feet, and turn and tear you to pieces.

When confronted with those who are so hardened, we are challenged to decide whether or not it might be time to move on. When would this teaching indicate that it is the appropriate time to abandon missions to Islamic countries or personally sharing the good news with Muslim friends closer to home? Before answering, what is the next verse following this verse of resignation just mentioned? I have been in rooms with significant numbers of biblically knowledgeable people, and extremely few know what verse follows. I did not either until God led me to this next truth. Typically, there is a paragraph break in Matthew 7 between verse 6 and verse 7, but the original Greek does not have paragraphs. I have come to believe our Lord Jesus never intended a paragraph break there. It is no accident that these two verses are together. In the greatest sermon ever preached, these two thoughts were coupled together, but we have lost this profound truth given to us by our Lord Jesus Christ. This time read Matthew 7:6-7 together:

> [6] Do not give what is holy to dogs, and do not throw your pearls before swine, or they will trample them under their feet, and turn and tear you to pieces. [7] Ask, and it will be given to you; seek, and you will find; knock, and it will be opened to you.

Without prayer, any conversation is meaningless. This may seem obvious, but I often found myself in discussions with Muslims, never having once prayed for them. This is inexcusable. One of the many things Jesus gives to us is the ability to ask for something in His name. Aren't we called to pray for the salvation of those who have not yet heard His message? What could be more honorable than asking for the salvation of our Muslim friends?

More specifically, our Lord tells us not to give what is holy to dogs, but that if we ask, we shall receive! What else could He mean but that only by prayer can the impossible become possible. I cannot overstress this point. To some extent, I am forced to remind myself of this fact over and over again. There are many people like myself who often consider themselves smart enough to reach anyone through logic and reason. We need to come before the Lord and admit that if the Holy Spirit is not working, we will accomplish nothing. When God is forced to teach us this lesson experientially, it will be a lesson that comes with much pain.

Not only do these two verses speak to those of us with the pearls, but they have a double meaning. They also speak to the dogs. For those who obstinately refuse to hear the gospel, there is yet hope. If they will but ask, Jesus will answer them and they can receive a place in the kingdom of our Heavenly Father by the grace of Jesus Christ.

So does this verse suggest moving on? It is not clear. What is clear is that we are to pray, and let God answer. Remember that the Holy Spirit will guide our prayers (Romans 8:26). Do not forget that this same Holy Spirit who has called us to speak to Muslims is the Spirit who gives the gift of compassion, the gift of tears for fellow humans who are lost. If that point does not hit hard enough, remember that this same Spirit was intertwined with Jesus as He lived a life of tragedy. He was called a "man of sorrows," and rightly so (Isaiah 53:3). God could have chosen to stay aloof, but instead experienced the life of a human, full of joy as well as sorrow. He never cheated nor took the easy way out for Himself. He accepted every ounce of pain, excruciatingly so, as He accepted death in the most torturous way ever invented by man. Yet after all that, He did the one thing that made it all worth every tear; He rose again. By rising again, He opened the floodgates of salvation to all of us.

These verses together tell us not to go before those who are hostile without prayer. We are not to just throw out pearls of wisdom to those who are unreceptive, but rather we are to ask in prayer for the Spirit to be at work. So listen to this Spirit. If the Holy Spirit says to mourn, mourn. If the Holy Spirit says rejoice, rejoice (Ecclesiastics 3:1-8). If the Holy Spirit is not there, continue to pray.

The Word of God Always Has an Answer

As we have seen in previous chapters regarding the true identity of Jesus, the Bible does a wonderful job of convicting Islam of antithetical thinking. The Bible is always the first place to turn for answers. No matter what the allegation, the Bible comes through with piercing and relevant clarity. It does so even in cases that are not immediately obvious, such as Middle East politics. As an example, Muslims are quick to climb on the Palestinian bandwagon. Here is a typical quote:

> It is time for the whole world to know that the land of Palestine was unjustly and forcefully taken away from its righteous owners in defiance of a covenant that God had made with the seed of Abraham.[10]

The author of this quotation means to suggest that the covenant of Abraham is being extended through Ishmael, and as such, Israel is the nation that does not belong there. Incredulity at the audacity of such error makes it hard to respond due to shock. Always remember that the Bible is the first place to regain composure after hearing such things. A quick peek at Genesis 17:18-19 confirms our suspicions:

> **[18]And Abraham said to God, "Oh that Ishmael might live before You!" [19]But God said, "No, but Sarah your wife will bear you a son, and you shall call his name Isaac; and I will establish My covenant with him for an everlasting covenant for his descendants after him."**

Remember, this is not about the politics of Middle East land ownership. It is not even about the fact that Islam inserts Ishmael where Isaac belongs. It is about the Word of God being the defense against this kind of ridiculous musing. Whether or not to debate this particular point by use of the above Scripture is a decision that will require spiritual discernment. Typically, such a point-by-point rebuttal does not help show truth unless the other person is genuinely curious. However, in this case, such Scripture reference might be able to launch a broader discussion of what God's covenant is.

Let us examine another similar example where the Word of God comes to the rescue. Muslims will often say that the covenant with Israel has been broken. This shouldn't be surprising, as even some Christians have adopted a replacement theology, believing that the church has replaced Israel as the covenant holder. This errant theology has a foothold despite such Biblical passages as 1 Samuel 12:22, Jeremiah 33:25-26, and Romans 11:1-5. Some Muslims will even go as far as to say that the covenant has been transferred to the Arabs. Again, the Word of God is there for us to help shed light on dark and inverted doctrine. God specifically says Israel will always exist as long as there is a universe for it to exist in. He goes on to clarify that the covenant will also remain. As shown in Jeremiah 31:35-37:

> [35]Thus says the LORD,
> Who gives the sun for light by day
> And the fixed order of the moon and the stars for
> light by night,
> Who stirs up the sea so that its waves roar;
> The LORD of hosts is His name:
> [36]"If this fixed order departs
> From before Me," declares the LORD,
> "Then the offspring of Israel also will cease
> From being a nation before Me forever."
>
> [37]Thus says the LORD,
> "If the heavens above can be measured
> And the foundations of the earth searched out below,
> Then I will also cast off all the offspring of Israel
> For all that they have done," declares the LORD.

Approaching such a subject requires great care and discernment. Remember, Muslims do not value Scripture as authentic. Also, any mention of the Jewish right to Israel is a disaster waiting to happen. Whether to bring this passage up depends on how much of an audience has been gained, and how open they are to hearing the Word of God. It is likely that discussing these passages right away would not be a good idea. Rather, I present them to remind you that the Word of God always has an answer for such ridiculous assertions. No matter what, do not lose sight of that.

We are now ready to analyze an example of the typical ways Muslims bend the truth. It is time to get down to business and start flipping inversions right side up.

Salaam Alaikum

With all this preparation in hand, we are ready to take an in-depth walk through another inversion to better get a handle on what they are, and how the Bible helps untangle them. An inversion is a theological tenet that illustrates a diametrically opposite theological principal when comparing Islam and Christianity. These differences are neither just details of observance nor minor issues of practice. Rather, these differences are profound and yet subtle enough that they require a bit of investigation to bring them out. When viewed in succession, they reveal a sinister pattern that becomes clear to the thoughtful reader. More importantly, they provide a path to discuss the gospel in surprising ways.

If you have ever been to a mosque or even just been hanging out with a group of Muslim friends, *As-salaam alaikum* is an expression that will be heard time and time again. As-salaam alaikum is the standard greeting Muslims share with each other when meeting. This expression is Arabic for "Peace be upon you." The common response back is a similar return greeting of peace, Wa alaikum assalaam (and upon you be peace). Even in this innocuous and harmless method of saying hello we find an interesting spiritual inversion. Sharing the peace might seem a place where Christianity and Islam look similar at first glance, but what might we find upon further investigation?

With a cursory look, a person would note that Jesus brought peace (John 16:33). Paul talks about the peace that passes all understanding (Philippians 4:7). So too a Muslim will tell you plainly that the word Islam, which means submission, comes from the same Arabic root word as peace, salam. It is right about here where any conversation will get sidetracked with whether or not Islam is truly a religion of peace. While those conversations have value, they are a detour to be avoided. By keeping on topic, a much more subtle yet profound truth will come to light. So here we stand, both Christians and Muslims claiming that each religion is one of peace. Muslims are even quick to cite such passages as John 20:21 as evidence that Jesus was a Muslim, since he gave the traditional Islamic greeting of peace. Muslims often argue that since Jesus greeted others with something akin to the traditional Islamic greeting of peace, and Christians do not, it is Muslims who follow Jesus more closely.[11]

Most people hear such an assertion, and then begin fumbling around for a response, and miss the opportunity provided here. Remember, the Word of God will always have an answer, so it is the first place to go to make sense of this assault. To unravel this confusion, look at greetings in the Bible in more depth. Paul has the greatest number of epistles, so there are myriad examples of greetings there. To get a flavor for these, examine 1 Corinthians 1:3, Romans 1:7, or Galatians 1:3. What pattern emerges? Additionally, consider the greetings of Peter in 1 Peter 1:2 or 2 Peter 1:2, or again those of John in 2 John 3 or Revelation 1:4. Seventeen times in the Bible there are greetings of both grace and peace. However, in each circumstance, notice that the order is always the same. In each case, the grace comes before the peace. Not even once does peace come first before grace.

This raises the question of whether it is possible for peace to ever come before there is grace. In the book of Philippians, the context of the passage discussing the peace that passes all comprehension is that such peace comes after rejoicing, prayer, and offering thanks to God. We are only able to do these because of God's grace to bring us to Himself in the first place. In John 16:33, the context is that peace will be given because Jesus has overcome the world, and He has just told His disciples plainly who He is, and therefore how He has the right to grant this peace. He grants it by the fact that He will return to the Father in order to be the instrument of grace to those who believe.

So again the question must be asked if there can even be peace without grace. There is surely no peace between God and any individual human until a person accepts the reconciliation that God offers via Jesus Christ. That peace between God and man comes only by grace alone and not by merit (Ephesians 2:8-9). For our relationship with God, peace comes as a result of God's grace. Peace between individuals, groups, or nations can be achieved temporarily and to a limited extent. However, history shows us clearly that strife between nations has been a permanent fixture of our world. Personal experience teaches us that maintaining peace with family members and friends is a constant battle. Indeed, maintaining that peace often requires showing the grace of forgiveness to those who have harmed us. Here too, often peace comes as a natural consequence of extending grace to those we encounter.

Yet what about the claims by Muslims that Jesus offered the traditional Muslim greeting of peace? Indeed, the Bible records four times when Jesus offers this greeting; Luke 24:36, John 20:19, John 20:21, and John 20:26. What commonality do all these verses share? In each case, this greeting comes after the resurrection! Jesus only gives this greeting after He has died on the cross and returned to the Father, healing the fractured relationship between God and man! The greeting of peace only occurs after Jesus has accomplished His mission of allowing us to receive God's grace to its fullest measure. Once again, peace follows grace.

So before discussing this in detail, the question for the Muslim who presents this argument is whether or not they believe the timing and manner of these greetings by Jesus are genuine, or whether these verses have been corrupted. If they answer that these greetings are indeed accurate, they admit to the resurrection, the core truth of Christianity. If they instead say these verses are not genuine, they undermine their own argument that Muslims more closely follows Jesus compared to Christians based on greetings. Which will the Muslim choose, to torpedo their entire religion, or sabotage the argument they just presented?

Identifying the Islamic inversion lets you get right to the heart of the matter. However, this must be done with love, care, and finesse. Nobody likes being painted into a corner, particularly when you realize your entire worldview is coming apart at the seams. Therefore, kindness is essential.

In this simple example, we see a marked difference between Islam and Christianity. In Islam, peace is put first and foremost and yet is attempted without grace. In Christianity, peace comes only after grace, never before. Jesus' greetings of peace first come after the resurrection, confirming the peace that came from His reconciling work on the cross.

In the next chapter, we will further expose the Islamic inversion by examining inversions specifically related to Jesus. As we learn to diagnose these inversions, we can better and more systematically turn them back on themselves, exposing the reality of Christ.

Section 4

Exposing the Islamic Inversion

We are destroying speculations and every lofty thing raised up against the knowledge of God, and we are taking every thought captive to the obedience of Christ

2 CORINTHIANS 10:5

Chapter 7

Inversions Relating to Jesus Christ

Inversions are often hard to spot and therefore tricky to expose because they are embedded deep inside a larger argument. However, once understood, they can be recognized and later we will see how they can be utilized. Thankfully for us, God is amazing! No matter how complex the lie, no matter how clever the assault, or no matter how devious the deception, God gives us His Spirit and instructs us in Truth. From John 14:26:

> 26 But the Helper, the Holy Spirit, whom the Father will send in My name, He will teach you all things, and bring to your remembrance all that I said to you.

So let the Holy Spirit work as the pattern of inversions begins to be revealed. In this chapter, examples of inversions will be presented specifically relating to Jesus. Remember, Satan's first tactic was to attempt to obscure and obfuscate Jesus' identity. All of the inversions listed in this chapter are variants of this one tactic.

Did Jesus Accept Worship?

Often, Muslims will bring up the fact that Jesus worshiped God the Father (Matthew 4:10, 22:37). Therefore, Muslims argue, devoted followers of Jesus should worship only God the Father, as well. After all, Muslims say, a true follower of Jesus should mimic His actions by worshiping the Lord God only. While this topic has already been discussed from the angle of Jesus being both man and God, let's now put our inversion detector into practice with regards to this latest assertion. Remember that an inversion is a truth examined from a backward perspective, or a lie coated with enough truth to make it sound plausible on the surface. To find an inversion, take the argument provided, turn it inside out, and examine it from a reversed perspective. The result will point back to the truth of Jesus, typically in an ironic way.

Getting back to the argument at hand, Muslims posit that if Jesus worshiped the Father, then this proves that Jesus and the Father are not one. Moreover, the argument asserts that Christians do not obey Jesus in that they do not follow his example of worshiping God the Father only. The Muslim logic goes as follows: Jesus commanded His followers to worship God only. Christians worship Jesus. Therefore, we are being disobedient to Jesus' command.

Rather than get into an argument with our Muslim friend, stop and note the point of agreement. It is true that only God is worthy of worship. Every Muslim will agree with this. Once that is established, we can invert the argument to expose reality.

The sword of the Spirit, which is the word (*rhema*) of God, helps us resolve this apparent dilemma. Clearly only God should be worshiped. Invert the Muslim argument. Rather than look at worship proceeding from Jesus, look at worship proceeding toward Jesus. If only God is worthy of worship, what would it mean if Jesus accepts worship? Moreover, what if Jesus not only accepts worship, but also never corrects or rebukes the people worshiping Him?

From Matthew 14:31-34:

> ³¹ Immediately Jesus stretched out His hand and took hold of him, and said to him, "You of little faith, why did you doubt?" ³² When they got into the boat, the wind stopped. ³³ And those who were in the boat worshiped Him, saying, "You are certainly God's Son!" ³⁴ When they had crossed over, they came to land at Gennesaret.

From Matthew 28:8-10:

> ⁸And they left the tomb quickly with fear and great joy and ran to report it to His disciples. ⁹And behold, Jesus met them and greeted them. And they came up and took hold of His feet and worshiped Him. ¹⁰Then Jesus said to them, "Do not be afraid; go and take word to My brethren to leave for Galilee, and there they will see Me."

Finally, Jesus talks to a blind man He had healed in John 9:35-39:

> ³⁵Jesus heard that they had put him out, and finding him, He said, "Do you believe in the Son of Man?" ³⁶He answered, "Who is He, Lord, that I may believe in Him?" ³⁷Jesus said to him, "You have both seen Him, and He is the one who is talking with you." ³⁸And he said, "Lord, I believe." And he worshiped Him. ³⁹And Jesus said, "For judgment I came into this world, so that those who

do not see may see, and that those who see may become blind."

Jesus accepts worship in these and several other instances. While the full number of these passages is not listed, others include Matthew 2:11, Matthew 15:25, Matthew 28:17, and Luke 24:52. A more subtle but equally profound truth emerges when looking carefully at the verses immediately following where the individuals worship Jesus. Note that in all these passages, never once does Jesus rebuke the person worshiping Him. In other words, Jesus never says "Hey, quit worshiping me, worship God." Instead, He accepts the worship and then directs the people with new and further instruction. Muslims believe Jesus is a prophet only, but such acceptance of worship would be arrogant and blasphemous for a prophet. Therefore, what is the logical conclusion? After all, the argument was that only God is worthy of worship. If only God is worthy of worship, and Jesus willingly accepts it, He claims to be God.

To see this more clearly, contrast the response when an angel is given worship in Revelation 19:10:

> [10] Then I fell at his feet to worship him But he said to me, "Do not do that; I am a fellow servant of yours and your brethren who hold the testimony of Jesus; worship God. For the testimony of Jesus is the spirit of prophecy."

This refusal to be worshiped is recorded again in Revelation 22:8-9:

> [8] I, John, am the one who heard and saw these things And when I heard and saw, I fell down to worship at the feet of the angel who showed me these things. [9] But he said to me, "Do not do that.

I am a fellow servant of yours and of your brethren
the prophets and of those who heed the words of
this book. Worship God."

We see clearly that Jesus accepts worship and never corrects
the person doing so. This seems obvious enough in itself, but
sometimes people would rather argue than listen to the truth.
Muslims focus on who Jesus worshiped. The real issue is Jesus'
reaction to being worshiped. By turning the viewpoint around and
looking at it from the other direction, the truth of Jesus asserting
his deity by accepting worship stands out. It is hard to recognize
this pattern of inversion, but after doing so enough times, it gets
easier.

These examples are given to show the pattern. Here is the
pivotal point to remember with this and every other example
given in this book. Muslims start with a direct frontal assault on
Christianity, in this case regarding Jesus and worship. Put aside
the particulars and move from the concrete to the abstract. Listen
to the Muslim argument, and then flip it upside down, inside
out, and backward. Spin it around and invert it. The result will
be spiritual revelation and enlightenment regarding an aspect of
the Triune God you may not have considered before. Previously
unknown truth about the nature of God will be staring you in the
face. What begins as the Muslim trying to destroy Christian faith,
when properly inverted, ironically will ultimately lead to profound
truth about the God of the Bible. Whether the Muslim is ready to
hear that truth is left to the Spirit.

On a side note, in conversations that I have had with Muslims
regarding Jesus and worship, I have been guilty of pursuing
unproductive avenues of dialogue. For example, the perpetually
recalcitrant Muslim may cite the difference between the Greek
words *sebomai* and *proskuneo*, both of which are sometimes
translated as worship, but have different connotations. Then they
will claim the Bible talks about one type of worship when Jesus

did it and another type of worship when it was done to Jesus. Now, upon further investigation, such arguments are easily shown to be in factual error. The words have different connotations, but the same word, proskuneo, is used when Jesus worships the Father as when people worship Him. It is exactly these types of conversations that are fruitless detours and should be avoided. While such a study of Greek word usage is interesting and educational, the point is not to win the debate, but to share Christ with those Muslims who have an open heart.

It is easy to get off track into topics such as the Greek word study example above. Such esoteric criticisms are not the reason that people choose to reject Christ. Why exactly is the Muslim even bringing up such an obscure grammatical argument? In my experience, it is to sidetrack the discussion or to send you on a time-consuming theological wild goose chase. How many Christians can read New Testament Greek, or want to learn it? The farther we drift from the crucifixion and resurrection of Christ, the less likely our efforts will bear fruit.

We need to avoid such pointless diversions. Investing time in Greek studies only to find out that the Bible means what it says gets nowhere in a discussion with Muslims. Rather, turn the argument back on itself, and as a result, consider what it meant that people worshiped Jesus. What was His response to it, and what was the significance of His accepting worship? Shift the focus away from the action of Jesus performing worship, and toward the act of Jesus accepting worship. The Islamic argument that only God accepts worship surprisingly strengthens the case for the deity of Jesus rather than weakening it. The very same Muslim logic used to topple the identity of Jesus Christ, when applied to the situation in reverse, serves as a path to reveal Jesus as God Almighty, the only one worthy of worship.

Another variant of this inversion is as follows: Muslims will say that Jesus prayed to His Father, thus confirming that He is not God. This type of flipped Islamic logic is similar to the last example. Employ the same inversion detector on this criticism. The criticism is that only God is worthy of prayer. This seems to be a logical assumption. So looking at Scripture, here is what we find. John 14:13-14:

> ¹³ Whatever you ask in My name, that will I do, so that the Father may be glorified in the Son. ¹⁴ If you ask Me anything in My name, I will do it.

So we see that Jesus wants us to pray in His name. Yet only God is worthy of prayer. Jesus claims He has the ability to answer prayer, which only God can do. The conclusion is obvious. As C.S. Lewis pointed out in *Mere Christianity*, making such outrageous claims means that Jesus is either a liar, a lunatic, or Lord. A simple messenger or prophet of God is not one of the possible options.

Now that we have more of a taste of what constitutes an inversion, we will look at Satan, the master inverter himself. Even when in the presence of Jesus, Satan uses some bizarre logical twists and turns.

Should Jesus Worship Satan?

We have already examined the third temptation of Christ as it pertains to the nature of temptation itself. Yet there is even more truth buried in this passage. As always, the Muslim attacks only go to illustrate something profound that most Christians have overlooked. In Matthew 4:9, Satan offers Jesus all the kingdoms of the world if He would worship him. Muslims often quote Jesus' response to Satan. After all, didn't Jesus say to "worship the Lord your God, and serve Him only"? Specifically, Jesus says in Matthew 4:10:

> ¹⁰Then Jesus said to him, "Go, Satan! For it is written, 'YOU SHALL WORSHIP THE

LORD YOUR GOD, AND SERVE HIM ONLY."'

Muslims harangue Christians for not following this advice. Jesus responds that we should worship the Lord our God, and so Jesus chose to worship His Father, the Lord God in heaven. Again, apply the inversion analysis to the Muslim argument so that we may learn the truth. Focus on the offer rather than the response. What offer is Jesus responding to? The issue is not primarily who Jesus is telling us to worship. Neither is the issue whom Jesus was telling Satan to worship. The point is that Satan was offering Jesus the choice to worship Satan. We all know that worshiping Satan is wrong, yet somehow such an obvious fact gets buried, overlooked, and inverted into a discussion of the finer points of Trinitarian doctrine. Of course, Jesus would respond that He should worship His Father. Nobody would suggest that worshiping Satan was the appropriate action.

It may be claimed that this does not address the issue of why Jesus does not worship Himself if He is God. Jesus, being one aspect of God as well as being human, would not worship Himself. Rather, He would worship the aspect of God who was in heaven, the aspect who sent Him. Jesus' ministry was just getting underway, and Satan was trying to undermine Jesus' future actions. Keeping that fact in mind will help keep this passage in perspective. As usual, the Islamic inversion of the passage clouds the issue. The issue is that Jesus was not telling Satan whom to worship. Rather, Jesus was rebuking Satan for suggesting Jesus worship him. This instruction from Satan was not to be followed.

Notice how what seemed an unanswerable challenge boiled down to Jesus' choice not to follow Satan's suggestion. What starts as a Muslim assault on Christianity winds up exposing something obvious yet profound. The Muslim starts by assaulting the Christian's actions of worshiping Jesus, and does so by quoting His response to Satan. Yet the response to Satan was a rejection of worshiping Satan. Even though Jesus is God, what other choice did He have?

Some might suggest Jesus should have used this opportunity to instruct Satan. However, Satan had already committed an unforgivable act; it was too late for Satan to worship God. Jesus would not instruct Satan to worship Him because even if Satan had then chosen to worship Jesus, it was too late. Satan's destiny had long ago been determined. People are redeemable, but fallen angels are not. Scripture speaks to this concept in Hebrews 2:16 and 2 Peter 2:4. This may seem an odd detour, but it is not. Remember the conversation is about whom Jesus is going to worship; it is not about whom Satan should worship, or about whom we as people should worship. Jesus was being tested here; not Satan, not you, and not me.

Some Muslims will suggest that Satan would never have the audacity to test God in the first place. What could be gained? Why would Satan choose to do this? Flip this over as well to see what is true. Rather than looking at what could be gained, examine the opposite question. What could be lost? The real question is why wouldn't Satan test God? Satan already knows he is banished to an eternity of fire. What possible disadvantage was there to Satan testing God?

Moreover, Satan knew everything was at stake. Satan never tempted the other prophets in such a way, yet Satan was willing to bet all he had when dealing with Jesus. Why was He so special? What was so unique about Jesus that Satan was willing to relinquish his rule on earth just for one moment of worship? If Jesus could remain sinless, then He could pay for our sins, but if Satan could make Jesus sin, then Jesus could not be the perfect sacrifice. There had never been a God-man before. Realistically, a non-omniscient Satan would be certain to make an attempt to unravel God's plan. This temptation only continues to underscore the reality of who Jesus is.

It is true that Satan trying to test God is outrageous!

Ironically, that is the whole point. Any normal human being or even a prophet could sin.* Only God Himself can ultimately resist Satan. Only God, the creator of all, could resist such an outrageous and incredibly devious bribe. Don't ever forget who Jesus is. In any discussion, it is of the most critical importance. From 1 John 5:20:

> ²⁰**And we know that the Son of God has come, and has given us understanding so that we may know Him who is true; and we are in Him who is true, in His Son Jesus Christ. This is the true God and eternal life.**

There are many inversions directly relating to Jesus. The next section examines how Muslims turn Jesus' atoning sacrifice upside-down by exploring the Muslim view of His death.

The Injustice of Punishing Jesus.

As we continue these examples, the distinct pattern of the "Islamic Inversion" will more clearly emerge. Again, to summarize, the Muslim takes a truth of Christ, and twists it around backward, inside out, or otherwise distorts it in order to make it sound reasonable, whereas in actuality the assertion is diametrically inverted from reality. The inversions are obscuring the nature of Jesus, taking Scripture out of context, or taking shortcuts to an end. We are still squarely immersed in the first of these tactics.

Here is yet another example of how it works. Muslims tend to think that the Christian view portrays an unjust God because He executed His own Son for someone else's crimes. What could be more unjust than punishing person B for a crime committed by

---

* A Muslim would likely disagree on the point of whether a prophet would engage in such an egregious sin.

person A? Here is an example of a typical quote from a Muslim directed at me during a conversation: "Instead of me being punished, the judge orders his innocent son who did nothing, by the way, to be punished because of a crime I committed!" Similarly, this Muslim author declared, "To demand the price of blood in order to forgive people's sins demonstrates complete lack of mercy, and to punish a guiltless person is undoubtedly the height of injustice."[12]

The temptation is to defend God's just character and engage in a debate. The good news here is that the Muslim in some way understands that Jesus died for our sins. This Muslim line of reasoning is an approximation of the substitution theory, one of the widely accepted views of the atonement. There certainly is validity in the fact that our sin is deserving of divine punishment, and that Jesus was and is our substitute. There are many other views of the atonement which carry validity as well and help us gain insight into what Jesus accomplished on the cross. It isn't so much that this Muslim line of reasoning is incorrect and needs to be debated; it is rather that the view is incomplete and needs to be amended by viewing it more thoroughly.

The question on the table is whether punishing another person is ever a just response? As usual, invert the Muslim line of thought to find a more profitable response. Rather than looking at it from the perspective of God the Father, we can expand our understanding by viewing it from the perspective of God the Son. Rather than God punishing an innocent man, Jesus freely donated his life as a ransom. In other words, God did not force punishment upon Jesus, but Jesus submitted to God's plan of salvation by obeying His Father. Rather than a judge passing sentence on an innocent person instead of you, an innocent person stepped forward to accept your sentence on your behalf. Of course, Scripture backs this up in John 10:17-18:

> [17] For this reason the Father loves Me, because
> I lay down My life so that I may take it again. [18]

> No one has taken it away from Me, but I lay it
> down on My own initiative. I have authority to lay
> it down, and I have authority to take it up again.
> This commandment I received from My Father.

A slightly different way to think of it is that the death of Christ was not a punishment imposed upon Jesus, it was a gift given by God through Jesus. The wrath of God is against us the sinner, and the gift of grace is thus also for us.

Notice how the Islamic adaptation has completely inverted the truth of the gift of the cross. They mix up what, why, and who the cross was all about. Not only that, but the analogy treats the subject as if God passed judgment on an innocent and unrelated third party. It is true that Jesus was innocent- sinless in fact- but He was not an uninterested third party. As God Himself in flesh, the choice to lay down His own life means that the so-called punishment was not perpetrated on anyone. Satisfying the wrath of God was achieved by God Himself. To be clear, starting with the assumption that Jesus was not God in the flesh inevitably leads to reversing these concepts completely. The Muslim turns the view of the cross from grace given to punishment doled out, twists it from obedience to forced execution, and switches the ultimate act of love to injustice perpetrated on an innocent bystander.

This ultimate act of sacrifice comes to us not only as an act of love but as an example of to what ends we must be willing to submit ourselves should God ask us to do so. How ironic that we as Christians must submit to this ultimate level, yet Muslims are so proud that being a Muslim means "one who submits." The Bible speaks to this clearly in Ephesians 5:2:

> [2] and walk in love, just as Christ also loved you and
> gave Himself up for us, an offering and a sacrifice
> to God as a fragrant aroma.

This attitude of Jesus going to the cross can be inverted in plenty of other ways as well. One such way is that a Muslim typically will view Gethsemane as the place where Christ begged for mercy, a place where Christ acted in a cowardly fashion. However, reading John 10:17 shows that He was willing to accept the onslaught of insults, torture, and death. He asked His Father that if it were possible, to remove this cup from him. Yet ultimately, He had the courage to embrace His role as the salvation of mankind. From John 18:11:

> ¹¹ So Jesus said to Peter, "Put the sword into the sheath; the cup which the Father has given Me, shall I not drink it?"

Don't allow the Islamic inversion to turn the cross into anything that it was not. Jesus was not killed against His will; He allowed Himself to endure the cross (Isaiah 53:10, Hebrews 12:2). He gave up His own life for us. It was the pivotal moment in history, and it represents God in more ways than this humble servant could ever convey.

Remember that the way Muslims invert the cross is by starting with an assumption that Jesus is human only. This changes all of their conclusions. Muslims invert the cross by looking away from Jesus rather than toward Him. Spotting these arguments takes practice. Keep focused on Jesus Christ, but more importantly, remember that it is all about Him, so view it from His perspective. With this in mind, let's recap this point. As has been said, it is not that God the Father punished Christ; it is that Christ, who is God in the flesh, was willing to provide payment for sin for His own sake. Isaiah 43:24-25:

> ²⁴ Rather you have burdened Me with your sins,
> You have wearied Me with your iniquities.

> ²⁵ **I, even I, am the one who wipes out your transgressions for My own sake,**

Again, the logical problem with the Muslims arguing a divinely unjust punishment is that they start with an assumption, that Jesus is human only. Starting with that assumption necessarily leads to the wrong conclusion. Of course, it is unjust to punish some random third party for the crimes of others. It is not logically sound to start a proof with a faulty assumption, as it will lead to a faulty conclusion. If Jesus were human only, then His suffering on the cross would have no meaning; in fact, it would be "the height of injustice" as our Muslim friend suggests. So this whole topic brings us back to the deity of Christ. It always winds its way back to Him, in one form or another.

Was Jesus Omniscient?

Some Muslims will grasp on to the fact that while on earth, Jesus was not all knowing, all powerful, nor all present. For example, some Muslims will say that since Jesus asked questions, he could not be all knowing (Mark 5:30). The faulty logic states that since Jesus had to ask questions, it would mean that He does not know the answer. Such logic is so far off center, most Christians do not even consider such ridiculous statements. Of course, we know God asks questions for a variety of reasons, such as to get people to commit to a response. When talking to Muslims, often the Christian is found defending the flawed interpretation that asking questions proves lack of omniscience.

Once again, flip the argument around to test its reliability. This whole style of conversation undermines Islamic doctrine itself. There are a variety of places in the Qur'an where Allah asks a question (Qur'an 69:2-3). By the logic presented, if Allah must ask a question, it would show he was not all-knowing. Therefore, if Muslims truly believe that asking a question proves the lack of omniscience, they must deny the omniscience of Allah. If they admit that asking questions is a valid method of interacting with humans, they undercut their original argument.

Again, take this wherever it makes sense, but being able to share Scripture and focus on Christ is usually much more productive than criticizing the Qur'an. Muslims know what it says, and they will defend the Qur'an with their life, even if it means denying logic itself. Just bringing up the issue of whether or not it is legitimate for an all-knowing God to ask men questions will get the point across.

When Jesus says, "What is it you want?" He already knows the answer. In order to communicate with human beings who are not omniscient, He must engage in human conversational style. So here is our hook. Again, we see the beauty of what it meant for God to truly become human and interact with us on the most personal level. Part of what we do as human beings is ask each other questions in order to help each other understand what we are thinking and saying. In human form, God did this as well. Experiencing humanity on every level paved the way for Him to go to the cross to pay the price for our sins. This bridged the gap between humans and God.

It is true that God took on certain limitations by becoming human. For example, as a human, Jesus had a physical constraint of not being able to be everywhere at once. As for any limits to his power or knowledge, it is not so obvious, but the Scripture speaks to this in Philippians 2:6-8:

> [5] Have this attitude in yourselves which was also in Christ Jesus, [6] who, although He existed in the form of God, did not regard equality with God a thing to be grasped, [7] but emptied Himself, taking the form of a bond-servant, and being made in the likeness of men. [8] Being found in appearance as a man, He humbled Himself by becoming obedient to the point of death, even death on a cross.

The preceding section of Scripture is one to get well acquainted with. It brings out a fascinating theological question of whether or not God has any limits, or rather whether God can choose to constrain Himself. Taking the example of God as all knowing, Muslims will assert that if God is omniscient and Jesus is God, then shouldn't Jesus be omniscient? The answer would seem to be yes, but Scripture tells a different story. Muslims often leap on the following Biblical verse and consequently enjoy misinterpreting it. Matthew 24:26:

> [36] But of that day and hour no one knows, not even the angels of heaven, nor the Son, but the Father alone.

Did Jesus just admit ignorance? We have already discussed what it means for God to assume human form. We have seen how often a seeming contradiction regarding the nature of Christ fails to take into account that Jesus was God in human form. In this verse, we need to take into account that Jesus was also a human in God form. In other words, back in chapter three we saw that misapplication of logic when we treated Jesus as human only and not God. Similarly, now we see the misapplication of logic when we treat Jesus as God only, and not human also. The question is not whether Jesus knew the answer, but whether God allowed Himself to know the answer while in human form.

In order to sort out the particulars of this nettlesome question, we must put on our thinking caps. The question is whether or not God has limits. It is certainly true there are things God cannot do because He is God. For example, God cannot cease to exist. Doing so would logically contradict the nature of an eternal being. There are many such actions that God cannot perform. These correspond to God's eternally unchanging character. For example, God cannot break His promises or lie. However, pondering these limitations due to His divine nature lead us directly to who God is. God's attributes by necessity constrain Him.

While God is constrained to be God in accordance with His attributes as discussed above, the issue at hand is how God's omnipotence asserts itself when He interacts with His creation. Can God choose to temporarily constrain Himself to become man and enter His own creation? The Muslim assertion is that a limitless God is too powerful to be able to constrain Himself in such a way. However, we find the exact opposite to be true. A truly limitless God would have the power and ability to enter His own creation. If He is not able to enter His creation, then we know God is not powerful enough to successfully interact with His creation in every way logically consistent with His attributes. In the same vein, a truly sovereign God somehow has the capacity to remain in control after the creation of free will. If God cannot stay sovereign over beings with free will, then there would not be anything for Him to be sovereign over. If God cannot create beings with free will to be sovereign over, He would be just a watchmaker viewing His mechanized universe tick away.

Getting back to the inversion at hand, does an all-knowing God know how to limit His own knowledge when human? This may be a confusing question, so ponder it again. Does a truly limitless God have the capacity to temporarily constrain Himself? At the root of this question is the issue of what a limitless God can and cannot do. A truly limitless God has the power, ability, and resource to temporarily constrain Himself. If God is unable to limit Himself, God is limited in that we have discovered something He cannot do. For one unique time in history, and for this time only, Jesus emptied Himself in order to be simultaneously all-man and all-God. A God who does not have this capacity to temporarily limit Himself is not a limitless being, and is then by definition, not God.

Again, we see the Muslim view and the Christian view of God are exactly opposite. Muslims define a limitless God as one who cannot limit Himself by becoming simultaneously human. Christians define the limitless character of God to mean that He can do all things in accordance with His character. Those things include temporarily suspending or restraining Himself while in human form. By claiming Allah cannot become man, the Muslim inadvertantly exposes the limitation of Allah. The Muslim by definition states that Allah did not have the capacity to make himself a God-man.

In the next chapter, we examine the most frequent rebuttal by Muslims, that the Bible cannot be trusted due to corruption. Dealing with the historicity of Biblical accuracy is wonderful, but ineffective. Therefore, we will tackle this common rebuttal in a slightly different and more effective way.

Chapter 8

The 1ˢᵗ Retreat: The Bible Is Corrupted.

One common position presented by Muslims is that the Bible we have today has been corrupted. No serious conversation with a Muslim will go on before stumbling over that one sooner or later, likely sooner. There are a variety of approaches in response to the allegation that Scripture has been corrupted, and they involve recognizing the inversions. Just as everywhere else, a little inspection reveals the same pattern of inverted thought resides here as well. To get started, we must first take a look at the bigger picture of unraveling circular logic with respect to Holy Scripture.

The Testimony of Two Witnesses

Back in chapter one, we introduced one of the typical Muslim approaches, "The Qur'an says so." Both the Bible and Qur'an claim to be God's Word. How does anyone determine whether a book is God's Word just because it claims to be? It is easy to go around in circles wasting energy on this one and never spot the inversion. Both the Qur'an and Bible claim to be from God and claim to be truthful, so both Muslims and Christians believe their respective holy books to be from God. This is called circular logic, and we will need to dig deeper to find our way out. To begin, look closely at what the Bible and Qur'an say about themselves.

The Bible claims to be the Word of God. From 2 Timothy 3:16-17 we read:

> [16]All Scripture is inspired by God and profitable for teaching, for reproof, for correction, for training in righteousness; [17]so that the man of God may be adequate, equipped for every good work.

Hebrews 4:12:

> [12] For the word of God is living and active and sharper than any two-edged sword, and piercing as far as the division of soul and spirit, of both joints and marrow, and able to judge the thoughts and intentions of the heart.

Just as the Bible claims to be the word of God, so too the Qur'an similarly claims to be the word of Allah.

Qur'an 12:2-3

> We have sent it down as an Arabic Qur'an, in order that ye may learn wisdom We do relate unto thee the most beautiful of stories, in that We reveal to thee this (portion of the) Qur'an: before this, thou too was among those who knew it not.

Christians claim the Bible is from God because it says it is, and therefore anything it says must be true because it is from God. Muslims claim the Qur'an is from Allah because it says it is, and therefore anything it says must be true because it is from Allah.

So what can break us out of this never-ending revolving logical impasse? If each claims to be the word of God, and there is no other way to confirm or counter the claim, then we have reached a deadlock. To break out, we must get confirmation from another source. Here we will see one of many places where YHWH, the God of Israel, and Allah differ.

The Qur'an is forever locked within its own internal system of self-confirmation. The only criteria by which to determine the truth of the Qur'an is the Qur'an itself, which is what we are trying to analyze. If the Qur'an is the only standard to judge the Qur'an, then of course it would be incorrectly judged as true, just as any other self-referential text would be. In fact, there cannot be outside confirmation for the Muslim, because Allah does not provide any direct communication other than the Qur'an. While Islam is not clear within itself about how Allah communicates with mankind in the present day, it is clear that Allah does not offer any second witness to the authenticity of the Qur'an. The only witness to the truth of the Qur'an is the Qur'an. So there it ends for the Muslim.

Interestingly enough, the Bible teaches that to determine truth, at least two witnesses are needed (Deuteronomy 19:15, Matthew 18:16). While it may initially seem we are again using the Bible to confirm the Bible, in reality the Bible is forcing us to find a higher standard of corroboration to ascertain the truth of the Bible. Jesus Himself notes this when confronting the Jews regarding His identity. By necessity, Jesus was always faithful to the Scripture, and that Scripture requires two witnesses. John 8:16-18:

> [16] But even if I do judge, My judgment is true; for I am not alone in it, but I and the Father who sent Me. [17] Even in your law it has been written that the testimony of two men is true. [18] I am He who testifies about Myself, and the Father who sent Me testifies about Me.

If we want to be certain that the Bible is true, we are looking for two witnesses to its truthfulness. How are we to find a second witness for confirmation? As it happens, not only does God the Father testify to the truth of His Word, but God the Son also testifies to the truthfulness of Scripture. Jesus constantly references the Scripture as He has altercations with the Pharisees and teachers of the law (John 5:39, Matthew 19:3-4) as well as when He is illustrating parables (Matthew 13:14-15, Mark 12:10). On the road to Emmaus, Jesus explained the Scripture with reference to Himself (Luke 24:27). He makes such statements with the presumption of validity, considering the Scripture a solid and accurate reference with respect to what God has said. Yet, He goes much further than this. Jesus talks about the fact that Scripture cannot be broken (John 10:35). Many, many more times He talks about how the Scripture must be fulfilled (Matthew 26:54, John 13:18). In Matthew 22:31, Jesus specifically states that the Scripture that he is quoting is "what was spoken to you by God". These passages categorically speak to the truthfulness and reliability of Scripture. Finally, and most emphatically, Jesus leaves no room for doubt when in John 17:17 He says "Your Word is Truth."

Moreover, Jesus informs us of a third witness who will disclose the truth of Scripture, the Holy Spirit. In passages such as John 15:26 and 16:13 Jesus instructs his disciples about a future day when God the Spirit will guide them, and all believers, to the truth. This is the Spirit of God that lives within every born again Christian (Acts 5:32, Acts 15:8, Hebrews 2:4, Hebrews 10:15-16, Romans 8:16, 2 Corinthians 1:21-22). If a person is saved through the redemptive work of Jesus Christ, then the Holy Spirit that lives within each of us testifies to the truth of God's Word (John 14:17, John 14:26). While all these verses speak to this subject, Ephesians 1:13-14 summarizes best:

> [13] **In Him, you also, after listening to the message**
> **of truth, the gospel of your salvation--having also**
> **believed, you were sealed in Him with the Holy**

> Spirit of promise, [14] who is given as a pledge of
> our inheritance, with a view to the redemption of
> God's own possession, to the praise of His glory.

This point cannot be overstressed. After being saved, it is the
Holy Spirit that is given as a pledge, a down payment, confirming
the reality of our redemption. We are not left wondering whether
the Bible is true; the Holy Spirit is given to us as a corroborating
agent, certifying our redemption. Such certainty is definitely
cause for the praise of God's glory!

The previous exposition may have raised some eyebrows. After
all, doesn't Muhammad testify to the truthfulness of the Qur'an
just as Jesus testifies to the truthfulness of the Bible? Certainly this
is the case. There is a big difference between these two situations,
though, that would miss most cursory inquiries. Muhammad is a
human being and a human being only. A human has neither the
authority nor capacity to testify with respect to an infinite God and
His message to humanity. Muhammad claimed that he heard the
message from the angel Gabriel, and he had to assume the veracity
of the messages and even the identity of the supernatural being
speaking to him for that matter. However, in the case of Jesus, He
isn't just a human. He is the Son of God. Here God is providing a
second witness to God the Father. So too the Holy Spirit provides
the third witness. Someone may argue that God the Father, God
the Son, and God the Spirit are all one God, so it is just one witness.
Ah, but the Trinity means that God is three in one. When all three
persons of the Godhead testify to the truthfulness of Scripture, we
have multiple corroborating witnesses, and they all can be given
the utmost confidence since they all come from God Himself! It
is exactly because Allah declares himself an indivisible unity that
disallows him from providing a second witness to the truthfulness
of the Qur'an. Yet the God of the Bible, who exists in three persons,
independently corroborates Scripture by way of all three aspects of
the Trinity each testifying in their own unique way.

We have exposed a number of inversions; so this one might be anticipated. As mentioned, the Bible confirms multiple witnesses are needed to determine truth (Numbers 35:30, Deuteronomy 17:6). So what does the Qur'an say regarding the necessity of multiple witnesses? Specifically, how many are required to corroborate a contract, settle a criminal conviction, or enact a will? Sure enough, two male witnesses must be present (Qur'an 2:282, 4:6, 4:15, 5:106, 24:4, 65:2).. Yet, for some unexplained reason, Allah is exempted from this requirement (Qur'an 3:18, 4:79, 4:166, 48:28). Is it surprising that the Qur'an undermines its ability to be examined by multiple witnesses, even though that is its internaly recommended truth-testing requirement? In matters of practical living, everyone knows the value of multiple witnesses, apparently even Allah. Yet when it comes time to determine ultimate truth about God, the most important aspect of life, Allah switches standards and uses criteria that are neither testable nor provable.

It is true some of the verses of the Qur'an mentioned above make reference to angels as other witnesses. However, angelic witnesses are not verifiable witnesses. Ultimately, Muhammad is the only witness who heard an entity claiming to be Gabriel, a spirit being who had no way to prove his identity. Gabriel claimed to bring words from the creator but again offered no outside witness to corroborate. In court, this would be called triple hearsay testimony and would be soundly rejected, and rightly so. The Qur'an demands two witnesses to confirm truth for everything except itself! Muslims are trapped to believe the Qur'an because the Qur'an says it is the truth even though by its own definition, it provides no outside method for confirmation, and therefore fails the very truth-testing criterion it puts forth.

Muslims confronted with this line of reasoning will run a million different directions. Be careful to watch for the addition of an unnecessary layer of abstraction. In other words, do not let the conversation back up an extra level without dealing with the issue. For example, a Muslim may say, "Well, the author of a book is its best witness, so of course Allah is sufficient for a witness." The question, though, hasn't been answered; it has just been diverted up one level. Specifically, now how do we tell who the author is? If a book claims to be from someone who is unreachable, another witness is needed to confirm the author's true identity. The argument takes the focus away from finding the truth of the content and moves it to finding the truth of the author's identity. Nothing has changed, but an opportunity to get lost in the fog has been provided. This example illustrates how an attempted detour can be easily seen and averted. Backing up one layer of abstraction does not change the issue; it just gives an opportunity to get sidetracked.

This is deep, and getting a Muslim friend to grasp this may not be practical. It is offered here to help anyone exit the circular logic loop and establish the Bible as true. When it seems circular logic was the end of the road, God shows why and how He confirms His own Word, and the inversion of the Islamic doctrine oddly agrees while simultaneously undermining itself.

Corrupted by Whom, and When?

As has been previously stated, Muslims allege that both the Old and New Testaments have been corrupted. It is well known that manuscripts exist from the Dead Sea Scrolls found in the caves of Qumran in 1947. It is also well known that most of those Old Testament manuscripts are dated before Christ, and are identical to those we have in our possession today. However, we are not going to linger on such obvious facts, for such incontrovertible truth tends to have a chilling defensive effect on the Muslim, who needs more time to come to these conclusions on his own.

With that in mind, any Christian who has dialogued with a Muslim has learned that Muslims believe that the Bible has been changed through deletion, interpolation, and addition beyond reconstruction. This begs several questions that can be posed to Muslims. Exactly how was it changed? When was it changed? What changes took place? These are the questions that can be asked even though the Christian knows that the Muslim will not likely have coherent answers. It will get them to think some things through on their own in a way that doesn't involve an "us vs. them" mentality.

The most critical issue is that of timing. Just when does a Muslim believe the Old Testament theoretically changed? There are three possibilities to consider. The first is that that the Old Testament was altered before Christ. Secondly, it was changed after Christ but before Muhammad. The final option is that it was modified after the time of Muhammad. When the Muslim attempts to pinpoint the time of corruption, the Qur'an hems him in to the last two possibilities, after the time of Christ. The Qur'an clearly teaches the Bible was intact at the time of Jesus. The Qur'an, speaking of Jesus, says:

Qur'an 3:48

> And Allah will teach him the Book and Wisdom, the
> Law and the Gospel...

So we see according to the Qur'an, Allah taught Jesus through the Law, which must have been uncorrupted at Jesus' time. Otherwise, Allah was teaching Jesus from a corrupted Torah, which makes absolutely no sense whatsoever. A Muslim may say that the Torah had already been corrupted and that Allah taught the Torah directly to Jesus. This then leads to the question of why didn't Jesus' followers produce revised, unaltered copies of the Torah at that time? Either way, the implication is that the Old Testament was known at the time of Christ.

Yet the Qur'an goes even further than declaring the Torah was intact to teach Jesus (Qur'an 5:68, 5:110). It states that the Scriptures were intact at the time of Muhammad (Qur'an 2:40-41,

2:136, 2:285, 3:3, 3:93, 4:47, 4:136, 5:47-48, 6:91, 10:37, 10:94, 29:46, 35:31, 42:15, and 46:12) . The Qur'an tells Muhammad that he can ask Christians about the Scriptures to corroborate the truthfulness of Islam. Therefore, the underlying assumption is that the Scripture held by Christians at the time of the Qur'an had not been tainted in any way. The following passages in the Qur'an illustrate this point.

Qur'an 5:48

> Let the people of the Gospel judge by what Allah hath revealed therein. If any do fail to judge by (the light of) what Allah hath revealed, they are (no better than) those who rebel.

And:

Qur'an 10:94

> If thou wert in doubt as to what We have revealed unto thee, then ask those who have been reading the Book from before thee: the Truth hath indeed come to thee from thy Lord: so be in no wise of those in doubt.

Here the Qur'an instructs Muhammad to judge the revelation of the Qur'an by using the Gospel at the time of Muhammad.* One might argue this is an improper interpretation of the Qur'an. To determine whether or not this is the case, we can

---

* Some Muslims might argue this verse is a hypothetical, and isn't about Muhammad having any doubts. Additionally, some may interpret this verse as being directed at Christians rather than Muhammad. Whether Muhammad did or did not have doubts is not the point. Who the verse is directed toward is not the point. The point is what the Qur'an states about the veracity of Scripture, not Muhammad's mental certainty of Islam.

consult learned and respected Islamic scholars to hear what they have to say regarding this verse. I have chosen to quote highly esteemed Qur'an commentators, Al-Jalalyn, Ibn Kathir, and Al-Tabari. Each of these three authored a respected *tafsir*, or Islamic commentary. Any of them would stand by reputation on their own, yet I will quote from all three.

The Al-Jalalayn commentary on this verse notes that Muhammad could hypothetically "question those who read the Scripture, the Torah, before you, for it is confirmed [therein] with them and they can inform you of its truth."[13] Another Islamic commentator, Ibn Kathir speaks to the veracity of previous Scripture when referring to verse 3:3. In this verse, the Qur'an states that it is "Confirming what came before it." Ibn Kathir says this "means, from the previous divinely revealed Books, sent to the servants and Prophets of Allah. These Books testify to the truth of the Qur'an, and the Qur'an also testifies to the truth these Books contained..."[14] As yet another example, the renowned 9th-century Islamic commentator Al-Tabari comments on Qur'an 2:101 where it says "when there came to them a messenger from Allah, confirming what was with them." Al-Tabari exegetes this phrase to mean, "Muhammad confirmed the Torah."[15]

Consistently, early Islamic scholars asserted the truthfulness and veracity of the New and Old Testament. These commentators quoted here are renowned within Islam, and they never wondered why Allah would advise looking at past Scripture. They interpreted the Qur'an as validating their integrity. Why would Allah ever suggest ultimate truth be determined by looking at corrupted books? As a Muslim, being asked such a question creates a tremendous amount of discomfort, so the question should only be asked if the questioner is prepared for an intense reaction. Again, we ignore the mounds of textual evidence of Biblical manuscripts that predate Muhammad. Rather, we focus the Muslim on their own holy book, which strongly asserts the Bible should be used by Christians of Muhammad's time as a judge of true revelation.

So we are left to conclude that the Gospels were changed after the time of Muhammad. However, this also raises obvious anomalies. Firstly, if the Gospel (Injil) was intact at the time of Muhammad, where was the Islamic effort to safeguard it? It seems odd that neither the last prophet of God nor his companions made any attempt whatsoever to track down a copy to ensure its preservation. Did the previous words of God mean so little to Muhammad and his followers that they were content to let them fall into historical obscurity?

Another problem with taking the approach that the Gospels were changed after the time of Muhammad is figuring out who corrupted them. Specifically, consider the Old Testament. Was it corrupted by the Jews or by the Christians? Regardless of which one is chosen, what would be the response of the other group? Since both the Jews and Christians regard the Old Testament as Scripture, how is it possible for one group to change it without the other group realizing it? Remember, both Christians and Jews have a vested interest in maintaining an intact and unaltered set of Scriptures. Since both treat the Old Testament as sacred, it would be impossible for Jews to alter the Hebrew Scriptures without Christians objecting, as Christians already had translated the Old Testament into various languages. Similarly, had Christians altered the Old Testament, surely the Jewish people would have soundly objected to the desecration of their Holy Book by Christians.

The only way out of the fallacy is to conclude that Jews and Christians coordinated a corruption effort. This is the most untenable position that can be taken. If Jews and Christians were in collusion, in just what way did they change the writings? Did the Jews agree to change them to make Jesus appear to be the Messiah? Did the Christians agree to change them to make Jewish prophecy point away from Jesus as Messiah? Such statements implying a level of conspiracy by two separate groups with opposing agendas are absurd and ludicrous at face value.

When an argument followed to its logical end lands at an obvious contradiction, it means that the original assumption was incorrect. This is referred to as *reductio ad absurdum,* a form of indirect proof, and is a staple of mathematical and logical constructs. It is constantly used to prove theorems and suppositions. Start with an assumption, and if a logically reached conclusion is contradictory, then the initial assumption cannot be valid. Our assumption was that the Scriptures were corrupted. Trying to figure out when and by whom leads us nowhere but to confusion and inconsistency. Our conclusion is that the initial assumption was wrong; the Scriptures must NOT have been corrupted.

All this line of reasoning is done without once referencing the fact that we do posess manuscripts from before Christ confirming the reliability of the Old Testament. It avoids detailed discussion of manuscript evidence. The use of such facts can be appropriate for those Muslims seeking the truth. The use of logical questioning to bring them to the point of asking for such facts also has value, and that is the point being made here.

The Qur'an: Confusion and Confession

The Muslim views the Qur'an as ultimate truth. Interestingly enough, the Qur'an has quite a bit to say about the Bible. We should be well acquainted with what it says. As usual, it undermines its own position upon careful examination. First, it claims that God gave His prophets the earlier books. Then the Qur'an claims that such words are unable to be altered. To begin, in the following verses the Qur'an confirms that previous revelations are Allah's word.

Qur'an 2:87

> We gave Moses the Book and followed him up with a succession of messengers

Again we read:

Qur'an 4:163

> and to David We gave the Psalms.

The Qur'an even goes on to say that the information given to these early prophets was guarded until the time of Jesus.

Qur'an 5:46

> And in their footsteps We sent Jesus the son of Mary,
> confirming the Law that had come before him: We
> sent him the Gospel: therein was guidance and light,
> and confirmation of the Law that had come before
> him: a guidance and an admonition to those who fear
> Allah.

As we see, the Qur'an clearly establishes previous Scripture as from Allah. Next, the Qur'an does a wonderful job of heading itself off at the pass, ambushing itself yet again by claiming Allah's words cannot be altered in several verses, such as Qur'an 18:27.

Qur'an 18:27

> And recite (and teach) what has been revealed to thee
> of the Book of thy Lord: none can change His Words,
> and none wilt thou find as a refuge other than Him.

Some Muslims will claim these only apply to Muhammad and the Qur'an, but the Qur'an says otherwise.

Qur'an 6:34

> Rejected were the messengers before thee: with
> patience and constancy they bore their rejection and
> their wrongs, until Our aid did reach them: there is
> none that can alter the words (and decrees) of Allah.
> Already hast thou received some account of those
> messengers.

This clearly states that nobody can alter God's words. The Qur'an denies that corruption of God's Word is even possible. In context, this verse is referring to how Muhammad sometimes was suffering rejection for bringing Allah's word just as other prophets had before him. The Qur'an clearly teaches that the previous messengers had also been given Allah's word. Of equal importance, this verse of the Qur'an expressly says that such words cannot be changed, by anyone. Again, in the Qur'an we find:

Qur'an 6:115

> The word of thy Lord doth find its fulfillment in truth
> and in justice: None can change His words: for He is
> the one who heareth and knoweth all.

This ringing endorsement of the accuracy of the Bible offers Muslims quite a dilemma. In fact, there is only one possible avenue of retreat. The only exit is to claim that these passages are making reference to "Allah's perfect word," which wasn't shared with humanity until the Qur'an was revealed. In other words, the Muslim will state that Allah's words only exist within the Qur'an itself; everything before was just a foreshadowing of what was to come. The real book of Allah's word was stored in heaven, and not revealed until given to Muhammad. A variant of that same theme is that Allah's words cannot be changed, but earlier Scripture was misreported or misinterpreted by those people who listened to God's prophets and subsequently wrote down the message. Both versions of this same argument back the argument up another level of abstraction, that God's words are only found to be in perfection when viewing the Qur'an.

In an effort to disprove the veracity of the Bible, Muslims must undertake some mental gymnastics to attempt to refute the previously cited verses about Moses and David being given the Books of God's Word. This is especially true given that the Qur'an says that those words cannot be altered. Sure enough, again the Qur'an undermines this distorted line of reasoning by making sure Muslims know the Qur'an does not disagree with those revelations.

Qur'an 5.48

> To thee We sent the Scripture in truth, confirming the scripture that came before it, and guarding it in safety:...

According to this and other verses in the Qur'an, the Qur'an confirms previous scripture. It goes so far as to say a Muslim who disbelieves those writings has gone astray (Qur'an 4:136). It commands Muslims to follow previous scriptures (Qur'an 6:90). Additional confirmation can be found in Qur'an 5:43-44, 5:68, 10:64.

It is true that this line of reasoning is not a logical proof since it assumes the truth of the Qur'an as a starting point. However, the point is that a Muslim is required to believe that the Qur'an is reliable. Therefore, he must accept the evidence provided by the Qur'an regarding the Scriptures. To deny the veracity of the Scriptures is to deny the veracity of the Qur'an. This leaves the Muslim in a quandary, as denying the Scriptures opposes what the Qur'an teaches about them.

The Qur'an preaches that the earlier Scriptures were kept intact. This topic needs to be handled delicately. Muslims are not keen to hear that their beloved Qur'an is working against them. So when bringing up such topics, make sure to use decorum and compassion. Nobody likes it when their entire worldview comes crashing down around them. Denial is usually the first stage of any such process involving major upheaval, and it is no different when confronting a Muslim with the reality of such an obvious contradiction.

Once the topic of Scriptural inerrancy is discussed, the next major fallback position by the Muslim is that both Christians and Muslims worship the same God. The Muslim will say that the Christian worships Allah, but does so in an incomplete manner. This line of reasoning can leave the uninformed quite exasperated, so the time has arrived to apply some mental energy to this next attack to see where it breaks down.

Chapter 9

The 2ⁿᵈ Retreat: Muslims Worship the Same God

In today's world, many individuals find it fashionable to talk about multiple paths leading to the same God. There are entire books written to refute such ideas, and this book is not intended to duplicate them. However, the purpose of this book is to help develop a technique of recognizing the backward nature of Islamic thought. Therefore, in this chapter, we will apply this technique to the question of identifying the God of Christianity and the god of Islam.

We are well acquainted with the concept of identification. We all have an ID card that allows officials to determine our true identity. Those documents typically contain our name, address, and some physical attributes such as height, weight, or picture. Similarly, we wish to identify the true God using these same features. We will examine His name, where He lives, and His attributes. Since God does not have physical attributes, we must revise our strategy. Yet the revision is only switching from identifying physical characteristics to spiritual characteristics. The same techniques will apply, but rather than comparing height, weight, and hair color, we will compare inherent attributes of God.

What's in a Name?

In an attempt to convince the Christian that Allah and God are the same entity, most Muslims will be quick to point out that the Arabic term for God is Allah. Since Muslims may have never distinguished the generic use of "God' from His personal name, the argument seems like a logical one from the Islamic point of view. Many Christians even fall into this trap and repeat this soundbite as if it were a reasonable assertion. Some Muslims know that Christians as a group are not educated enough to perceive the logical implications of distinguishing between God's personal name and generic name. After all, from the Islamic point of view, any Christian cannot be very well informed on Islam, because a truly educated Christian would have already converted to Islam. The reality is that many Christians are indeed not informed enough to know God's personal name or its meaning.

The most predominant method people use to determine identity is by name, so this issue requires some deep analysis. The name God gives Himself is "YHWH," sometimes rendered Jehovah, which is a transliteration of the Hebrew words for, "I AM who I AM." While God has many attributes such as love, holiness, transcendence, mercy, omniscience, and many others, none of these could even be possible without His being self-existent. While we exist through His creation, God has the unique attribute of never having been created. His existence was, is, and will be eternal, thus the name. In fact, God went so far as to make sure people knew that His name, "I AM," would never be changed. In Exodus 3, Moses is arguing with God about whether he should be the one to help Israel escape from their plight in Egypt. Here is how God tells Moses to address Him. Exodus 3:13-15:

> [13] **Then Moses said to God, "Behold, I am going to the sons of Israel, and I will say to them, 'The**

God of your fathers has sent me to you.' Now they
may say to me, 'What is His name?' What shall I
say to them?" [14] God said to Moses, "I AM WHO
I AM"; and He said, "Thus you shall say to the
sons of Israel, 'I AM has sent me to you.'" [15] God,
furthermore, said to Moses, "Thus you shall say
to the sons of Israel, 'The LORD, the God of your
fathers, the God of Abraham, the God of Isaac,
and the God of Jacob, has sent me to you.' This is
My name forever, and this is My memorial-name
to all generations."

What does "all generations" mean? It means that God as
a being does not change, and His name that reflects His self-
existence will never change either. If this issue seems trivial or
unimportant, then search for a Muslim who would be willing
to pray to "I AM" rather than Allah. When a Christian prays
to God, the generic word for the omnipotent, omnipresent, and
omniscient being, he knows that his name is "I AM," or YHWH
in Hebrew.

Nowhere in the Old Testament does God specify that His
name is Allah. However, the pre-Islamic Arabs had a specific
moon god named Allah who had three daughters.* Muslims,
of course, will say that Allah is just another word for god. In
one sense this is true. Baal is another word for god too, but what
Christian would ever consider praying to Baal?

We need to examine the statement that Allah is just the Arabic
word for God. Muslims argue that even Arabic Bibles contain
the word "Allah" when referencing God. While this is true, the
statement blurs and obfuscates the point beyond recognition. This
specific aspect of the argument is particularly exasperating for

---

* Coincidentally, Muslims often decorate mosques and flags with pictures of a
crescent moon.

Christians to respond to. The difficulty lies in the double usage of the word Allah. Allah is both the generic Arabic word for "God" as well as the specific name given to that God by Muslims. When discussing this point, it must be clear which usage is being put forth to avoid confusion. So the question must be asked: When the term Allah is used, does its use refer to the specific name of the god of Islam or the generic name for God? As an example, an Arabic copy of the New Testament will use the term Allah, just as a Hebrew New Testament will use Elohim, but only in the general case. For specific references, Arabic Bibles still refer to God's specific name as something entirely different. God's name "I AM" is translated in Arabic Bibles as أهْيَة, which is not Allah, الله. The original Hebrew is transliterated into English as YHWH. These four consonants represent God's name, which the Jewish nation considered too sacred to even pronounce. This word is typically rendered in English Bibles as LORD in capitals. This term is different from the generic word for God, whether in Hebrew, English, or Arabic.

Do not be surprised if all this seems perplexing. Some illustrations might help to clear up the confusion. One of my coworkers goes by the name "Buddy". I remember once being in his office, and I said "You got that right, buddy." I suddenly realized that my statement was ambiguous. Was I using the expression as slang indicating a general sense of agreement with a friendly colleague, or was I saying that he, Buddy, was correct? While that story actually comes from my personal life experiences, consider another more contrived example. Imagine a married couple has a child, their first daughter. The couple is rather quirky, and names their daughter "Woman." Now this child grows up and finds a nice young man and gets engaged. The fiancée comes over to meet his new in-laws and says "Woman, come over here for a moment." The woman's parents get outraged because the fiancée made a derogatory remark by referring to their daughter by the generic use of the word meaning female. Was he genuinely being insulting, or was he calling her by her specific given name? The answer is uncertain. Since the same language can refer to general or specific, the issue is muddied beyond most people's ability to clarify. God is not the author of confusion, so wherever such befuddlement exists, we can be certain of its origins.

The bottom line is that the confusion over the word Allah as both specific and general masks the Muslim dilemma in recognizing that Muhammad changed God's name. For all the allegations that Christians corrupted Scripture, the fact remains that it is the Muslims who have changed Scriptures by changing God's name from YHWH to Allah. Again we are at a place where reality has been turned inside out. Muslims state we all worship the same God while simultaneously changing God's personal name. It is the Muslims who claim the God of Israel has always been named Allah, where in reality it has been they themselves who have been continually referring to a god of a different name. Unless Muslims want to start worshiping the great "I AM," or YHWH, we must conclude it is a distinct and separate being of a different name.

Who Needs Directions?

Another mechanism to determine identity is by address. There are at least five other people in the United States who have the same name that I do. However, each of them lives in a different state. The location of existence or residence can help determine identity. Should anyone wish to contact me, that person would not only need to know my name but what state I live in as well.

The question at hand is, "Where does God reside?" or "What is God's address?" Everyone knows that God is omnipresent, so this may seem a non-starter. However, God often constrains Himself in certain ways to make interaction with humans possible. Since we are finite beings, the infinite God sometimes operates in our finite physical realm in order to allow us to comprehend certain aspects of His nature. One such example has to do with the fact that God adopted a hometown while His presence was in Israel. That hometown was Jerusalem. In 1 Kings 9, after Solomon's prayer dedicating the temple, God declares that Jerusalem is to have special significance from that time forward:

> [3] The LORD said to him, "I have heard your prayer and your supplication, which you have made before Me; I have consecrated this house which you have built by putting My name there forever, and My eyes and My heart will be there perpetually.

That choice was not one of expediency, but rather contained substance of lasting significance. God's Word speaks to this point in a passage about events yet future. Isaiah 2:2-3:

> [2] Now it will come about that in the last days the mountain of the house of the LORD will be established as the chief of the mountains, and will be raised above the hills; and all the nations will stream to it. [3] And many peoples will come and say, 'Come, let us go up to the mountain of the LORD, To the house of the God of Jacob; That He may teach us concerning His ways and that we may walk in His paths.' For the law will go forth from Zion and the word of the LORD from Jerusalem.

God established his permanent place of residence in Jerusalem. The religion of Allah takes Mecca for the place of greatest significance. Once again, we see Muhammad changed God's address from Jerusalem to Mecca. Indeed we see that Christians and Muslims are not worshiping the same God. Some readers may view this as a trivial point, but God spends a great deal of time emphasizing this point throughout Scripture.

Many passages make it quite clear where God intends His earthly residence to be. These passages that reinforce this point of eternal residence in Jerusalem include 1 Kings 11:13, Jeremiah 3:17, Zechariah 3:2, Zechariah 8:2-3, Ezekiel 43:7, Micah 4:7, and Matthew 5:35. Another such passage is Joel 3:16-17:

> [16] The LORD roars from Zion
> And utters His voice from Jerusalem,
> And the heavens and the earth tremble
> But the LORD is a refuge for His people
> And a stronghold to the sons of Israel.
> [17] Then you will know that I am the LORD your God,
> Dwelling in Zion, My holy mountain
> So Jerusalem will be holy,
> And strangers will pass through it no more.

And more succinctly in Psalm 132:13-14:

> [13] For the LORD has chosen Zion;
> He has desired it for His habitation.
> [14] This is My resting place forever;
> Here I will dwell, for I have desired it.

For some, this truth may be lost, as they do not know exactly what Zion means. While the topic of what Zion fully entails is beyond the scope of this book, it is imperative that we talk about its geographical aspect. The term Zion, while a heavenly concept, has an earthly counterpart. In the present, it is inseparably linked to that geographical area known as Mount Moriah. It is commonly known from Genesis 22:2 as the place where Abraham was to sacrifice Isaac. It is the place where David bought the threshing floor from Ornan the Jebusite to build the temple (1 Chronicles 21:22, 2 Chronicles 3:1). Today we refer to this spot as the Temple Mount. While the exact location is only known to within a few hundred yards, it is the place near where the Dome of the Rock currently stands within the Al-Aqsa mosque complex. *

So not only has Islam changed God's name, but His earthly address as well. The Muslims assign God's location of record as Mecca. However, the Bible is clear that Jerusalem is God's permanent earthly dwelling place when He chooses to make Himself known on this terrestrial globe.

Attributes Matter

To continue, we need to lay some groundwork regarding one particular attribute of God, his immutability. This may first appear to be a slight detour, but it is an important one. To keep this as clear as possible, we will keep our focus on this one attribute. Immutability of God means that God is the same yesterday, today, and tomorrow. The Bible, in such passages as Psalm 102:27 and James 1:17, declares that God does not change. Malachi 3:6:

> ⁶ For I, the LORD, do not change...

The Bible goes even further and states that God's purpose does not change either. These passages can be found in Psalm 33:11 and Hebrews 6:17.

Do Muslims believe Allah is immutable? Strangely enough, the answer varies depending on the Muslim. Some Muslims will state that one of the 99 names of Allah is Al-Baqi, which some Muslims translate as immutable (but perhaps more accurately, the one that cannot not exist). Additionally, the Qur'an speaks to the immutability of Allah's purpose (Qur'an 17:77, 35:43, 48:23). However, not all Muslims would agree. Many Muslims disagree regarding the translation of Al-Baqi. They translate it as "The

---

* It is true that Muslims consider the site holy, but its religions significance is tertiary behind that of Mecca and Medina. Mecca is the undisputed center of Islam.

Everlasting." As such, Muslims are loathe to attribute anything to Allah that the Qur'an does not directly attribute to him. So we see a division between Muslims as to whether Allah is immutable or not. Regardless, both these assertions can be examined to see where they lead.

At this junction, we need to recognize where we are. If Muslims deny that Allah is immutable, then straightaway we note that Allah and YHWH have different attributes. In other words, if Allah is not immutable and YHWH is immutable, then by definition they are described differently. The fundamental rule of logic says that a thing cannot be true and not true at the same time. Saying that God is simultaneously immutable and not immutable defies all logic and reason. If Allah and YHWH have conflicting attributes, how could they be the same entity?

Alternatively, examine the case where some Muslims do believe Allah is immutable. If they believe this, then we need to examine that claim in detail. The Qur'an cites an interesting passage regarding the mercy of Allah. Read the next passage of the Qur'an, bearing in mind the immutability of Allah:

Qur'an 6:54

> When those come to thee who believe in Our signs,
> Say: "Peace be on you: Your Lord hath inscribed for
> Himself (the rule of) mercy:

Other translations say that Allah "ordained" mercy upon himself. Moreover, multiple Hadith discuss that when Allah created mercy, he divided it into 100 parts, keeping 99 for himself, and giving one to mankind. There are numerous such Hadith appearing in the most respected collections, two of them being Sahih Bukhari, Volume 8, Book 76, Number 476 and Sahih Muslim, Book 37, Number 6629.

So it is very clear that the Islamic literature teaches Allah created mercy, giving most of it to himself. This means that mercy is not part of Allah's essence, but is rather a created attribute. Before the time of its creation, mercy was not an aspect of Allah. Allah somehow made the decision to grant himself mercy, meaning that before that decision, he had none. The skeptical reader may question this line of reasoning since time does not have much meaning in eternity past. However, such a rebuttal misses the point. An infinite and eternal God does not create His attributes. He "is" the collection of His attributes. In other words, God does not have holiness because he chose to give it to Himself. Rather, God embodies holiness. Holiness is who He is, who He will always be, and who He always was, because His essence is to be holy.

So we are left with two choices. Muslims may state that Allah is not immutable, in which case we immediately see a clear differentiation between Allah, the god of the Qur'an, and YHWH, the God of the Bible. Alternatively, Muslims may state that Allah is immutable, which is clearly contradicted with reference to Allah's mercy. We see from the Bible that God is mercy, whereas Allah had to create it for himself. This discrepancy between the attributes of the god of Islam and the God of Christianity instantly marks them as separate beings.

Commands, Statues, and Practice

The differences between the God of the Bible and the god of the Qur'an also come out when viewing the doctrines and practices of each religion. The way that Allah and YHWH command us and explain concepts to us are also 180 degrees apart. The differences are so prolific it is impossible to provide an exhaustive list or to cover them in the detail they deserve. However, the following are several rapid-fire examples to illustrate. For brevity, the following are paraphrased. The verses of the Bible, and corresponding verses, or *ayat*, of the Qur'an are not quoted *per se*. However, the citations are given for those who want a full view of the context in which the various doctrines are espoused.

- **Prayer.** Muslims are instructed to rehearse the same prayers five times daily (Al-Bukhari Volume I, Book 8, 345). Jesus instructs his followers not to be repetitive (Matthew 6:7).
- **Sacrifice.** Muslims are instructed to shed the blood of others in jihad to achieve paradise (Qur'an 2:154, 3:157-158, 3:195). Jesus instructs his followers that His blood is shed for them (Matthew 26:28, Acts 20:28, Romans 3:25).
- **Self-improvement.** Muslims are instructed to purify themselves from the outside in (Qur'an 2:222, 9:108). Christians are purified by faith in God from the inside out (Acts 13:39, Galatians 2:16, Galatians 3:11, Philippians 3:9).
- **Abrogation.** The Qur'an teaches *nasik*, that some parts of it are superseded by others (Qur'an 2:106, 13:39, 16:101). The Bible teaches that not one jot or tittle will be changed (Luke 16:16-17).
- **The Jewish nation.** Muslims are told Jews are apes and swine, and must be slaughtered before the last day can come (Qur'an 2:65, 5:60, 7:166, Sahih Muslim Book 041 Number 6985). The Bible says that God's love for the Jews and His covenant with them is everlasting (Genesis 17:19, Zechariah 2:8).
- **Heaven.** Islam teaches Muslims will have wives in heaven (Sahih Bukhari Volume 4 Book 54 Number 476). Jesus teaches there is no marriage in heaven (Matthew 22:30).
- **Original sin.** Muslims deny the existence of original sin. They believe that all children are born pure (Qur'an 30:30, Sahih Bukhari Volume 2 Book 23 Number 440). In fact, Muslims will say that one never converts to Islam,

but only returns to his or her original nature. The Bible says everyone is born with original sin (Romans 5:12).

- **Love.** Allah loves those who do not fight against Islam (Qur'an 2:192), those who are careful (Qur'an 9:4), those who purify themselves (Qur'an 9:108), and those who fight in His way in ranks as if they were a firm and compact wall (Qur'an 61.4). God loves unconditionally and without partiality (John 3:16, Ephesians 6:9, 2 Peter 3:9).

The similarities are few and far between, but the differences jump out from all directions. There are many, many, more of these, but perhaps the most telling difference is how Jesus and Muhammad responded at the pivotal moment of each religion.

The Hijra and the Cross

The common avenue of argument that Christians and Muslims worship the same god is presented by attempting to prove that Islam is just an extension of Christianity. The goal for the Muslim is to convince the Christian that they both worship the same god, doing so by providing any number of activities or beliefs that Christians and Muslims have in common. For example, both pray, fast, and read a book considered holy. It is true that there are many surface similarities. However, such comments completely miss the mark. Ravi Zacharias once said "I often hear the question posed wrongly. They'll say, 'Aren't all religions fundamentally the same and superficially different?' No. They are fundamentally different and at best they are superficially similar."[16]

Fundamentally different is a grand statement. To test such a hypothesis, we can look closely at the pivotal event of each religion and contrast them. Let's identify the defining moment of each religion and then put them side by side. How would these two events oppose or parallel one another?

The foundational event in Christianity is the crucifixion

(and subsequent resurrection) of Jesus Christ. Everything in the Gospels leads up to the cross. Each Gospel devotes an especially inordinate amount of space to Jesus' last few days on earth. The cross is pivotal; for it is by the atoning death of Jesus that our sins can be forgiven. It is His subsequent resurrection that proves Jesus is who He claimed to be, and that He has the authority to forgive sins. The crucifixion is the pinnacle of Jesus' work, for by it finally He could say, "It is accomplished." From the standpoint of the earliest apostles, it was of prime importance (1 Corinthians 15:3-4). Indeed, the cross is emblematic of Christianity more than anything else. No other event in Jesus' life approaches the significance of what He achieved on the cross.

What is the pivotal moment in Islam? Was it perhaps the birth or death of Muhammad? Was it the day he first claimed to have received revelations from an angel who identified himself as Gabriel? As it turns out, the critical moment in Islam is the *hijra*, or migration. Muhammad originally lived in Mecca and suffered various forms of persecution. He became aware of a plot to assassinate him. Muhammad slipped away that very night and with a small band of followers fled from the city of Mecca to Medina. After arriving at Medina, Islam as a faith began to grow, Muhammad gathered many more followers, and years later, triumphantly returned to Mecca with an army. The hijra was the turning point in Islam, and Muslim scholars uniformly acknowledge the centrality of this event. In his comments on verse 9:22 of the Qur'an, for example, Ibrahim B. Syed, Ph. D. says, "There is no doubt whatsoever that the migration of Prophet Muhammad (peace be upon him) to Madinah was the crucial event, which established the Islamic civilization."[17] Shamim A Siddiqi makes the case that the hijra "... is a corner stone or the turning point of the process of the Islamic Movement for the establishment of Allah's Deen," adding this support from Mohammad Hussain Haikal: "Caliph Umar took Hijrah as the greatest event of the Islamic history when Rasulullah [the prophet of Allah] migrated from Makkah to Madinah."[18] The hijra is the central event around which the Islamic calendar starts. From an Islamic point of view, this book was completed in the year 1439 A.H. The abbreviation A.H. stands for Anno Hegirae, the Islamic year. Starting a calendar by this event certainly testifies to its place of prestige in the Islamic mindset.

So what happens when the cross and the hijra are considered simultaneously? The cross is all about Jesus embracing persecution. The hijra was about Muhammad fleeing from it. When Jesus' disciples learned of His impending death (Matthew 16:21), they wanted Jesus to glorify Himself without the cross (Matthew 16:22), but Jesus would have nothing of it (Matthew 16:23). He was willing to accept the Father's plan, regardless of the cost (Luke 22:42). In contrast, Muhammad, when confronted with paying the ultimate price, planned his getaway. He hatched a plot to have one of his followers take his place at his house to divert attention while he made his escape.[19] His response could not have been any more dissimilar to that of Jesus. Since Jesus' death served a greater purpose, the redemption of sinners, His death had purpose. In Muhammad's case, escaping a meaningless death would make sense from a human perspective.

Some people may argue that there were times when Jesus avoided being captured by the crowds, and indeed this is so (Luke 4:29-30). So too there were times when Muhammad, with an army behind him, was courageous in the face of battle. However, such objections miss the point entirely. Regardless of any of these specific times or places, what is being discussed is the pivotal moment, the central event, upon which each religion hinges. For Christianity, it is Jesus accepting the persecution which awaited Him. In Islam, it is Muhammad running from it. Upon inspection, we find the religions are not just different, but that they are totally opposite. The defining moments in each religion are a complete antithesis of each other. What Muhammad did at the critical juncture of Islam is the exact reversal of what Jesus did at the pinnacle of His time as God on earth.

Such a stunning discrepancy is not something to be argued in a debate. It is a question that can be posed. Why such a difference? The Muslim will be keen to defend Islam, so the question stands, why would running from persecution be superior to accepting it? Herein awaits opportunities to share the gospel.

All of these examples have established that Christians and Muslims clearly worship a different being who claims to be the Creator.

Equating Inequalities

The previous sections have approached the identificaiton of God through several vantage points; name, location, attributes, practice, and fundamental message. To appreciate how we will summarize these discrepancies between the Christian God and Islamic Allah, first imagine wanting to learn about a specific unmet person. Call him "Mr. X." To recognize him, we gather information from two different acquaintances who know this mystery person. So we talk to our first informant, and they describe Mr. X as Fred from Colorado, thin, loyal, talkative, a little goofy, but good-hearted. To get more information, we go to our second informant, and he describes Mr. X as Joe from Florida, short, stocky, stern, introverted, and self-serving. Getting two variant descriptions of Mr. X is a bit disconcerting, to say the least. We might conclude one of our informants is lying, grossly mistaken, or that they are describing two different people. Since we have gotten two completely variant descriptions of our mystery person, Mr. X, what would be our conclusion? There are five possibilities.

1. One or both of our informants is purposely lying to us.
2. One or both informants have mistakenly assessed Mr. X's qualities.
3. Mr. X is schizophrenic.

4. We have an incomplete description.
5. Our informants are referring to two separate people.

So it is with YHWH and Allah. If a Muslim tells us about Allah, and the description differs from that of YHWH, there are these same choices. The first option is that the Muslim or Christian is purposely lying. Second, it is possible that either or both Christians and Muslims are off base in their analysis of who God is. Third, it could be that God is schizophrenic. Fourth, it is possible that Christians and Muslims are describing the same being, but the descriptions sound incompatible because they are incomplete. Fifth, Christians and Muslims might be referring to different entities who both claim to be God. We must probe each of these options in detail one by one.

Is one group intentionally lying about the nature of God? As Christians, the witness of the Holy Spirit gives us confidence that we are presenting the true gospel. If Muslims are purposely being dishonest in their description of God, we would immediately conclude their assertions that Allah and YHWH are one in the same could not be trusted either. In other words, we know God values truth (John 14:6, Ephesians 4:25). By definition, both Muslims and Christians cannot worship the same God if either group is systemically deceitful about His nature.

The second choice, that either or both Christians and Muslims are off base in the analysis of who God is, is one that many New Age adherents cling to. These New Agers believe that somehow God does not fully reveal Himself to everyone, but reveals Himself partially to each religion, thus the discrepancies. Such an approach asserts that God has not sufficiently revealed Himself in the Bible, and thus we are mistaken about who God truly is. While it is true that there are mysteries not yet fully revealed, (Revelation 10:7) the Bible declares itself a revelation suitable enough to allow us to recognize God as much as possible on this side of the grave. We understand God as much as we as we are able and as is necessary at this point in time (Galatians 1:8, Revelation 22:18). Additionally, Jesus declares Himself the first and the last (Revelation 1:8). He states the Scriptures testify about Him (John 5:39). The Muslim viewpoint also rejects this New Age way of thinking, as the Qur'an also claims it is the final and solely reliable revelation as well (Qur'an 5:3). The point is that within the theology of both Christianity and Islam, each religion teaches that it has a sufficient and adequate view of God to allow its followers to recognize Him.

The third choice of a schizophrenic God should be immediately and soundly rejected as an absurdity beyond discussion (Hebrews 13:8).

The fourth option immediately presents problems in that many of the aspects of YHWH and Allah that we have been discussing are in direct contradiction to each other. According to logic, this presents us with a nonstarter. Logically speaking, an object or person cannot be a thing and not that thing simultaneously. Yet some people will yet claim this is a viable logical option in that God is too big for any one description to be complete. One often cited analogy used to support that God is beyond full description is that of the three blind men and the elephant. As one man feels the tail, another feels the body, and the last feels the trunk, they give seemingly conflicting reports. This anecdote is used in an attempt to posit that God is bigger than any of us can wholly describe, and therefore shows how all religions have part of a greater truth too big for any one religion to contain. Such an analogy easily breaks down, however, when we consider that God is uniform in His essence. While an elephant has different parts, God is God through and through. He does not have some holy parts and some unholy parts. He does not have some immutable parts and other changeable parts. He is what He is in totality and entirety. Again, since God is who He is in all regards, we cannot support a conclusion that two conflicting descriptions could relate to different parts of God. Both Christians and Muslims recognize

God is neither discontinuous nor heterogeneous. The indivisibility of Allah is a major theological position in Islam, so if a Muslim were to argue down this path, they would be undermining the very religion which they are trying to support.

Only the last possibility remains. We are forced to conclude that the descriptions are of two separate entities. Allah and YHWH have different names. They have different addresses. They have different attributes. Regarding practice, many of the particulars of Islam and Christianity are not just different but are diametric opposites. The pivotal moment of Islam and Christianity are also exact opposites of each other. Allah and YHWH must be different entities. No other explanation is sound.

The next batch of inversions is related to another frequent tactic of Muslims, the misuse of Scripture.

Chapter 10

The 3rd Retreat - Scripture out of Context

Once you have established a friendship with your Muslim neighbor, there are many times he or she will cite Scripture to prove the Muslim case. Typically, these Biblical citations come out of context and thus may catch the unsuspecting Christian off guard. However, when a true ambassador for Christ is properly prepared, these conversations will be the most fruitful. If the Muslim is trying to use the Bible to assert a point of view, the door is open to continue forward using God's word. These assaults are the most counterproductive for the Muslim because God's Word will not return void. Any time that any person is in the Word of God, it can effectually work to pierce the heart. From Isaiah 55:10-11:

> ^{10} For as the rain and the snow come down from heaven,
> And do not return there without watering the earth
> And making it bear and sprout,
> And furnishing seed to the sower and bread to the eater;
> ^{11} So will My word be which goes forth from My mouth;
> It will not return to Me empty,

> Without accomplishing what I desire,
> And without succeeding *in the matter* for which
> I sent it.

Never underestimate the power of God's Word. Once the inversion is exposed, God's Word will always provide an answer. With that in mind, it is time to look at how and why Muslims take the Scripture out of context.

Exegesis Inverted

In many conversations with Muslims, sometimes the Scripture will be taken so far out of context that it will be hard to recognize its original meaning. The Muslim will conclude the exact opposite of what the Bible actually says. To understand why Muslims misinterpret the Bible, we must compare the Bible to the Qur'an. Reading the Qur'an is often difficult for most Christians. The reason is that we are accustomed to reading the Bible, which contains contextual clues to help show us the message that God has for us. We read books of history, books of poetry, books of wisdom, books of prophecy, and letters. We place the Scripture within the context of the literary style in which it is written, as well as the section in which it is located.

In contrast, the Qur'an contains few such contextual clues or themes in any of its chapters. It is simply a congealed heap of warnings, words of guidance, and stories interspersed with whatever comes next in the text, often with no connection. For example, the second chapter of the Qur'an, Surah 2, is called "the Cow," but it is not really about a cow. The chapter contains 286 verses that cover a variety of unrelated topics, but seven verses, or about 4%, talk about the sacrifice of a cow.[20] Nothing else notable stands out as a theme, so thus the chapter name, such as it is. Even the chapters themselves are organized longest to shortest without regard for content or sequence. So don't be surprised that

Muslims are not trained even to understand what it means to put a verse in context. They have never done this before, so making that intellectual leap is not easy. Remember that students of the Bible are trained how to interpret within context. Our Muslim friends have no such practice.

To be fair, during a debate it is easy for either side to "cherry pick" verses that prove whatever point they want to drive home. Just as a Muslim can surgically extract a Biblical verse out of context, so too a Christian could selectively pluck verses from the Qur'an to undermine the Islamic message. This is one of the many reasons why it is imperative to move from debate to more targeted dialogue. Additionally, this is why early Islamic commentators are cited throughout this book. It would be easy to fall into such a trap, and it is this author's intention not to drive home a point by cherry picking verses from the Qur'an, but by exposing Islamic theology for what it is, as defined by trusted and respected Islamic theologians.

Back to the topic at hand, any diligent Christian wanting to understand more about the Bible uses a process called *exegesis*. Exegesis is defined as "critical explanation or interpretation of a text or portion of a text, especially of the Bible."[21] So when examining a verse, there are defined steps to take in order to correctly and accurately understand the Word of God. For example, first pray before beginning. Then read the verse to see the meaning. Then read the surrounding paragraph to get the general idea of what is being talked about, and thus see where the specific verse fits into the larger picture. Also, remember what book we are reading. For example, the book of Acts is a historical account of the formative years of the church, whereas 1 John is a letter of admonition to the early believers. Finally, remember the author in order to ascribe even more context to our analysis. For example, the Gospel of Luke was written by an author renowned for historical accuracy within the book of Acts, thus providing us an even larger picture of what is being read. At that point, we might examine individual words to see their other uses, do a topical search to see if we can examine a more obscure verse in light of more straightforward passages, or learn more about the people involved in the historical account we are analyzing.

If we dare to take a single verse and run with it, we do so at our own peril. Such behavior is indicative of cults. While it is true that some Christians will attempt this for their own gain, the seasoned Bible reader recognizes the folly of such an approach. We should view any verse that sparks controversy in light of the surrounding passage, the context of the message, the genre of the book, and the alignment of the verse with respect to a topical search.

Welcome to our next inversion. Muslims approach the Bible in a manner that is the antithesis of exegesis. They do not read the Bible to see what they might get *out* of it, but rather to see what they might put *into* it. This process is called *eisegesis*. This process involves combing the Bible to find verses that in isolation might reinforce the Qur'an. When found, the Islamic spin is inserted, regardless of the actual meaning of the passage. Reading something into (eisegesis) the passage that reinforces the Islamic worldview is what many Muslims are interested in doing.

The astute reader realizes this seems contrary to the Muslim notion that the Scriptures have been corrupted. The Muslim argument is that those verses matching Islamic doctrine are uncorrupted verses, and all the others that do not reinforce Islamic thought are the corrupted ones. This process allows them considerable latitude in misrepresenting Scripture. From the point of view of debate, it is impossible to dialogue with someone who makes up the rules as they go along. You cannot effectively communicate with someone who picks and chooses individual verses of a larger text as the Word of God while ignoring the rest as man-made.

Consider a real-life example to illustrate the point. Many Muslims believe that at the time of the crucifixion, Judas was made to have the appearance of Jesus, and thus it was Judas who was crucified and not Jesus.[22] This errant theology is linked to the account of Peter's denial of Jesus in Mark 14:54-71. A Muslim will quote Mark 14:71 where Peter says:

[17] I do not know this man you are talking about.

The Muslim will conclude Peter must have been truthful, and therefore must have meant that Judas had been made to look like Jesus. Then they will quote the Qur'an:

Qur'an 4:157

> That they said (in boast), 'We killed Christ Jesus the
> son of Mary, the Messenger of Allah'; but they killed
> him not, nor crucified him, but so it was made to appear
> to them, and those who differ therein are full of doubts,
> with no (certain) knowledge, but only conjecture to
> follow, for of a surety they killed him not.

The Muslim will then conclude that this proves Judas was made to appear as Jesus and then killed in place of Jesus. They come to this conclusion because the Qur'an implies it (Qur'an 4:157), and they use Peter's denial out of context to corroborate the supposition. Forget for a moment that the body of the person crucified was never found. Forget that Peter knew Judas, and so the denial still wouldn't make any sense. Forget the reports of direct interaction with the risen Christ by the apostles, including Peter himself. Pursuing these tactics with a Muslim may be appropriate, but could be fruitless. Any fanatical conspiracy theorist can explain away any combination of facts with enough effort. So what do we do?

Once we recognize the tactic of eisegesis, either we can discuss the example to determine how serious the Muslim is about seeking truth or we can examine the process of eisegesis itself to help the Muslim understand how to obtain truth from the Bible. In this way, we may find out the person we are talking to does not genuinely want to know what the Bible says but is just using some Islamic talking point that he does not even care about. In other words, asking the Muslim to dive into the Bible to examine the context in an effort to refute such accusations can be a very effective filtering mechanism to find out who is serious and who is not.

Nevertheless, it is important for our own understanding to stop the eisegesis process. Remember, we have already discussed that it was this same eisegesis process that Satan used to tempt Jesus by quoting Scripture out of context. Satan cited a passage in Psalm 91 outside the context of the promise in which it was contained (Matthew 4: 6). When anyone employs the technique of eisegesis, recognize it for what it is – a satanic tactic.

The Bible clearly presents the resurrection of Christ, but in the light of eisegesis, anyone can make the Scriptures say anything they want. In our example above, one verse was taken out of context to try to validate the Qur'an without looking into the whole story. Instead, we will perform some **exegesis** and see what comes out. First, we see Mark 14 is a prelude to the death of Jesus (Mark 14:8). So everything we read must be viewed in that light. Next, the account is about a brash man who claimed he would never abandon Jesus (Mark 14:31). However, Jesus told Peter that he would deny Him that very night (Mark 14:30). Indeed, that is exactly what happened, and Peter wept because of his disloyalty by abandoning Jesus (Mark 14:72). But we also know that Christ later led him to restoration (John 21:15-19). We can also do more research and learn that Peter claimed that Jesus was the Son of God before the crucifixion (Matthew 16:15-17). He saw the empty tomb (John 20:6-7). He also claims after the resurrection that Jesus is Lord and Savior, so much so that he begins his epistles with it (1 Peter 1:3, 2 Peter 1:1). To sum up, Peter says who Christ is in no uncertain terms in Acts 4:10-12:

[10] let it be known to all of you and to all the people of Israel, that by the name of Jesus Christ the Nazarene, whom you crucified, whom God raised from the dead--by this name this man stands here before you in good health. [11]"He is the STONE WHICH WAS REJECTED by you, THE BUILDERS, but WHICH BECAME THE CHIEF CORNER stone. [12]"And there is salvation in no one else; for there is no other name under heaven that has been given among men by which we must be saved."

In context, the denials of Peter are a perfectly fitting puzzle piece. Bible readers can then apply larger lessons to their own lives. We learn about how Peter was humbled. We also learn from looking at Peter's epistles that God uses fallible people, such as Peter. This encourages us to remember that any lack of faithfulness on our part can be forgiven, and that our relationship with Jesus can be restored. But the bottom line is that outside of context, citing this one passage referencing Peter's denial of Jesus is a poor and misleading attempt at falsification and conspiracy.

The particular example is not the point. The point is to be aware of the Islamic eisegesis of the Bible. When you are alert to it, you can then combat it in a more appropriate way. Debating the individual point may or may not be right. This particular example has power because it leads directly to the truth of the resurrection. In other cases, it may be better to ask the real question, how do we evaluate Scripture? By getting the Muslim to understand contextual issues, it might be possible to head off the next dozen frivolous debates before they start.

Let's dive into some more examples in order to help circumvent typical Muslim attempts at eisegesis. Remember that the point is to learn the general way to handle these, not the specific examples. We need a few examples though to get our minds around the problem.

What Does "Not Everyone" Mean?

We view this next example because it is one Muslims frequently quote out of context. Muslims often cite this particular section of the Sermon on the Mount, and it is a sobering call to all of us who claim Jesus as Lord and Savior. So, before we look at the Islamic interpretation, read these verses carefully. Matthew 7:21-23:

> [21] "Not everyone who says to Me, 'Lord, Lord,' will enter the kingdom of heaven, but he who does the will of My Father who is in heaven will enter. [22] Many will say to Me on that day, 'Lord, Lord, did we not prophesy in Your name, and in Your name cast out demons, and in Your name perform many miracles?' [23] And then I will declare to them, 'I never knew you; DEPART FROM ME, YOU WHO PRACTICE LAWLESSNESS.'"

The Muslim attitude is that Christians will approach Jesus for intercession, at which point He will tell the Christian to "depart from Him." They will harp on the fact that we should be doing the will of the Father, which is true. We should be doing the will of the Father. Muslims will gleefully point out that the people being rejected are those who did things "in the name of Jesus," i.e. Christians. It is easy to get caught up in the fact that Muslims do not understand Scripture, but to be fair, there are many Christians who do not have a thorough grasp either. Rather than focusing on the misuse of the passage, we will take another route.

Remember that our goal is not to argue the point, but rather to bring the conversation back to the redemptive work of Christ. So where do we go with such a partial interpretation? First, let's ask ourselves what "not everyone" means. Does it mean most, some, few, or none? In the most general sense, "Not everyone" means "not everyone." Therefore, by definition, some who do call Jesus

"Lord" will enter. A Muslim must believe that NO ONE who calls Jesus Lord will enter, but here Jesus clearly indicates some, if not most, will. This provides a wonderful avenue to now ask the Muslim "Why are some who call Jesus Lord saved?"

Moreover, here Jesus says, "I never knew you." What does it mean for Jesus to know us? How could He know us if He is dead? Apparently, this passage implies that He is not dead, and He does know some people personally. Therefore, Jesus must still be alive and active in our lives! Then He says, "depart from ME." Why didn't He say "depart from Allah"? Why instead is the direction of the departure away from Himself? All these questions are great conversation starters without being confrontational. Of course, the answer is because Jesus is God, and making us depart from Him is the punishment for not knowing Him, i.e., not having that personal saving relationship. As LORD, Jesus is one to whom we answer and one who is responsible for salvation through His death and resurrection.

Don't be flustered. Recognize that there is a general confusion within Islamic apologists about these verses. One Muslim apologist states his interpretation this way:

> Further the verse implies very convincingly that those were not ordinary nominal Christians with indifferent faith, but they would claim to have been blessed with the powers of working miracles in the name of Jesus. Claiming to have done many wonderful works in his name itself is self explanatory that they had confessed Jesus before men. [23]

This is one of the aspects of Christianity that Muslims just don't understand. This criticism is not meant to be derogatory. Again, here is an opportunity. What does it mean to perform miracles in Jesus' name openly, yet not to have a personal relationship with him? It just means saying some words, regardless of whether or not the person truly believes them (Acts 19:13-16). What if a person confesses Jesus before men, does not actually believe it, and then builds an orphanage to show others his (supposed) love for Jesus? Do such works earn rewards? Here is an opportunity for a launching pad to discuss the plan of salvation through grace rather than works.

Such a person who has confessed Him may have done wondrous works for Him, and yet still does not "know" Him. Jesus, the same God who created the heavens and earth, cared so much about everyone that He came down to earth as an example. This same God wants to know each and every human. He desires to come into close proximity with us and know each of us on our most intimate level.

Look carefully at what the Bible is teaching here. In this one simple passage, there are so many clues that are left pointing toward Jesus' identity and the true avenue of salvation. The very verse used to attempt to disprove Christian doctrine points squarely back to the gospel message. Yes, the analysis of Matthew 7 by the Muslim twisted the passage out of recognition. Yet the door has swung wide open! Just because a person confesses Jesus before men and does something "in His name" does not mean the person truly knows Him. It is our relationship that is paramount, and this passage expressly demands that Jesus "know" us! Many Biblical passages can now be brought to bear on what it means to have a relationship with Jesus! So don't get caught up in the apologetics of the verse, but rather use it to bring the discussion to bear on the relevant topic of knowing Christ.

Muhammad in Deuteronomy?

Another example of Muslim misuse of Scripture is an attempt to find Muhammad in prophetic passages. Muslims will take passages that clearly point at the Messiah, and insist that they point at Muhammad. While the Bible references Jesus as the Son of God consistently and frequently throughout the text, Muslims scour the Scriptures looking to find a reference to Muhammad. When they get something that they can shoehorn into Islamic theology, they run hard with it. One such favorite verse that Muslims enjoy citing is one that came through Moses, and is found in Deuteronomy 18:18:

> ¹⁸ I will raise up a prophet from among their countrymen like you, and I will put My words in his mouth, and he shall speak to them all that I command him.

Muslims claim this verse points directly to Muhammad. Careful and thoughtful individuals who bother to read the next few verses will have the information for more fruitful discourse. Deuteronomy 18:19-22:

> ¹⁹ It shall come about that whoever will not listen to My words which he shall speak in My name, I Myself will require {it} of him. ²⁰ But the prophet who speaks a word presumptuously in My name which I have not commanded him to speak, or which he speaks in the name of other gods, that prophet shall die. ²¹ You may say in your heart, 'How will we know the word which the LORD has not spoken?' ²² When a prophet speaks in the name of the LORD, if the thing does not come about or come true, that is the thing which the LORD has not spoken. The prophet has spoken it presumptuously; you shall not be afraid of him.

Verse 22 defines the litmus test for identifying prophets. If anyone speaks prophecy that is not later fulfilled, God says such a person should not be considered a prophet. Do Muslims who refer to this verse also point to Mohammed's prophetic utterances and their corresponding fulfillment? If not, why not? The answer is because there are none! The same verse, cited by Muslims in an attempt to claim we were foretold about Muhammad is immediately followed by one that condemns him as a false prophet. This pattern often repeats itself. While Muslims point to a scriptural reference in an attempt to justify some Islamic doctrine, the next few verses will undermine that very same doctrine. After a while, the alert Christian will come to appreciate the power, reliability, and perfection of God's Word.

Not only does Deuteronomy 18:19-22 reference the necessity of fulfilled prophecy, but it goes much deeper. In Acts 3:22 Peter references this verse making clear it referred to Jesus. Jesus Himself points out that Moses was referencing Him in John 5:46. An even more in-depth study reveals more truth that is often lost. These verses say the prophet will be like Moses. Here again, we have a huge opening to ask "What does it mean to be like Moses?" Examining both Jesus and Muhammad in light of this statement -- "like Moses" -- illustrates the shallowness of the Muslim use of this verse:

1. Moses prophesied about the nation of Israel (Leviticus 26:42, 44-45). Jesus also prophesied and noted its importance (Matthew 24; John 14:29). Muhammad never prophesied.*
2. Moses established a blood covenant with God (Exodus 24:8-10). Jesus did the same (Matthew 26:28:30). Muhammad did not.
3. Moses talked directly to God (Numbers 12:6-8). Jesus spoke directly to God the Father (John 12:28, John

---

* As with most such generalizations, there is more to the story here. Some Muslims would disagree with this statement. However, a deep dive into Islamic theology will reveal the accuracy of the assertion.

14:10). Muhammad was required to have an intermediary (Qur'an 42:51).

4. Moses was in the presence of God, and his face glowed as a result (Exodus 34:5, 29-30). Jesus' face also glowed at the transfiguration (Matthew 17:1-2). Muhammad was only allowed to see Allah in a vision, and even this is disputed among Muslims (Qur'an 17:1).

5. Moses performed miracles (Exodus 14:21-22). Jesus also performed many miracles (John 21:25). Muhammad's only purported miracle was bringing the Qur'an.[24]

These examples* illustrate two key points. First, the Islamic pattern of quoting Scripture out of context always presents an avenue to reference the surrounding Scripture. Not only will undertaking these exercises of examining nearby Scripture help maintain a level of composure for the Christian, but it will also allow the truth to be revealed to the few Muslims that are seriously seeking. Secondly, Islamic doctrine has a tendency to contradict itself and illuminate its own inconsistencies. Once trained to watch for it, the pattern becomes more and more obvious. We should always be cautious so as not to beat them over the head with this type of material because many Muslims are not ready to handle such a cudgel of truth.

The point is that Scripture itself combats its misuse when specific passages are misapplied. Further, there is a larger issue of Biblical authorship as well, which will be tackled next.

That Renegade Paul

Since we are in the business of looking at the Muslim misuse of Scripture, we need to take a look at the Muslims' favorite man

---

* This information has been restructured and extended from the original cited source.

to criticize, Paul. Muslims will often imply that Paul preaches a different gospel of Christ than did the other apostles. Again, while debating this point is typically fruitless, the Christian should be prepared to understand why this assertion has no merit. The Bible itself deals with this ridiculous assertion. As always, the Word comes fully prepared to refute these attacks, showing itself for what it is, the Word of God. To see this fully, we will examine three scriptures: one with words from a fellow apostle, one with words from Paul, and finally one from the Holy Spirit.

First, Peter references Paul's epistles as in agreement with that of the rest of the apostles in 2 Peter 3:16:

> [15] and regard the patience of our Lord as salvation; just as also our beloved brother Paul, according to the wisdom given him, wrote to you,

In this passage, Peter confirms that Paul has received wisdom and that he preaches the same message. Paul himself states that he must deny his own authority except for that which points back to God. 1 Corinthians 3:4-6:

> [4] For when one says, "I am of Paul," and another, "I am of Apollos," are you not mere men? [5] What then is Apollos? And what is Paul? Servants through whom you believed, even as the Lord gave opportunity to each one. [6] I planted, Apollos watered, but God was causing the growth.

Finally, The Holy Spirit authorized Paul and Barnabas to continue the work as recorded by Luke in Acts 13.2:

> [2] While they were ministering to the Lord and fasting, the Holy Spirit said, "Set apart for Me

> **Barnabas and Saul (Paul) for the work to which I have called them."**

So what does this all mean? It means that when confronted about how Paul allegedly corrupted the Scriptures, it must be asked how the doctrine he wrote about is any different than what is written by the other apostles. If this were not enough, John speaks of how to identify false prophets in 1 John 4 1-3. In this passage, John notes that anyone who proclaims Jesus Christ has come in the flesh is from God, which Paul does, and so again we see confirmation of the message. Finally, Jesus Himself tells us that "by their fruits you shall know them" (Matthew 7:16). We know Paul preached Jesus Christ to the Gentiles and changed the world.

Trumping Scripture with Pseudepigrapha

As we have seen, not only do Muslims assault the Bible on the micro level but many Muslims assault the Bible on the macro level as well. Muslims will often quote a variety of passages from the pseudepigrapha. That is just a fancy word referring to dubious sources such as the Gospels of Thomas, Phillip, or Barnabas. No Christian denomination accepts these as authentic given their later date and their theological inconsistencies. Some of the verses in these spurious texts are nothing less than outrageous. Quoting any of these in full from their source would serve no purpose for this writing other than distraction. There are verses about Mary being transformed into a man, Jesus committing adultery, a giant cross coming to life, and other such egregiously anti-Christian expositions. Occasionally a Muslim will bring some of these stories to bear, catching most Christians unaware.

It is so easy to get caught up in the unprofitable details of these types of arguments. For example, the Gospel of Barnabas was first discovered in the 16th century and was written in Italian at that. Trying to imagine a Muslim accepting some new Surah found today written in Urdu or Turkish would be an analogous situation. Spending hours researching the unreliability of these texts will only result in finding out that the Muslim friend likely does not care anyway. While it is often helpful to know something about how the Bible was codified and how to identify false Gospels in order to maintain one's own composure, having a debate about the authenticity of Scripture is typically unprofitable. Does your Muslim friend have a genuine interest in the theological strategies of identifying false Gospels? Even most Christians have not undergone a deep study into such topics.

Yet there are intriguing points to inquire about here. Why does the Muslim choose to present the information? Does the Muslim believe the quoted text is valid? If so, why? If not, why not? In other words, why does the Muslim accept the Gospel of Barnabas as valid, but not the Gospel of John? The answer will typically reside in that the Gospel of Barnabas says what the Muslim wants to hear, while the Gospel of John does not. The Muslim will counter that the Christian does the same; he accepts the Gospel of John because it says what the Christian wants to hear and rejects the Gospel of Barnabas because it does not. So we have reached a stalemate. Perhaps the Muslim's point of view is that all of these writings are fruit from a poisonous tree, thus invalidating the whole bunch.

So the question remains. Why is the Muslim presenting such material? If the Muslim does not believe the texts are valid, then the likely motivation to bring them up is to disprove the gospel. However, as Christians, we know how to determine the truth of Scripture. We know the Bible was canonized after centuries of the Holy Spirit's leading. So the question must be turned back around. What does the Muslim believe about the validity of Scripture? Since we know which Scripture is true and which is not, now is the time to ask the Muslim how anyone would make such determinations. This will likely only be a filtering mechanism. By asking questions about how the Muslim tests Scriptural integrity, you can learn whether he is seriously asking questions, or is just running interference. Perhaps the Muslim is not interested in knowing how to determine whether the Bible is true. If this is the case, perhaps it is time to move on.

There is always room talk about Islam itself. As with any false religious system, the doctrines of Islam, when put under full scrutiny, will show themselves as internally inconsistent. In the next chapter, some of the most prominent of these will be discussed.

Chapter 11

How Islamic Doctrine Collapses on Itself.

Sometimes inversions are uncovered just by examining Islamic doctrine with respect to the rest of the religion. Typically, an argument will be put forward and it will make certain assumptions or use certain points of information to assert the conclusion. However, the very same assumptions will often result in undermining Islam itself. Just following the Muslim argument to its logical conclusion will disprove the very item they are trying to assert. Alternatively, the same information, when considered in light of other passages in the Qur'an, corners the Muslim into very precarious positions. It is this last situation that must be handled with care. Nobody likes to feel cornered, especially when it has to do with a religious system they have bet their whole life on. With that in mind, it is time to look at some of these in detail.

Self-Inflicted Wounds

One Muslim miscue to be aware of is that Muslims will undermine their own doctrine when attempting to disprove Christianity. Watch for this, because it is a common thread. To illustrate this point, consider the Islamic view of the subject of sin and the justice of God. Dealing with sin is one area where Islam struggles to find consistent answers. Islam views the justice of God as scales weighing good and bad. Those whose good deeds outweigh their bad deeds go to Paradise, while those whose bad deeds are heavier wind up in hellfire (Qur'an 7:8-9). This raises the question of why God punishes people. As Christians, we know that an eternity in hell separated from God is what the unbeliever has chosen. God satisfies His justice and simultaneously grants the wishes of the person who never wanted to know God in this lifetime. However, the Islamic view of hell is somewhat different.

The words of Muslims themselves illustrate how Islam undermines its own doctrines in an effort to prove Christianity wrong. One Islamic author, attempting to refute the atonement, feels that it is unfair for God to punish anyone who has performed more good than evil. He goes on to assert that if a person wants to overcome his evil part, irrespective of Christ, punishment would be unfair. He puts it this way:

> After all, the only proper motive for punishment is to check evil and reform the offender. To punish a person for his past sins, even after he has repented and reformed himself, is a sign of vengeance, not justice. [25]

Remember that our goal is to take the inverted statements of Islamic thought and use them to lead the Muslim to a full understanding of Jesus Christ. Interestingly enough, the last sentence of this Muslim's quote points directly to the gospel. The author cites the only reason for punishment is to provide a method of reforming the person punished. In an attempt to defraud the Christian doctrine of atonement, the author undermines the very reason for hell within Islam, his own religion. After all, if the only proper motive for punishment is reform, then hell would be a place of reformation, which the Qur'an definitely does not teach. In Islam, hell is a place a person goes forever; there is no reform possible. The Muslim's logic to discount Christianity forces him to deny what his own Qur'an teaches him about hell.

If that were not enough, examine the second sentence in close detail. Note the focus on repentance. Is it at all possible for an unrepentant person to be forgiven? In Islam, the scales for judging eternal destination mentioned in the Qur'an say nothing about repentance. Yet the issue of repentance manages to come up anyway. What is repentance? How do we achieve it? How does it work? These questions come flying out of the original attack against Christianity. Yet Islam never addresses the issue of how repentance works, or how much of it is necessary. The attack against Christianity undermines Islamic doctrine while simultaneous points back to Jesus' atoning work on the cross.

This pattern of Islamic talking points undermining Islam itself is often seen. The irony of abandoning one's own beliefs to disprove the gospel is a theme often seen both today and in Jesus' time. For example, to crucify Jesus, the Jews had to verbally state their allegiance to Caesar (John 19:15). Again to arrest Paul, the Jews had to submit to Roman authority, the government they loathed (Acts 17:7). Trying to tear down the message of who Christ is will often require someone to disavow their own beliefs.

In all of these previous examples, it is the concept behind them that is more important than the example itself. The previous example was not given primarily to understand one Muslim's view of atonement, but rather to become more cognizant of what to watch for. Remember to be in prayer. The Word of God is consistent, always corroborating itself. Don't ever abandon the Word of God, as it is the first place to look for answers. Undermining one's own doctrine to win a debate is a sure sign something is inherently wrong. Again, the goal here is not to win a debate but to use Muslim arguments to point back to Jesus. Another excellent example of this type of inversion drops out from one of the Muslims' favorite topics, the Crusades.

Christianity Meets Jihad

In a previous chapter, we saw that the God of Christianity and Allah of Islam have different names, different addresses, and different characteristics. A pertinent question to ask is whether we see any difference in the followers of each religion. Jesus said, "by their fruit you will know them," (Matthew 7:15-20) so it would seem logical that we should examine the actions of those following the religion to gauge the nature of that religion. If we compare the milestones of Christianity and Islam, it will be quite revealing. However, any such dialogue with a Muslim will quickly migrate to one particular time in Christian history, the Crusades. This next Islamic talking point must be exposed for the inversion that it is.

Both Muslim and Christian alike are aware of the Crusades, unarguably one of the greatest Christian atrocities of all time. When confronted with the topic of the Crusades, most Christians will respond that the actions of those at the time did not reflect the teaching of Christ. Christians may also point out that there are good Christians and bad Christians, just as there are good Muslims and bad Muslims. These statements are true, but they miss a deeper irony.

A little closer look uncovers what instigated the Crusades. While the global politics, societies, and events of the time were complex, there is a critical moment to note. This watershed moment was when Pope Urban II gave his speech in Clermont in 1095, asking Europeans to retake the Holy Land as Christian territory. Here is an excerpt from his speech, as recounted by the chronicler Fulcher of Chartres and adapted from Thatcher:

> All who die by the way, whether by land or by sea,
> or in battle against the pagans, shall have immediate
> remission of sins. This I grant them through the power
> of God with which I am invested.[26]

By this point, thoughtful readers might spot this irony more clearly before it is explicitly spelled out. What Pope Urban II did in this speech was introduce the concept of forgiveness of sins via death in battle into Christianity. This decree by the Pope came nowhere from Scripture and was a result of human error. Nowhere does our Lord Jesus Christ teach remission of sin for dying in battle. Rather, this teaching comes from Islam! It is unclear whether the Pope knew he was taking this teaching from Islam, but the reality is that it is an Islamic teaching nonetheless. Those who disagree should ask themselves what other religion preaches salvation for dying in battle? Obviously, Christians are disgusted at the concept of jihad within Christianity. It is embarrassing and distasteful when considering the mandate of Pope Urban II. He deviated from the teachings of Christ and imitated an element of Islamic doctrine. It may be argued that I am overemphasizing the theological aspects of the launch of the Crusades compared to the political, cultural, and military movements of the day. That is a fair argument, but we do not want to underestimate the theological significance either.

At any rate, the events that followed this speech were disastrous. Christians melded an aspect of Islam into Christian thought wholesale, and Christians are still apologizing for it almost a millennium later. What is critical here is not that individual Christians of the 11th and 12th centuries engaged in brutal acts. What is critical is that Biblical ideology itself was viciously altered. This perverted ideology caused its followers to act in horrible ways. By papal decree, the concept of jihad, though not specifically named, was smuggled into a place where it never belonged, and never will belong.

So what is the point? The point is that the Crusades started as a result of jihad being declared. Does the Muslim applaud the teaching of jihad or not? This is a question that every Muslim should be asked. If they applaud jihad, then they should not be against the concept of the Crusades. If they denounce jihad, then they do not follow Islam. Many Muslims may react viscerally to this line of reasoning.

Muslims may counter that jihad is only warranted against infidels, so jihad is acceptable when perpetrated against others, but vicious and unwarranted when perpetrated against them. But why is this so? The concept of treating others as you wish to be treated as a moral code is one most people can relate to and will agree with (Luke 6:31). Why is it moral to treat someone else differently than you yourself would wish to be treated? Here the teachings of Jesus can be brought to bear on the topic. Notice that we have moved from arguing over the rightness or wrongness of the Crusaders, and gotten back to Jesus' message and its relevance for everyone.

To recap, in the case of Christianity, the height of brutality came when the Pope took a page from Islam and tried to shoehorn it into Christian theology. It is just too ironic to watch Muslims harangue Christianity for the one instance when it attempted to adopt an aspect of Islamic teachings. The question must be asked: Do Muslims applaud the inclusion of this Islamic teaching into Christianity or do they denounce adopting this piece of Islam into Christianity? I hope this irony is not lost on you. Muslims condemn Christians of the 11th and 12th century for trying to adopt a tenet of Islam.

The Trinity in the Qur'an?

Continuing to examine how Islamic doctrine collapses on itself will lead us to a more in-depth view of the Qur'an, and the oddities therein. Our first oddity relates to the many references to the lack of Oneness (tawhid) of Allah. Remember that Muslims believe Allah possesses a singular type of oneness of nature, essence, and purpose. That oneness, or tawhid, is a major point of contention when compared to the Christian view of God having a triune nature. Strangely enough, when we begin to examine the Qur'an in more detail, a conflicting story emerges. To see this next inversion fully, we must also take a small detour to discuss the Holy Spirit.

If it has not been made clear yet, remember this is not about trying to show a Muslim the contradictions in his holy book. That typically leads nowhere. Muslims are convinced that the Qur'an tells them that Allah is indivisible, and their view of God hinges around that fact. Assaulting that belief head on is usually not an effective approach. Therefore, this section is rather about finding a hook by which to share the story of Jesus. As it happens, the Qur'an has some interesting verses which do just that.

One thing Muslims do not understand is the indwelling of the Holy Spirit. This should not be a surprise, as Jesus Himself told us that the world cannot know or receive this Spirit of Truth (John 14:17). We should expect that Muslims do not grasp who the Holy Spirit is. As one of my newly saved friends commented, "In this world, you begin to learn after you are born, so why would you ever expect to learn about spiritual matters before you are born spiritually?" It is quite the profound statement for someone who only knew Jesus for two weeks. As an unbeliever myself until the age of 33, I certainly did not understand the working of the Holy Spirit. So this is not a criticism; it is just spiritual reality. Muslim or not, a person cannot understand the Spirit until after having felt the Spirit.

The Qur'an also talks about a Holy Spirit, but most Muslims disagree on what or who the Holy Spirit is. Most will say it is Gabriel (Qur'an 16:102). However, we will read some of the other verses from the Qur'an and Hadith to see if we can figure out what or who the Holy Spirit is.

Qur'an 97.4

Therein come down the angels and the Spirit by Allah's permission, on every errand:

Qur'an 5.110

> Then will Allah say: "O Jesus the son of Mary!
> Recount My favor to thee and to thy mother. Behold! I
> strengthened thee with the holy spirit,

(Sahih Muslim, Book 4, Number 0987)

> Narrated Aisha: The Messenger of Allah (PBUH)
> used to pronounce while bowing and prostrating
> himself: All Glorious, all Holy, Lord of the Angels
> and the Spirit.

So we can sense the ambiguity and understand why there might be a debate within Islam itself. How can we make sense of the Islamic mindset in order to reach our Muslim friends? With this in mind, consider perhaps the most illuminating clue in the Qur'an is the very verse cited in an attempt to disprove the Christian concept of the Trinity.

Qur'an 4.171

> O People of the Book! Commit no excesses in your
> religion: Nor say of Allah aught but the truth. Christ
> Jesus the son of Mary was (no more than) a messenger
> of Allah, and His Word, which He bestowed on Mary,
> and a spirit proceeding from Him: ...

Here we see an interesting aspect of Allah. First, the Qur'an states that Jesus is some type of Word from Allah. This may be a hook right into John 1:1, because if you ask a Muslim what it means for Jesus to be a Word from Allah, most have no idea. Additionally, we hear Jesus described as "a spirit proceeding from Him." Now clearly this spirit cannot be Gabriel here, because otherwise Jesus was Gabriel, which makes no sense. Rather, the Qur'an implies the spirit to be some aspect of Allah's personality. Here again, the Qur'an undermines itself in the very verse cited to disprove the Trinity. In this very same verse where the Qur'an attempts to disprove the deity of Christ, it discusses three different aspects of Allah: Allah, Word, and spirit. It would be humorous if it were not so convoluted.

Now one can go out on a limb and still claim the spirit mentioned above could be Gabriel. Somehow Gabriel strengthened Jesus, and somehow Muhammad prayed to Allah, "the Lord of Gabriel." A little more digging dispels this notion quickly. If the spirit of Allah were Gabriel, this next verse would imply that Gabriel visits every Muslim.

Qur'an 58.22

> Thou wilt not find any people who believe in Allah and
> the Last Day, loving those who resist Allah and His
> Messenger, even though they were their fathers or their
> sons, or their brothers, or their kindred. For such He
> has written Faith in their hearts, and strengthened them
> with a spirit from Himself. And He will admit them to
> Gardens beneath which Rivers flow, to dwell therein ...

So this spirit comes from Allah and strengthens those who have faith. This verse is one that could be used as a means to inquire about the nature of that spirit. What is the proper interpretation of this verse? Does Allah have a spirit, and if so, how can this be and yet Allah still maintain his oneness (tawhid). Asking such a question may wind up causing the Muslim to explain the concept of the Trinity to you!*

---

* On a personal note, I once had a Muslim explain to me that Allah operated in paradise, but also sent his perfect word, the Qur'an, as a manifestation of his will, and thirdly his spirit to guide mankind.

Yet it gets even stranger.

Qur'an 38:71-72 (See also 15:29)

> Behold, thy Lord said to the angels: "I am about to
> create man from clay: When I have fashioned him (in
> due proportion) and breathed into him of My spirit, fall
> ye down in obeisance unto him."

Qur'an 21:91 (See also 66:12)

> And (remember) her who guarded her chastity: We
> breathed into her of Our spirit, and We made her and
> her son a sign for all peoples.

Surely the Muslim does not believe part of Gabriel was breathed into Adam and Eve. Surely they do not believe Mary had intimate relations with Gabriel. So in what other way can such verses be interpreted? The only logical answer is that Allah has some kind of spirit, uncreated and absolute. Even many Muslims are forced into this conclusion. Al-Shaikh Muhammad al- Hariri al-Bayyumi is quoted by Sam Shamoun in the source cited in the section entitled, "Spirit of God" as saying: "The Holy Spirit is the Spirit of God and the Spirit of God is not created."[27] In this quote, a Muslim is unwittingly arguing that these attributes show that the spirit mentioned is also Allah, as only Allah is uncreated.

We need to be careful. It is not our goal to preach the Trinity out of the Qur'an. Quite the reverse, exposing the conflicting nature of the Qur'an may lead the Muslim to discussions of absolute truth, and what the Spirit is. The Qur'an yet again undermines itself by disavowing tawhid when it introduces this spirit of Allah as another aspect of Allah. This spirit of Allah shares the characteristics of Allah, yet somehow is acting in conjunction with Allah as another aspect and agent of his existence. If this sounds familiar, do not be shocked. This is the Trinity, and the Qur'an asserts it.

I do not point out this fact that the Qur'an supports the Trinity as proof of Christianity. Of course, we know the Qur'an is a fallible document, as evidenced by its inability to maintain internal consistency. Rather, the Qur'an itself can be used to point to the true nature of God if the Christian is well educated. Accordingly, neither is exposing the Trinity within the Qur'an done for the sake of showing a contradiction, as there are many more obvious examples. Rather, I illustrate this example as an avenue to breach one of the most taboo subjects for a Muslim and a way to do so from their own scriptures. The important part for the believer is not to go too fast here. Ask the Muslim what the Holy Spirit is, wait for them to answer, and listen. If the answer is Gabriel, then ask them what the subsequent verses mean. They are quite familiar with tawhid, the oneness of Allah. So the point will be obvious enough without being explicitly stated. Now with guidance from the real Holy Spirit, perhaps you can engage the Muslim in profitable dialogue.

To Hadith or Not to Hadith

One of the most complicated aspects of the Muslim faith is the Hadith. As you may remember, the Hadith are a collection of sayings about the life of Muhammad. There are thousands of these, with various levels of authenticity. Knowing which teachings from the Hadith should be followed, which are of prime importance, and knowing how various teachings intersect is a monumental task. In order to avoid the complexities of authenticity, we will focus on two collections of Hadith that are universally considered by Muslims to be reliable. Therefore, Sahih Bukhari and Sahih Muslim will be the two collections referenced in this book.

The Hadith is the vehicle by which Muslims are able to pick and choose which parts of their religion they wish to follow, and still reside under the banner of Islam. For any given Hadith and any given Muslim, there is no way to determine whether or not they follow that particular Hadith. Some Muslims will say that they accept the entire Hadith, although no human life would be capable of living out the requirements listed therein. Of course as Christians it is impossible for us to live out the example set by Jesus, but Muslims trying to live out the example of Muhammad face a problem of a very different nature.

Most Muslims will admit that the Hadith should not be taken as seriously as the Qur'an itself. Careful observation uncovers another interesting logical fallacy of this assertion. The Qur'an commands a Muslim to follow Muhammad's example (Qur'an 33:21). However, following Muhammad's example means following the Hadith, the record of his life and times. Since no human being could follow the entire Hadith, it means Muslims are not following their own laws. Some Muslims will try to escape by citing the unreliability of some of the Hadith. Yet if some Hadith are unreliable, why would the Qur'an order Muslims to adhere to it? Allah's perfect word orders Muslims to obey a guidance that is neither reliable nor valid!

The paradox is one that many Muslims have not considered. The Qur'an orders Muslims to follow a set of rules which is not only unworkable but more importantly under dispute. If following the full Hadith is unattainable, two questions must be asked: What religion gives its members unachievable standards? How does a holy God view such failure? One might argue that the standard set by Jesus is impossible to follow as well. So it is, yet this comparison provides another hook into the concept of grace, which we examine in more detail in the next chapter. The difference is that the Christian has an avenue to deal with failure to meet Jesus' standards. In Christianity, our inability to live up to God's perfect standard is the entire reason for grace, and pursuing that avenue could lead to sharing what the gospel is. The Muslim not only has such no such pathway to peace, but also doesn't even know which rules to follow, nor which can be broken.

But on another note, if the reliability of some Hadith are under dispute, why would a perfect revelation from God instruct people to follow invalid guidelines? In contrast, the life of Jesus is written within the Bible itself, circumventing such a paradox. We do not have one book telling us to follow the life of Christ and another less reliable book with the details of the life of Christ. The Bible is self-contained. It tells us to follow Jesus, and at the same time how to do so. The example of Jesus is contained within the same infallible Word which gives the command to be imitators of Christ. In Islam, the examples of Muhammad are contained within a mishmash of potentially dubious sources.

Bless You, You Unforgivable Wretch.

When Christians first grab the Qur'an, it is difficult to get a coherent picture from it. We have discussed this lack of context before, but the point is that these inconsistencies expose some massive theological holes.

One thing the Muslim is sure about is that assigning partners to Allah is the unforgivable sin, shirk. This is what the Muslim views Christians as doing with regard to Jesus, committing this unforgivable sin of shirk.

Qur'an 4.48

> Allah forgiveth not that partners should be set up with Him; but He forgiveth anything else, to whom He pleaseth; to set up partners with Allah is to devise a sin Most heinous indeed.

For a Muslim, committing shirk is the sin most abhorred by Allah. There could be an entire section devoted to the irony of the road to true salvation being the biggest sin within Islam, but we will instead focus on the inconsistencies within the Qur'an regarding shirk. The Qur'an teaches that shirk is forgiven if a Christian become a Muslim, yet shirk is still considered the most serious sin that can be committed. Christians are constantly accused of committing this gravest sin. For example, a guide to the different kinds of shirk, found on various Islamic websites, describes the Christian's misbehavior in the following way:

> A classic example of this is the Christian concept of Trinity. Christians believe that God (Allah) alone does not regulate the affairs of mankind. They believe that the other two parts of the Trinity, Jesus (as) and the Holy spirit, also play a part in worldly affairs e.g., Jesus pronounces judgment on the world and the holy spirit helps Christians through their daily lives.[28]

On the one hand, the Qur'an condemns those who commit shirk with the harshest possible tone. At the same time, while the Qur'an harshly condemns Christians for this most heinous sin, it turns around and discusses Christians in a favorable light. For example:

Qur'an 3:55

> Behold! Allah said: 'O Jesus! I will take thee and raise thee to Myself and clear thee (of the falsehoods) of those who blaspheme; I will make those who follow thee superior to those who reject faith, to the Day of Resurrection: Then shall ye all return unto me, and I will judge between you of the matters wherein ye dispute.'

The Qur'an says that the followers of Jesus are superior to those who reject faith, or to put it simply, Christians who commit shirk by following Jesus are superior to atheists. This is a great place to start, but we should not stop there. As noted before:

Qur'an 61:14

> O ye who believe! Be ye helpers of Allah: As said Jesus
> the son of Mary to the Disciples, 'Who will be my
> helpers to (the work of) Allah?' Said the disciples, 'We
> are Allah's helpers!' then a portion of the Children of
> Israel believed, and a portion disbelieved: But We gave
> power to those who believed, against their enemies, and
> they became the ones that prevailed.

We come to the million-dollar question. Why does Allah
think so highly of people who assign partners to him relative to
those who just don't believe in him at all? It would seem logical
that those people who commit the most egregious sin would
be somehow cursed, yet the Qur'an indicates that they are not.
In fact, not only are those who commit shirk not cursed, but
they are somehow blessed by being exalted beyond others, and
allowed to prevail against their enemies. Wouldn't it be true that
an atheist who had not yet committed the gravest of sins would
be more easily saved, whereas a Christian, having committed
shirk, would be in the most perilous of positions? Why is it that
the Christian who has committed shirk is somehow in some
superior position?

The Qur'an goes on to describe those of us guilty of shirk in
this way:

Qur'an 5:82

> Strongest among men in enmity to the believers wilt
> thou find the Jews and Pagans; and nearest among
> them in love to the believers wilt thou find those who
> say, 'We are Christians': because amongst these are
> men devoted to learning and men who have renounced
> the world, and they are not arrogant.

Apparently at the time the Qur'an was written, people of the day who referred to themselves as Christians were nearest to Muslims. It is strange how a people guilty of the most odious crime against God would be nearest to the Muslims in both attitude and belief.

This is the inverted and confusing realm of Islamic thought. The Qur'an first says that Christians commit the worst sin imaginable, and then it turns around and says that Christians are superior to others and nearest to Muslims. Wow. Why do I bring this up? It is not so much to expose the lunacy of the Qur'an, but rather to allow the Christian to hook into what it means to be a Christian. It allows the Christian to discuss what it means to worship the one true God within the context of asking the Muslim to explain why the Qur'an honors those it claims are so despicable. If the Qur'an seems to contradict itself, so be it. At least now we can address the issues of shirk, and why Allah seems to bless those who commit it. That is the question that needs to be asked. Why does the Qur'an tell Muslims they are closest to people who commit the worst possible sin? Are Muslims truly nearest those who are the furthest from redemption?

These are perilous questions and must be handled with delicacy. Nobody likes being painted into a corner. All sorts of excuses will come forward about how the real followers of Christ were Muslims, and it is the Christians of today who have perverted the gospel and become blasphemers. Now is when the Christian can start quoting Scriptures by Paul, James, Jude, Peter, Luke, Matthew, Mark, and John regarding Christ, reminding our dear Muslim friends that these Christian leaders were the ones who prevailed. Who knows where such a conversation will land when the dust settles, but one thing is for sure, once again the Qur'an undermines its own position. Remember to use such potentially vitriolic assaults with restraint and compassion, as it is not our goal to debate. This kind of topic can often do more harm than good, and I provide it here with trepidation. I only do so as an example of some tough questions to ask should the time be right. To summarize, the Qur'an defines shirk as the worst thing one can do, and then exalts the very people who did it and tells Muslims it is these same people they are closest to.

Now that the ways in which Islam undermines its own doctrines has been probed, it's time to look at how Islamic doctrine plays out in real life. In the next chapter, we will take a spiritual tour of Islam, with a particular emphasis on worship.

Chapter 12

A Spiritual Guide to Islam

We have examined inversions relating to Jesus, inversions about the nature of God, and inversions within the Qur'an. The backward nature of Islamic thought is not a new concept that I have stumbled upon. Ex-Muslim Walid Shoebat pulls no punches when he describes Islam's approach as follows,

> Like their god, the accuser, the corruptors accuse the virtuous of corruption, the murderers accuse the innocent of murder, the haters accuse the righteous of hate, the warmongers accuse the peaceful of war, the lovers of death accuse those who love life with cowardice...**Everything is urned upside down.**[29]

It's time to take a look at some of the inversions relating to the overarching principles of Islam itself. We will consider Islamic ideology from the viewpoint of the religion as a whole rather than individual practices. Of course, no tour through how the inversions of Islamic theology undermine itself would be complete without a thorough examination of the worship of Muhammad. There are a few short detours to take first as we begin our spiritual tour through Islam as a system to help us better frame our understanding.

When Rules Outweigh Principles

The Qur'an says that Islam is the religion that is now perfected for mankind (Qur'an 5:3). Muslims are proud of this fact, and they base this belief on the myriad of rules that Allah has given them to lead a life pleasing to him. What does it mean to have a religion full of rules and how does that compare to Christianity? Might there be another subtle inversion to uncover?

Islam is great at micromanagement. It can tell the exact rule for almost any aspect of 7th-century life. A collection of all of these rules is the basis for Sharia law. For example, there are rules for inheritance (Qur'an 4:11-12, 4:176), rules for how to punish fornicators (Qur'an 24:2), and rules for how to wash before prayer (Qur'an 5:6). While the details differ considerably from the Mosaic law, the fact that the Qur'an and Hadith lay out their own structure of law is notably evident. Yet we know the law was never meant to be the doorway to salvation, but the means by which we recognized our need for a Savior. From Galatians 3:23-24:

> 23 But before faith came, we were kept in custody under the law, being shut up to the faith which was later to be revealed. 24 Therefore the Law has become our tutor to lead us to Christ, so that we may be justified by faith.

So while the Qur'an and Hadith map out a law to follow, principles such as doing good to others are relegated to secondary status. Remember, Muslims are instructed to follow the example of the life of Muhammad. Therefore, if Muhammad performed some specific kind act, then Muslims feel required to perform that particular act of kindness too. By negative inference, if Muhammad did not perform a specific type of good deed, Muslims do not feel required to do so either. This view of Muhammad as the ultimate role model is described in a section of his posting entitled, "The prophet's status as a role model and the practices of his companions," by Muslim author Rasit Küçük in this way: "The verses in the Quran that command belief in, obedience to, conformity with and submission to the Holy Prophet are unambiguously clear".[30]

Jesus was not concerned about religious customs, but rather on the relationship we have with Him, and the relationships we then have with others. Jesus came and taught principles, not rules. This is what any parent does with a child. When a child is young, the parent gives them rules but doesn't tell them why. Commands are given such as "Eat your vegetables," "Don't talk to strangers," and "Don't touch the hot stove." When the child does what is asked, he is given a reward; when the child misbehaves, punishment is meted out. This works for toddlers, but not for teens. As children grow, rules are not enough. Rules get replaced with principles on which to base decisions. Parents teach their children how to treat others, how to be polite, how to listen, how to respect, and how to evaluate risk. They do this because life is complicated, and no amount of rules can ever suffice for the nettlesome situations that we all eventually find ourselves in. Without principles, rules will always fail us.

Herein lies the inversion. A religion that teaches rules is for spiritual toddlers, while a religion that teaches principles has moved on to fully equip spiritual adults. Muslims claim their religion is perfect when in reality it takes a very immature approach. Any rules based system leads us to guess intent by looking at the individual rules. Following or rejecting those rules is straightforward obedience or disobedience with no understanding. While obedience is necessary for a relationship with God, when general principles such as love your neighbor as yourself enter the picture, spiritual maturity allows us to infer proper action based on principles.

While Muslims claim Islam is the logical culmination of the monotheistic religions, it has instead taken a major step backward.

Moving forward is going from rules to relationship, but Islam's replacement of Christianity regresses from relationship to rules.

Do What I Say, Not What I Do.

Another facet of Islam that is completely opposite of Christianity is how God equips His followers to allow them to obey. The Qur'an tells Muslims what do to, but it does not give any instruction as to how to accomplish it, nor provides the tools to do so. Telling someone what to do, and then giving them absolutely zero means for implementation is nothing less than cruel. When Jesus gives Christians commands to obey, He gives us the Holy Spirit as a Helper to accomplish that which is being required of us. However, without such a Helper, the commands of Islam do nothing but score success and failure. Allah just told people what to do. YHWH chose to come to earth to offer an example of how to live. Then, He sent His Spirit to enable us to do that which we were unequipped to do beforehand. The difference between the law and the grace given by the Spirit is put succinctly in the following lyrics, based on a poem originally attributed to John Bunyan.

> "Do this and live," the law commands,
> But gives me neither feet nor hands.
> A better way his grace doth bring,
> It bids me fly and gives me wings. [31]

The Bible speaks to this clearly in a number of passages. Notice the word equip here from Hebrews 13:20-21:

> [20] Now the God of peace, who brought up from the dead the great Shepherd of the sheep through the blood of the eternal covenant, even Jesus our Lord, [21] equip you in every good thing to do His will, working in us that which is pleasing in His

sight, through Jesus Christ, to whom be the glory
forever and ever. Amen.

This concept is one any parent is familiar with. Any decent
parent not only gives instruction but enables his child with tools
and skills that allow him to be capable of succeeding. We would
instantly see the folly in setting unrealistic expectations of our
children without offering them any method of success. Why is
it that Allah gives humans an impossible task, and then offers
nothing but warnings of eternal damnation if they do not succeed?
In other words, what is the point of talking about the evil of sin
without providing any remedy? This question reintroduces the
issue of salvation itself, and how we can be pleasing to God.

As we have already discussed, the Qur'an is not clear on how to
obtain salvation, as there are many conflicting passages. So it is no
wonder Muslims want to die in jihad. The Qur'an tells Muslims
that dying in battle is a sure way to paradise (Qur'an 3:157-158,
47:4). They want to go to paradise, and jihad looks to them to be
their best shot. It is disturbing that the Islamic teaching that offers
them the only real chance at salvation simultaneously expedites
the process of dying in their sins. Does the irony never cease?

This whole topic moves into the larger issue of how a Muslim
finds forgiveness for his sins when all is said and done. As previously
stated, entrance to paradise is ultimately set by the arbitrary will of
Allah. According to Islamic doctrine, forgiveness of sins comes from
works (Qur'an 11:115), dying in jihad (Qur'an 3:195), by giving alms
(Qur'an 2:271), or by performing the hajj (Sahih Al-Bukhari, Vol.
3, Book 27, Number 1). Ultimately, even among Muslims, there is
considerable confusion about how to get one's sins forgiven, or even
if they need to be. So yet again we see the problem of sin is outlined,
and the punishment for sin is conveyed, but there is no remedy
provided. There are multiple half-remedies suggested. The bottom
line is that everybody within Islam knows what sin is, but nobody
within Islam is certain as to whether or not they are forgiven.

Praise be to God we have been forgiven by being released from the law. From Romans 8:1-2:

> [1] **Therefore there is now no condemnation for those who are in Christ Jesus. [2]For the law of the Spirit of life in Christ Jesus has set you free from the law of sin and of death.**

These are delicate conversations to have, and again I caution not to go too fast, but the heart of the gospel can be approached from many different ways once the conversation gets to this level.

All Polytheists, Raise Your Hand

This next section will not serve you well in a debate. As we have discussed, winning a debate with a Muslim is easy, but often unproductive. So I include this next piece with an admonition. This is for edification only, to help illustrate the Islamic inversion. Remember, we are trying to understand the inverted and antithetical nature of Islam. Rarely would we use an example such as this as verbal ammunition. Trying to argue down this path will likely cause hard feelings. A Muslim will not wish to admit the irony of this point anyway. So be aware of this, and do not discuss this next concept unless the Spirit has clearly spoken that it is the right time.

Muslims complain Christians believe in and worship a man. Closer examination of how Muslims treat Muhammad offers yet another bizarre twist. While Muslims technically do not worship Muhammad, in many ways their actions tell a different story. The Islamic creed, the Qur'an itself, how Muslims behave in everyday life, and the Hadith all point toward something that appears a lot like Muhammad worship.

To start this line of investigation, consider the *shahada*, the Muslim creed. To become a Muslim, a person must recite the shahada in Arabic. Roughly translated, the shahada is as follows, "I bear witness that there is no god but Allah, and I bear witness that Mohammad is the messenger of Allah." Notice that this is a two-part testimony. Of course, Muslims believe that there is no god but Allah, but look at the rest of the shahada. Part two of the Muslim creed requires the additional belief that Muhammad brought the message of Allah. Consider these words within a Muslim tract discussing the shahada, "The second part of the Shahada means that Prophet Mohammad (PBUH) is the servant and chosen messenger of Allah. No one must have two opinions about this matter."[32]

Part of the Muslim creed is focused on Muhammad and his position and role. From the Muslim perspective, a person who believes in the oneness and uniqueness of Allah without believing that Muhammad brought the one true message is not a Muslim. In other words, believing in Allah is not enough to be called a Muslim. A Muslim must also believe that Muhammad is Allah's messenger. So what was that message? One part of it is that Muhammad's actions are to be followed as closely as possible (Qur'an 33:21). This means, by corollary, Islam requires belief in a man. Some readers may think this an overextension of Islamic doctrine. Yet consider what the Qur'an itself has to say on the issue of belief.

Qur'an 49:15

> The believers are only those who believe in Allah and
> His Apostle then they doubt not and struggle hard with
> their wealth and their lives in the way of Allah; they are
> the truthful ones.

In other words, a Muslim must not only believe in Allah but in his apostle, Muhammad, as well. Believing in what Muhammad did and obeying what he said is part and parcel of being a Muslim

(Qur'an 9:71, 24:51-52, 24:62, 33:31, 33:71, 48:17, 49:14-15, 58:13, 64:8). This means, by necessity, Muslims require belief in a man. It is true that the way in which Muslims are to believe in Muhammad is very different from the way a Christian is commanded to believe in Jesus. However, Christians are not required to state a creed that they believe that Isaiah and Haggai are prophets in order to be a Christian. Of course, we do believe they are prophets, but stating it is not part of any Christian confession. In contrast, if a Muslim does not believe in Muhammad, he is not a Muslim and cannot go to paradise, thus making the religion of Islam oddly coupled to a man. Not only is the belief in Muhammad as the messenger stressed from the positive standpoint as referenced in the previously cited passages of the Qur'an, but unbelief in Muhammad is emphasized from the negative standpoint in many passages as well. Hellfire is guaranteed for those who do not believe in and obey both Allah AND his apostle. (Qur'an 4:14, 9:63, 9:84, 48:13, 58:5, 58:20).

Qur'an 4:14

> And whoever disobeys Allah and His Apostle and goes
> beyond His limits, He will cause him to enter fire to
> abide in it, and he shall have an abasing chastisement.

Disobedience of Muhammad is just as much a ticket to hell as is disobedience to Allah. This is important because Islamic doctrine via the Qur'an gives Muslims no rules for life. The Qur'an gives some instructions, but in a vacuum. It does not have nearly enough detail to allow for a workable system to live out faith. The devout Muslim, therefore, must look to Muhammad, whose life is the only one believed to be of sufficient record to be followed as the premier example. The result is that the instructions Muslims receive on how to lead their lives result in the worship of Muhammad in every way but name only.* This is becoming obvious even to Muslims, and when a Muslim dares state it, he may be branded heretical. This next quote is from a Muslim, Anna Jordan. Please remember this is not some Christian author discussing perceptions of Muslims; this is a Muslim describing the state of her own religion within an article espousing Islam:

> While they have adamantly insisted they do not deify Mohammed, they have sought to supplement God's word by looking for guidance in the words and actions of Mohammed, thereby elevating the prophet to a status never ordained by God.[33]

Not only does the shahada throw confusion on whether Muslims worship Muhammad, but so too the Qur'an itself undermines its own position by lumping Allah and Muhammad into the same category on a variety of occasions. Muhammad and Allah are linked together in some rather awkward instances. Several verses will be presented here, but they are only a brief snapshot. Muhammad implied equality with Allah on a number of points, and we must not ignore them. While many of these passages do not necessarily conclude by themselves that Muhammad is deified, the set as a whole paints a very clear picture of the role of Muhammad within Islam.

For example, swearing allegiance to Muhammad is the same as doing so to Allah.

Qur'an 48:10

> Verily those who plight their fealty to thee do no less than plight their fealty to Allah:

---

* Even Muhammad itself in Arabic means "The praised one." Biblical prophets have names with meanings such as "God is salvation" or "God is judge," but never such a name causing a blatant refocus of praise away from God Himself and instead toward the prophet bringing His message.

As another example, obedience to Muhammad and to Allah are one in the same.

Qur'an 4:80

He who obeys the Messenger, obeys Allah.

In this following verse, notice that a Muslim's love for not just Allah, but Muhammad as well must surpass even that of his or her own family.

Qur'an 9:24

Say: If it be that your fathers, your sons, your brothers, your mates, or your kindred; the wealth that ye have gained; the commerce in which ye fear a decline: or the dwellings in which ye delight – are dearer to you than Allah, or His Messenger, or the striving in His cause;- then wait until Allah brings about His decision: and Allah guides not the rebellious.

There are quite a large number of verses that make these comparisons. Appendix A contains a comprehensive list of these verses to drive home the point more fully. To recap, the Qur'an states that a pledge to Muhammad is the equivalent of a pledge to Allah, commands the same level of obedience to Muhammad as to Allah, and requires love for both Muhammad and Allah to surpass that of anything else in your life, including family and spouse. If that is not worship, what is?

The shahada and Qur'an paint a tainted picture regarding the worship of Muhammad, but the worship of Muhammad comes into focus in some unusual places within Islamic practice as well. Consider the Islamic law relating to the image of Muhammad himself. Islamic law forbids that any representation of Muhammad be drawn, painted, or otherwise shown. Where does this prohibition come from? No verse of the Qur'an states that such representations of Muhammad cannot be made. Of course, the Hadith give more detail on what can and cannot be done within Islam. Strangely enough, when the Hadith are examined, no prohibition of drawing or painting an image of Muhammad is there either! Instead, we find a general prohibition against any images of human beings whatsoever.

Muslim Book 24, Number 5268

> Allah's Messenger (may peace be upon him) having said: Those who paint pictures would be punished on the Day of Resurrection and it would be said to them: Breathe soul into what you have created. [34]

Islamic law maintains that the prohibition extends to the representation of any person, not just Muhammad. Yet this Islamic tradition of not allowing images of people seems to get ignored with regard to the average person and amplified when applied to Muhammad, even though he is not singled out in any of the original Islamic texts. Then why do Muslims forbid any such representations of Muhammad? Muslim authors are quick to point out that the reasoning behind not having any images of Muhammad is to prevent later followers from worshiping him. That seems a fair statement, so where does such an assertion lead and how does it play out in real life?

Many people have discussed this issue in relation to the 2005 incident where Jyllands-Posten, a Danish publication, featured cartoons of Muhammad and the ensuing controversy. This event garnered significant press, but move past this controversy and on to a road less traveled. Rather than analyzing such a negative case, look instead at a positive example. In 1977, Anthony Quinn starred in a little-known movie called "Muhammad, Messenger of God," or alternatively titled "The Messenger." It was directed by a Syrian-born Muslim and approved by the renowned Al-Azhar University. In this movie, the personage of Muhammad is never shown. It is odd to watch an entire full-length feature film about Muhammad without ever seeing him. The movie shows the actions and movements of his followers and his enemies during the inception of Islam as a religion. Everyone else is represented, but not Muhammad. He is given unique status in that throughout the movie his character is never depicted on camera. The movie gives the following reason in its introduction:

> The makers of this film honor the Islamic tradition which holds that the impersonation of the prophet offends against the spirituality of his message. Therefore, the person of Muhammad will not be shown.

Here again, the irony of Islamic thought crashes straight to the forefront. In an attempt to prevent the worship of Muhammad, he gets elevated to a special status no other character is given. He has been raised to a level beyond any other man. Just as God Himself cannot be seen face to face, so too Muhammad receives the same status from the cinematography point of view. What likely started with genuine concerns has had massive unintended consequence. The very attempt to prevent the worship of Muhammad has caused his un-displayable image to become an object of worship.

Perhaps this seems a stretch to some readers, so consider how the Hadith describe Muhammad's physical appearance in Muslim, Book 30, Number 5772, "Allah's Messenger (may peace be upon him) had the most handsome face amongst men and he had the best disposition and he was neither very tall nor short-statured." [35]

His likeness is deemed so amazing that it surpassed all other men. Again, while this is not technically worship in a strict theological sense, it sure comes across as such. Perhaps most striking is a line from the movie itself. As the film unfolds where Muhammad goes unseen throughout, one of the characters aptly states, "The real god is unseen." What an appropriately ironic statement. This author is confident that the self-incriminating nature of the statement went totally unnoticed by most viewers.

Muslims grant Muhammad the same status as God Himself with regards to the representation of His image. In the Muslim attempt to avoid idolatry, they have inadvertently created a new and powerful unseen idol.

Now that we have examined the shahada, the Qur'an, and practice, consider the Hadith regarding Muhammad's status and role. They provide a strikingly unsettling picture as well. The following Hadith makes it more clear how early Muslims viewed Muhammad.

Bukhari Volume 1, Book 4, Number 171

> I said to 'Abida, 'I have some of the hair of the Prophet which I got from Anas or from his family.' 'Abida replied. 'No doubt if I had a single hair of that it would have been dearer to me than the whole world and whatever is in it.'[36]

Here we see the hair of a dead man's head is more valuable than the entire earth and its contents. Again, if this is not worship, what is? Even Muhammad himself claimed a unique capability relative to his followers. In Bukhari, Volume 1, Book 7, Number 331, Muhammad describes five things given to no other prophet but himself. The 4th one is that "I have been given the right of intercession (on the Day of Resurrection)."[37] There are other Hadith which claim Muhammad as intercessor for Muslims such as this:

Muslim, Book 30, Number 5655

> Abu Huraira reported Allah's Messenger (may peace
> be upon him) as saying: I shall be pre-eminent amongst
> the descendants of Adam on the Day of Resurrection
> and I will be the first intercessor and the first whose
> intercession will be accepted (by Allah).[38]

How ironic that Muslims revile at the idea of Jesus as intercessor, yet Muhammad, who never claimed deity as such, claimed he had the power to intercede for Muslims. Allah will make a decision, on everyone's eternal destination, but then Muhammad potentially has the right and privilege to alter that decision.

Could there be anything more God-like than having the power of intercession? It's hard to fathom, but Islamic theology goes even further with elevating Muhammad's status. A well-known Hadith called the "law laak" deals with Adam's first trespass and his subsequent request for forgiveness. The Hadith claims that when Adam repented of his sin, he did so for the sake of Muhammad, who of course was not even born yet![39] In other words, it was because of Muhammad that Allah chose to forgive Adam. For those readers confused by the anachronism of how Adam could have known about Muhammad, here is a relevant passage from the source cited above:

> Adam said: O Allah! When you created me and blew
> into me the spirit, I lifted my head and saw written on
> the 'Arsh 'La ilaaha illallah Muhammadur rasoolullah'.
> So, I got to know that you would only join your name
> with him who is most beloved to you.[40]

Yet one of the boldest claims comes from the words of a Muslim author from the same cited source discussing this particular Hadith. We find that Muhammad is the entire reason for creation itself!

> Indeed the Prophet of Allah (sallallahu 'alaihi wasallam) is the reason for the creation of Adam 'alaihis salam and the universe. If the Prophet of Allah (sallallahu 'alaihi wasallam) was not in existence, then the 'Arsh and Kursi, Lawh and Qalam, the Skies and the Earth, Heaven and Hell, the trees and stones and all other creatures **would not exist** (emphasis mine).[41]

How can a man be the sole reason for causing God to create the universe? Had Muhammad not existed, neither would all of creation. Again, if this does not deify Muhammad, what else could?

The skeptical reader may object that while these arguments are somewhat damning, today's Muslims do not truly believe Muhammad is a god. It is true no Muslim thinks that they treat Muhammad as a god. Yet Muslims unwittingly deify Muhammad with their own words.

> Prophet Muhammad (peace and blessings be upon him) practiced what he preached. He very carefully and meticulously followed the Qur'an, Allah's Word that was revealed to him. He followed and lived the Qur'an at every moment in every detail of his life. His life was the reflection of Allah's Words. He became the Qur'an in person, the embodiment of the Qur'an, or one may even say in a metaphorical sense 'the Word in flesh.'[42]

The term "the Word in flesh" should instantly call Scripture to mind. The true Word in flesh is described in John 1:14.

> [14] **And the Word became flesh, and dwelt among us, and we saw His glory, glory as of the only begotten from the Father, full of grace and truth.**

To recap, the shahada requires Muslims submit and believe in a man. The Qur'an equates Allah and Muhammad in ways that a man cannot be equated with God. Islamic practice elevates Muhammad to a level only worthy of God, and the Hadith portrays Muhammad's supremacy of status in ways no man could ever hold. What conclusion is ultimately to be drawn? Muslims can continue to claim that they do not worship Muhammad, and that is what is stated over and over again. However, their creed, the Qur'an, their actions, and the Hadith tell a very different story.

What is so ironic is that the Islamic religion, one so depending on a man, lambastes Christianity for worshiping a man. Of course, since Jesus is also God, Christians do not worship a mere man. Yet the tables have been oddly turned, in that Christians are falsely accused of the very thing Muslims do. Muslims decry polytheism as heresy, and yet Muhammad is the only human who gets many of the special exemptions otherwise due only to God.

Once again we see that Islam has taken Christianity and flipped it upside down, inside out, and irrevocably twisted it out of recognition. God became a man to deliver us, and as such, we worship God alone. So another inversion has been exposed. The same people who mistakenly accuse Christians of worshiping a man are locked into a system where they do not realize nor admit that they do exactly what they prohibit. The inversions just keep coming.

As a whole, it has been shown that Islam is a religion that emphasizes rules over relationship, cannot equip its adherents to follow the rules laid out, and spends a great deal of time focusing on the worship of a man. Hopefully, spotting these inversions is becoming easier and easier. In the next chapter, some quick examples of these inversions will be presented in order to further illustrate the technique for recognizing the twisted nature of Islamic assaults on the gospel.

Chapter 13

The Last Bastion of Islamic Hope - Obfuscation

Obfuscation is the term that best suits what Muslim apologists attempt to do. Obfuscation is the art of purposely obscuring and confusing an issue in order to make it difficult to understand. In today's world, there are countless resources on the Internet. These provide the novice debater with all sorts of material to use incorrectly. Cut and paste is the new misused and overused tool for young apprenticing online apologists. What begins as relatively clear information is twisted, muddied, and obscured to the point of non-recognition. While referencing seemingly reliable information, many people are not aware of the most basic logical flaws in their co-opted material. Those who seek wisdom must practice mining the nugget of truth that has been buried under a mountain of perplexity. What follows is an example where incomplete information leads to the obvious incorrect conclusion.

Is it logical that spending less time in a dangerous situation is good? Clearly, the answer is yes; spending less time in danger is a wise goal. Under such logic, can it then be said that while driving and approaching a dangerous curve, a person should accelerate in order to spend less time in the area of danger? The answer is clearly no. Where did the logic go wrong? Our assumptions were valid, and clearly going faster reduces our time in danger. What is wrong with that picture? Conclusions were drawn from information that was indeed factual, yet an important piece of threat assessment was missing and left unaddressed. Velocity is a component of the equation that was perilously ignored. In this example case, it is clear that the logic is incomplete and does not make sense because the topic is simple. However, logical fallacies are not so obvious when talking about issues of origin, death, sin, salvation, free will, sacrifice, heaven, hell, love, faith, prophets, and prophecy.

There are a variety of verses that Muslims tend to focus on. We have already spent time focusing on some of the more prominent ones, such as Matthew 7:25, Numbers 23:19, Deuteronomy 18:18, Matthew 26:39, and others. Many of these next inversions are infrequently cited and seemingly more esoteric. However, they are provided as examples to help the reader identify the pattern of spotting inversions, and then turning them right side up. So for quick practice, several rapid-fire examples are given in quick succession, applying the inversion detection techniques previously discussed.

Ten Examples of the Islamic Inversions

1. Christians are disobedient because they eat pork, which is prohibited in the Old Testament.

Muslims will cite a passage such as Deuteronomy 14:7, which prohibits the eating of pork. Next, they will claim Christians are not following God because we do not obey it. After all, don't Christians eat pork? Here is proof enough that Christians do not submit to Allah. Of course, as Christians, we read the entire Bible, including Matthew 15:17, where Jesus explains that what goes into the mouth is not what defiles us, but it is what comes out of our mouths that is the problem. Later, in Acts 10:15 we read again how the dietary law no longer applies, but arguing along this line is typically fruitless. So, instead watch how Islam undermines its own argument without any help from us.

Qur'an 22:36

> The sacrificial camels we have made for you as among
> the symbols from Allah: in them is (much) good for
> you: then pronounce the name of Allah over them as
> they line up (for sacrifice): when they are down on their
> sides (after slaughter), eat ye thereof, and feed such as
> (beg not but) live in contentment, and such as beg with
> due humility: thus have We made animals subject to
> you, that ye may be grateful.

The Qur'an specifically allows the eating of sacrificed camels.
Yet, in Jewish dietary law, the camel is as unclean as the pig.
In fact, the camel is explicitly mentioned. Where would we find
the specific reference to camels being unclean? To find the exact
reference outlawing camels, look back at the very verse the Muslim
originally cited, Deuteronomy 14:7! The same verse a Muslim
cites to try to undermine a Christian's faith shows the Qur'an as
violating the law they claim cannot be violated! Why does the
Muslim believe that Muhammad has the right to rewrite one part
of the law whereas Jesus does not? This is the question that can
now be asked. Why do Muslims no longer believe in the dietary
law when applied to camels, but do with regard to pork?

You might wonder what is the point of stating that Islam, just
like Christianity, does not require obedience to the dietary law?
Ah, but if that question arises, NOW you can show what Jesus
Christ did with regards to the law. Remember, it is the Muslim
stance that the Mosaic law is upheld and untouched in the Qur'an
and not in the New Testament. As Christians we know Jesus came
to fulfill the law and allows us to have a better understanding of it.
It was the law that was our tutor and led us to Christ, so that we
may be justified by faith (Galatians 3:24). The law was expanded
to include the spirit of the law rather than merely the letter of the
law. In some cases, such as the dietary rules, Jesus followed them

as the perfect example but instructed us that we were not under the same obligation. For a Muslim who is truly seeking, showing him that the Qur'an does not follow the Mosaic law might allow the possibility of discussing the progression from law to grace, what Jesus accomplished on the cross, and how it relates to the fulfillment of the law. Now the Muslim may seriously ask to understand this aspect of Jesus' teachings.

In other words, Muslims claim that they follow the law, while Christians do not. In actuality, it is exactly backward. We follow the law as given and fulfilled by Christ Jesus. Muslims do not follow the Mosaic law in this specific case, as well as others, because the Qur'an supersedes and tells them not to. So the question to Muslims is whether they should follow the Mosaic law or not. If they say yes, then ask them why the Qur'an tells them not to. If they say no, then ask them what was the point of their original argument.

2. Demons did/did not know who Jesus is.

Muslims always like to point out apparent contradictions in the Bible, and in doing so they constantly undercut themselves. Remember, this list is not about memorizing all of these verses, but rather learning to recognize the pattern. As an example, a Muslim may cite 1 Corinthians 2:6-8 and Mark 1:24 as contradictory verses. In 1 Corinthians, Paul says that the "rulers of the age" did not understand the wisdom brought by Jesus, or else they would not have crucified him. By "rulers of the age," many people believe Paul is referring to demons. However, in Mark's Gospel, demons do recognize that Jesus is the Holy One of God (Mark 1:24). Muslims argue that this is a contradiction, as one verse says the devils do not understand Jesus, and yet elsewhere they recognize Him for who He is.

Two items leap to mind. First, does "rulers of this age" truly refer to spiritual beings? Many people would justifiably argue that "rulers of this age" doesn't refer to demons at all, but rather to human leaders of the day. Such an argument, while quite valid, has gotten far off track from the truth of Jesus Christ. Pursuing such an esoteric point is exactly what should not be done. Second, it seems almost comical that Muslims would cite a verse such as Mark 1:24 which points directly to the identification of Jesus. Rather than dealing with these avenues, look a little deeper. Remember that our goal is to help our Muslim friend out of the trappings of Islam, not to win a debate.

It may seem we have been presented a contradiction here. In Mark, the demon recognizes Jesus as the Holy One of God, yet in Corinthians, they do not understand the wisdom He represented. Here is the hook. Just because the demons knew WHO Jesus is, didn't mean they understood the mystery of the atonement for sins, which was soon coming but as yet future for them. Is it possible for someone to know that Jesus is the Messiah, but not understand His plan of salvation? Can someone claim that Jesus is the Messiah, yet not acknowledge the crucifixion and resurrection? As a matter of fact, there is an entire religion founded on this premise -- Islam! By citing this contradiction, the Muslim inadvertently lays bare his own conflicted stance. On the one hand, the Muslim acknowledges Jesus as a messenger of God but does not understand the gift of salvation via the cross. Just like the demons, the Muslim claims to know Jesus and even calls Him Messiah, but yet does not know the mystery of His purpose. James speaks of such errant thinking in James 2:19.

> ¹⁹ You believe that God is one. You do well; the demons also believe, and shudder.

What initially looks to be a biblical contradiction is actually an indictment against the very religion that is bringing the charge. The contradiction perfectly illustrates the mistake of claiming to know who Jesus is, yet not understanding his true purpose. The very argument brought to disprove the work of Jesus Christ only reveals it more fully.

3. If Jesus is one aspect of the Trinity, why did He say God had forsaken Him?

One of the favorite verses Muslims like to quote is Matthew 27:46:

> ⁴⁶ About the ninth hour Jesus cried out with a loud voice, saying, "ELI, ELI, LAMA SABACHTHANI?" that is, "MY GOD, MY GOD, WHY HAVE YOU FORSAKEN ME?"

The argument goes that if Jesus were truly God in the flesh, why did He say this while hanging on the cross? It certainly is an intriguing and justified question. Now again, those of us well schooled in Christian doctrine like nothing more than to explain the need for a holy God to separate Himself from sin, and how that relates to the mystery of the Trinity. Before embarking down such a fruitless path, just stop for a minute and think. What is wrong with this picture?

Remember that Muslims do not believe Jesus was crucified! So if Jesus was never on the cross, how did He say this? So before launching into some complex theological treatise, just ask first if the Muslim believes Jesus did in fact say these words. If the answer is yes, then there was just an admission that Jesus was hanging on the cross. Such an admission denies the reliability of the Qur'an, and now some fascinating follow-up questions can be asked. If the answer is no, then why did the Muslim engage in this line of reasoning in the first place? If the Muslim does not believe Jesus said this, then the conversation might be over. If Jesus never said these words, as the Muslim might claim, then the whole argument is a non-starter from the Muslim point of view. In other words, if the only point of explaining complex theology is for defending your faith to a Muslim who does not even assert the validity of the question, what is the point? Focus on the real issue, how was it these words were said on the cross when the Qur'an denies Jesus that was ever crucified?

The Muslim may assert that even though he himself does not believe that Jesus spoke these words, that the Christian does, and therefore the statement attributed to Jesus undermines the Christian position. There is no reason to get into a big debate. Just ask the Muslim if he wants to discuss it. If so, here is a great opportunity to grab a Bible and read Psalm 22 together, stopping to note verses 8, 16, 18 and others. If the Muslim isn't willing to open the Bible with you, there is no need to refute the argument. Just let him know that you would enjoy answering but doing so requires reading God's Word. Reading the Psalm together allows the prophetic implications of these verses to point squarely to the crucifixion and need no complex exposition. Let God's Word do the work. If the Muslim is not interested in reading the Bible, the conversation is a non-starter.

If the point is strenuously pressed, by all means, take it to the next level. The question of how Jesus referenced God while on the cross exposes the reality of who Jesus is. There are several references to God, and by viewing each, Jesus' identity is well illustrated. First, in Matthew 27:46, Jesus uses the general Aramaic term for God, "ELI," most likely from which the generic term Allah came into use by Arabs. Additionally, in Luke 23:34 and elsewhere, Jesus refers to God as "Father," indicating the direct Father/Son relationship. Notice again how Jesus portrays His dual nature as both God's servant as well as God's Son.

In summary, ask some questions before getting into a theological debate. A Muslim must deny what the Qur'an says to assert that the verse cited is true. If he does not believe that Jesus said these words, do not waste too much time. If the Muslim honestly wants to pursue it, use the opportunity as a hook to study the Bible together and thus give the Spirit more opportunity to work.

4. Christians say Jesus is the Son of God while both Jews and Muslims do not. This leaves Christians as the only people with renegade theology.

This argument comes in various forms. Typically, Muslims play a kind of numbers game. They look at the three monotheistic religions and note that of the three monotheistic religions, only Christians stray down the path of saying "Jesus is the Son of God," so they must be wrong. They will triumphantly state that both Muslims and Jews recognize Jesus is not God's Son.

This argument is sneaky. As such, the inversion is much tougher to catch. To unravel this, we need to set a clear distinction. First, what did the Jews of 1st century Jerusalem believe that Jesus claimed? Second, what did the Jews believe about the accuracy of those claims? Confused yet? Put another way, there is the question of what Jesus stated regarding His identity, and there is the question of the veracity of those statements. While Jews disagree with Christians regarding the actual identity of Jesus, the Jews of Jesus' time were in complete agreement concerning whether or not Jesus claimed deity. This is observed from Scripture in Matthew 27:40, and continues in more detail in the next verse.

> [41] In the same way the chief priests also, along with the scribes and elders, were mocking Him and saying, [42] "He saved others; He cannot save Himself. He is the King of Israel; let Him now come down from the cross, and we will believe in Him. [43] HE TRUSTS IN GOD; LET GOD RESCUE Him now, IF HE DELIGHTS IN HIM; for He said, 'I am the Son of God.'"

The Jews did not believe Jesus was the Son of God, but there was absolutely no doubt that the Jews knew that Jesus said He was the Son of God (John 10:33, John 19:7). In fact, in some sense, the

Jews understood the meaning of Jesus' statements more than the disciples did. For example, Jesus said in John 2:19:

> ¹⁹Jesus answered them, "Destroy this temple, and in three days I will raise it up."

The Jews understood Jesus' comments regarding rebuilding the temple to refer to a resurrection. In fact, consider what the chief priest had to say in Matthew 27:63:

> ⁶³ ...Sir, we remember that when He was still alive that deceiver said, 'After three days I am to rise again.'

Even more dramatic is the reaction of the Jewish leaders to the news brought by the guards of Jesus' tomb. They did not doubt the story of the resurrection at all. In fact, they were expecting it. The key here isn't to look at what the Jewish elders said, but rather to look at what they did not say. From Matthew 28:12-14:

> ¹² And when they had assembled with the elders and consulted together, they gave a large sum of money to the soldiers, ¹³ and said, "You are to say, 'His disciples came by night and stole Him away while we were asleep.' ¹⁴ And if this should come to the governor's ears, we will win him over and keep you out of trouble."

The Jewish leaders did not for a moment doubt the story of the empty tomb. The reason that the guards were put there in the first place was to prevent any possible manipulation of events to support a resurrection account. Wouldn't the obvious reaction be to disbelieve reports that such a closely guarded body had disappeared? Rather, the Jews immediately trust the soldiers and start planning how to discredit what they knew had transpired. The conclusion is clear. The resurrection was no big surprise to them. The Jews of that day knew exactly what Jesus had claimed, even to the extent that they were not at all amazed when reports of the resurrection came in.

We arrive at the all-important question: So what? Remember the original distinction that was made. Muslims note that Jews and Christians disagreed about the identity of Jesus, which is true. However, Jews and Christians were in complete agreement that Jesus represented Himself as the Son of God. The Muslim viewpoint is that the claims of Jesus are ambiguous and unreliable since Muslims and Jews agree. In effect, Muslims view this from a kind of majority rules mentality. Since Christians are the ones who disagree, they must be wrong. The reality is that the confusion is over whether to accept the claims, not the existence of the claims. The existence of the claims is further illustrated by the charges directed against Jesus. If someone else was crucified in place of Jesus, as Muslims believe, just what were the charges brought by the Jews?

Islam is the only monotheistic religion that unequivocally denies the existence of Jesus' claims. Islam is the only monotheistic religion that alleges Jesus never even declared Himself to be God in the flesh. In this assertion, the Qur'an stands alone when viewed from every other historical document on record, whether Christian, Jewish, or even that of secular historians. Originally, the Muslim claim was that Christians are the lone holdouts concerning the identity of Jesus the Messiah. It turns out that Muslims are the lone holdouts concerning the existence of Jesus' assertions. So do Muslims believe that if one of the three major religions stands in opposition to the other two, that it must be wrong? If so, they need to acknowledge that Jesus stated He was God in the flesh. If not, then the original argument holds no weight even in their own framework of thought.

Of course, we know most Muslims do not believe that if two of the three major world religions believe something, it doesn't make it true. Since both Jews and Christians believe Muhammad to be a false prophet, Muslims will not come alongside the majority in such a case. However, exposing this inversion in such a straightforward manner may cause a visceral reaction, as Muhammad's honor and reputation are always fiercely guarded. It is much better to focus on who Jesus declared Himself to be, and how Christians and the Jews of Jesus' time are in perfect agreement regarding whether or not those declarations were made.

5. The Bible says that the coming prophet should be named Emmanuel, not Jesus.

This is another classic example of attempting to cite an apparent Biblical contradiction, and inadvertently proving the deity of Jesus. When Christians talk about fulfilled prophecy, Muslims will state that the Bible is contradictory because it says that the coming Savior's name was to be Emmanuel rather than Jesus (Isaiah 7:14). We know that Emmanuel means "God with us." What exactly do Christians proclaim about Jesus? We proclaim that He is "God with us." Literally, we proclaim that Jesus is Emmanuel. The Muslim's viewpoint is that since Jesus' name is Jesus and not Emmanuel, it shows that He cannot be God in the flesh, the prophesied one.

The Muslim argument maintains that Emmanuel and Jesus cannot be the same, and thus intends to show that Jesus is not "God with us." To prove that Jesus is not Emmanuel, they must start with the assumption that Jesus and Emmanuel are two distinct individuals. The technical term for this is circular reasoning.

Look at this from another angle. To try to convince Christians that Jesus is not Emmanuel, Muslims cite the passage from Isaiah and argue that Jesus was not named Emmanuel, and therefore cannot be the same person as prophesied. They attempt to show what they feel is a contradiction, but do not realize that Jesus claimed to be Emmanuel. What the Christian is saying is that Jesus is Emmanuel. Christians proclaim that Jesus and Emanuel are the same individual. When Muslims say that Jesus claiming to be Emmanuel is a contradiction, because the names are not the same, it displays an overly literal interpretation that misses Jesus' message entirely. Jesus and Emmanuel are indeed one, and this is the whole point. Jesus is "God with us." The Bible speaks to this point directly.

From Matthew 1:21-23:

> [21] "She will bear a Son; and you shall call His name Jesus, for He will save His people from their sins." [22] Now all this took place to fulfill what was spoken by the Lord through the prophet: [23] "BEHOLD, THE VIRGIN SHALL BE WITH CHILD AND SHALL BEAR A SON, AND THEY SHALL CALL HIS NAME IMMANUEL," which translated means, "GOD WITH US."

6. You cannot understand the Qur'an if it is read with preconceived notions.

Just keep turning these around. Assume the above is a true statement and that truly grasping the Qur'an requires that it must be read without preconceived notions. Since the vast majority of Muslims were taught to believe the Qur'an before being old enough to read it, they also have preconceived notions. Since Muslims have preconceived notions about the Qur'an, their own logic dictates that they cannot truly understand it. Would any Muslim freely admit to this?

What the Muslim means is that a person cannot have negative preconceived notions. Keep turning this around. Again assume this is true. The statement asserts that reading God's Word, while simultaneously contending that it is not, results in a complete misunderstanding of the message. Here is our opportunity to seek clarification. Do Muslims believe that reading God's Word with negative preconceived notions would result in a lack of understanding?

If Muslims hold to this position, which is the original argument, we must apply it to the Bible. If the Bible is the Word of God, and the Muslim were to read it assuming it was corrupted, what would be the logical conclusion? Remember, the conclusion is reached from the Muslim's own logical standard! The conclusion is that the Muslim would not understand the Bible's message if read from the wrong mindset. The irony is thick.

Typically, the Muslim will counter that the Bible is not the Word of God. The issue here is not to ascertain the veracity of the Bible, but rather to validate or invalidate the underlying logic. Does the Muslim truly believe the original assertion? The Muslim, by his own arguments, has inadvertently admitted he would not understand the Bible if it were God's Word. This now is the door to read the Bible and Qur'an together. The Muslim can be given the right to explain the Qur'an if the Christian is given the right to explain the Bible. The Christian can maintain his or her composure and now let the Holy Spirit be the guide as to how to proceed.

7. It is pure arrogance that Christians can know they will go to heaven.

Again, it is always easy to get lost arguing with a Muslim about how it is not arrogant to trust in God's promises. However, getting caught in the debate is not the point. Rather, find out if the Muslim is serious about finding God, or just sending up trial balloons to see what floats. The Muslim will state that the sovereignty of God is so grand that humans cannot know for certain what their ultimate destination will be. So, assume this statement is true. If a person were to know his ultimate eternal destination, it would be arrogance, and therefore any such religion with these teachings would consequently be incorrect.

What does the Qur'an teach about those who die in battle while fighting for Allah?

Qur'an 47:4c-6

> But those who are slain in the Way of Allah,- He will
> never let their deeds be lost. Soon will He guide them
> and improve their condition, And admit them to the
> Garden which He has announced for them

How fascinating! Allah makes a promise to certain Muslims about a sure way to get to paradise. The original statement, by the Muslim, is that any religion with such teachings is invalid. Does the Muslim still contend that any book that prescribes an assured path to paradise must be false? If so, he must jettison belief in the Qur'an. If not, then the original argument does not even stand against his own logic.

At this point, the real question can be asked. It is not whether God allows us to rely on His promises regarding our ultimate destination, but what are the promises that God has made?

8. The Old Testament demands that Jews kill apostates, just as Islam does.

This is another example of an inversion that is tricky to spot. The Muslim argument proceeds as follows. Muslims worship the one true God, which they assert is the same God worshipped by the Jews of the Old Testament era. The religion of Islam instructs its followers to kill apostates, which Muslims say is the same punishment that has always been a part of God's religion. They prove it by citing passages in the Bible that instruct God's loyal followers to kill those who stray from the one true faith (Deuteronomy 13:6-9). The Qur'an does not explicitly mandate death for apostasy. However, "The four major Sunni Madh'hab (schools of Islamic Jurisprudence) and the Twelve Shi'a Jafari

Madh'hab agree that any sane adult male apostate must be executed."[43] Since the rule requiring the death penalty for apostasy has been unchanged throughout history, this example serves to illustrate that it must mean Muslims worship the same God that Christians and Jews do.

What if we follow the logic and see where it leads? Even though we have shown earlier that Allah and YHWH are different beings, assume for a moment that Muslims worship the same God as Jews and Christians, as the Muslim line of reasoning asserts. If that is the case, then a Muslim turned Christian or Muslim turned Jew is worshiping the same God as a Muslim, just in a different way. Therefore, if a converted Muslim is worshiping the same God, albeit incorrectly, such a person is not an apostate and does not deserve death. The entire argument that the apostate requires death gets thrown out because they would be worshiping incorrectly, not worshiping a different God, and subsequently not deserving of the death penalty. In other words, Muslims assert that they worship the same God as Christians and Jews worship, but then simultaneous hold to a theology that demands death for conversion. Why have a law requiring the killing of apostates if those apostates are worshipping the same god? That punishment is because they would be worshiping a different God. In short, the proof that Allah and YWHW are the same is based on the requirement of killing an apostate for switching allegiance from Allah to YHWH.

If Christians and Jews worship the same God as Muslims, then Muslims who convert to Christianity or Judaism should not be killed. The particular Islamic tenet of killing apostates for rejecting God would be rendered invalid if each religion worshiped the same God. If Christians and Jews do not worship the same God, then the original argument undermined itself from the very beginning by setting out to prove the reverse of what it stated. Trying to prove that Muslims and Jews worship the same God by citing Scripture demanding the killing of people for worshiping another God makes no sense whatsoever.

217

9. Jesus cannot be God because He has a different will than God, and thus is a unique being.

Muslims are quick to cite the following verse in an attempt to show Jesus is not God. From Luke 22:41-42:

> [41] And He withdrew from them about a stone's throw, and He knelt down and began to pray, [42]saying, "Father, if You are willing, remove this cup from Me; yet not My will, but Yours be done."

The Muslim stance is that Jesus admits here that His will is different from that of the Father, thus proving Jesus cannot be God. We have already covered in-depth the dual nature of Christ, but there is something even more profound here. On the surface, we can return to the definition of the incarnation, that Jesus was a man with full human agency as well as being fully God. However, this raises the question of how His human will asserted itself. Even more to the point, did Jesus ever allow the will of His human aspect to override the will of His God aspect?

Jesus answers this question quite clearly, and in doing so reveals something astonishing about who He is. From John 8:28:

> [28] So Jesus said, "When you lift up the Son of Man, then you will know that I am He, and I do nothing on My own initiative, but I speak these things as the Father taught Me."

In this passage, Jesus explicitly says that He is not speaking on His own, but rather that His words are the same as those He received directly from God the Father. While it can be argued this verse does not state that Jesus was acting out the exact will of the Father at every point, the following verse does. From John 5:30:

> [30] I can do nothing on My own initiative As I hear, I judge; and My judgment is just, because I do not seek My own will, but the will of Him who sent Me.

What we see is that Jesus makes it known that His actions and words are not on His own initiative. Just what does Jesus mean by this? He is performing actions and saying words identically as God Himself would do and say them. In other words, there is no distinction between the actions and words of Jesus when compared to those of God (John 14:10). The conclusion is that the human will of Jesus was completely subservient to the will of God. No mere human can accomplish this, but the God-man could.

Even more intriguing though, is how Jesus then goes on to describe the Holy Spirit. From John 16:3:

> [3] But when He, the Spirit of truth, comes, He will guide you into all the truth; for He will not speak on His own initiative, but whatever He hears, He will speak; and He will disclose to you what is to come.

Just as Jesus asserts He and the Father are one because of the singular purpose of their collective will, so too He equates the Holy Spirit as another aspect of God for the very same reason! The Holy Spirit is shown to be God, because He will not act on His own initiative, but rather only repeat those things that God Himself is disclosing to us. Jesus again subtly clues us into the triune nature of God. God, Jesus, and the Holy Spirit all act out of one will. None ever wanders or veers from it.

What initially appears to show Jesus claiming to be separate from God, upon deeper investigation, actually reveals His assertion that the Father, He, and the Holy Spirit all have the same will. Jesus was indeed saddled with a human will, which lay in total subjection to the will of God. He claims that He and the Holy Spirit both share that will in its entirety, thus offering yet another claim of His deity and of the Trinity in general.

10. Jesus denies His deity before the rich young ruler.

For our last example, we will examine an encounter many Muslims are familiar with, where Jesus meets the rich young ruler. From Mark 10:17-18:

> [17] As He was setting out on a journey, a man ran up to Him and knelt before Him, and asked Him, "Good Teacher, what shall I do to inherit eternal life?" [18] And Jesus said to him, "Why do you call Me good? No one is good except God alone."

The Muslim position is that Jesus again separates His identity from God by noting that only God is good, thus saying by implication that He is not. What is perhaps so strange about this attack is that Muslims view all prophets as a higher caliber of human. In other words, prophets are a better class of people by birth and are therefore good and worthy of being listened to. So in order for a Muslim to claim that Jesus implies that He is not good, they do so at the expense of undermining their own view of prophets. This dismantles their own theology about Jesus, or any other prophet for that matter. So the question must be posed, does a Muslim believe Jesus is good? If not, then they have rejected the Islamic view of prophets. If so, they undermine the argument they are making regarding this verse.

Again, confronting a Muslim with this line of reasoning may not seem to get anywhere at first. The comeback may be that it is not about what the Muslim believes, but rather that a Christian must confront Jesus' words here. Yet this is no problem for someone who understands who Jesus is. The point being made is that Jesus was called "Good teacher", and he proceeds to give advice on that basis, noting that only God is good. The subject is eternal life and Jesus has much to say on the subject. Yet if Jesus is not good, why would anyone pay attention to what He has to say. It is only because He is the Good teacher and because only God is good that allows Jesus to respond with divine authority. The logical conclusion is that Jesus is God.

Learning to recognize these inversions is hard. However, once done, the work is not over. We must turn the inversions back upon themselves in order to point to the truth of Christ. In the last section, we will take this final step and illustrate how to keep the conversation focused on the redemptive work of the only one who can save us from our sin and reconcile us to God.

Section 5

Applying the Islamic Inversion

And when I came to you, brethren, I did not come with superiority of speech or of wisdom, proclaiming to you the testimony of God. For I determined to know nothing among you except Jesus Christ, and Him crucified.

1 CORINTHIANS 2:1-2

Chapter 14

From Common Criticisms to the Truth of Christ

The Qur'an contains a number of contradictions, and while exposing them can be rather gratifying in the flesh for the novice debater, such tactics completely miss the mark. Remember that our goal is not to win the debate, but to reach Muslims who are seeking the truth. Anyone who has experience interacting with Muslims knows that it is unproductive to launch into attack mode, as this is difficult to do with gentleness and respect (1 Peter 3:15). Therefore, since we have been practicing how to identify Islamic inversions, the next step is to learn how to apply these inversions in such a way to lead back to Christ, and Him crucified. How can we use the inversions that we now see to do this? How do we take this to the next level? From now on, do not just see the inversion; use it to hook back into the truth of Christ. As always, remember this is not a debate. From Colossians 4:6:

> 6 Let your speech always be with grace, as though seasoned with salt, so that you will know how you should respond to each person.

How can we prevent the conversations from going adrift? Keep the verse above in mind as we recognize the inversions, and then flip them back around to point toward Christ.

From Politics to Christ

If you want to get nowhere fast, have a political debate with a Muslim. Even well-meaning Christians disagree on the most effective way that governments should be run, how much they should intrude, and when they should act versus when they should not. And why shouldn't we disagree sometimes? Figuring out the best means to an end is hard enough, let alone when global issues and uncertain future consequences are involved. Toss into the mix the Islamic hatred of Israel, and you have a debate that will at best accomplish nothing, and at worst create hard feelings. So what to do? The answer is to watch for hooks.

For example, what if you find yourself in the uncomfortable position of defending the U.S. Middle East policy concerning the most recent U.S. war in Iraq? (If you vehemently disagreed with the U.S. policy in Iraq, then this just proves the point of the previous paragraph.) One counter argument that might arise would be for a Muslim to ask you how you would react if your country were invaded. Stop right there. Are you sure that you want to answer that question? Think first about what is being said.

What is happening here? What the Muslim is doing is asking you to put yourself in his shoes. Herein lies the inversion. A great teacher once taught this principle in Luke 6:31:

> [31] Treat others the same way you want them to treat you.

The Muslim is in truth citing Christian principles to defend his political position! Muhammad never taught this principle. Isn't it odd that everyone, whether Christian, Muslim, or atheist, is aware of this moral standard? It is so pervasive it even has a name – the Golden Rule. That is the inversion, but we can now turn up the heat. Here is our hook. The challenge itself of "How you would feel if" is the important thing, not the answer. The challenge presupposes the morality of Christ and the profound nature of His teaching over that of Muhammad! Here is your chance to ask questions. Ask your Muslim friend if treating others the way you want to be treated is indeed the 2nd highest commandment (Luke 10:27-28). Why or why not? Why didn't Allah reveal this in the Qur'an? Did Jesus teach this, and what does this say about His love for others and the love that we should imitate? So don't get bogged down in details. Such a question opens a great door, so be watching when the hook comes along.

Knowing God's Inner Thoughts

During any conversation, communication happens on a variety of levels. When any two people converse, they share experiences and thoughts as best they can. Yet at the end of the day, no two people can ever see the world exactly the same. People will hold differing views partly because everyone has had a unique set of experiences. A person will often say, "you cannot understand until you have walked a mile in my shoes," or "you cannot understand it until you have lived it." These statements can often be a roadblock to true two-way communication, yet that does not make them invalid. Muslims often raise this type of defense to derail the Christian's attempt to connect. This kind of fallback mechanism allows the Muslim not to get too close. It provides a shielding mechanism within Islam that allows the Muslim not to take anyone from another faith too seriously. In this way, the Muslim's true spiritual needs can get buried behind accusations of misunderstanding. How can we as Christians convert this potential roadblock to meaningful conversation and turn it back toward who God is and what He has done for us? As it turns out, examining what is required for significant and substantial communication itself will lead directly to how God interacts with us via His Spirit.

The reality is that when any two people communicate, in some ways they will connect and in others they will not. This balance is obvious when the nonsensical consequences of each extreme are considered. If it were impossible for two people to exchange meaningful information or to learn about each other on any level, what would be the point in any communication? Similarly, the ability to know someone fully, including their deepest inner thoughts requires a level of intimacy unattainable except for an omniscient being.

Enter our hook. When it is made clear that true understanding cannot be achieved, there is a level of agreement that can be reached. It is true that for ourselves, only our inner spirit can know the full depths of what is inside each one of us. As it turns out, the Bible speaks to this point, that this is how it is with God, too. From 1 Corinthians 2:10-12:

> [10] For to us God revealed them through the Spirit; for the Spirit searches all things, even the depths of God. [11] For who among men knows the thoughts of a man except the spirit of the man which is in him? Even so the thoughts of God no one knows except the Spirit of God. [12] Now we have received, not the spirit of the world, but the Spirit who is from God, so that we may know the things freely given to us by God,

When a Muslim discusses the inability of his Christian friend to truly understand him, it can be a segue into how this mirrors our relationship to God. Only a man's spirit can truly understand his innermost thoughts. So too only God's Holy Spirit can truly understand and convey God's innermost thoughts.

Any mature Christian truly knows this, and that knowledge comes from our personal relationship with Him. Many Muslims will proudly exclaim that they have the same kind of knowledge which comes from obeying the Qur'an. However, closer inspection shows that such a perceived relationship is entirely one way, and does not offer any insight into the mind of God.

To fully understand how Muslims communicate with their god, it would be best to draw an analogy. Imagine a father abandoning his child before birth. While the child has no direct memories of his father, the father leaves behind a list of rules for his son to follow. Then the son never sees his father or ever hears anything about him. Now the son is a faithful son, so he sends him letters all the time. He tells his father how he is doing, and always writes how much he loves him. He also writes to his father about how he follows almost all of the rules laid down for him. Now this son says, "I have a great relationship with my father. I obey the rules he left for me, and I know my dad by thinking about those rules that he left for me." The hollowness of this example is evident, and anyone hearing such a story would unequivocally call the child misguided, and rightly so.

From the Muslim perspective, Allah left behind a bunch of rules. The god of Islam no longer communicates with Muslims but expects them to engage in ritual prayer to him five times daily. He does not ever answer, but the Muslims will still tell you how great their relationship is with their god. Doesn't this seem just as ridiculous as the previous story? It is so much easier to see with the previous analogy. However, it is harder for Muslims to recognize this with regards to their own religion.

To review, Muslims will often say that we as Christians cannot understand them. The inversion is that it is true that perfect understanding between two fallible beings is impossible, but not so with God. He gives us albeit partial understanding, but on a level that we can handle and that resonates with His very inner Spirit. While it is true that finite humans are unable to grasp the full majesty, glory, and wisdom of God, He gives us rich and deep glimpses into who He is. The true God gives us this capability through the Holy Spirit. Here is the chance to talk about who the

Holy Spirit is and how He interacts with you. Hook into what it can mean to truly understand God, not just follow a bunch of rules you believe God left for you.

The Ultimate Jihad

Often Muslims will claim Jesus was a human sacrifice. They will then proceed to rant and rave about how human sacrifice is outlawed and so on. Now again you have a choice to either debate about how Jesus was not a human sacrifice in the way the Muslim intends or to expose the inversion and turn the tables.

From the Muslim point of view, a true human sacrifice is a person who dies in jihad. What if we travel down this road to its logical conclusion? First, we need to decide if jihad is a good example of human sacrifice, and thus serves as a workable definition. If so, and if human sacrifice is evil, then why isn't jihad as well? Here lies our first conundrum. Jihad is honored, and if jihad is a type of human sacrifice, then the Muslim must acknowledge that some forms of human sacrifice are not only acceptable but also venerable.

All we need to do is determine what type of human sacrifice is worthy of our respect. As a Christian, we immediately recognize the difference between killing someone else as a sacrifice and giving one's own life out of free will for another. Would a Muslim say it is worthy to die in jihad if you are advancing the cause of God? Perhaps yes; perhaps no. As Christians, we would agree that giving one's life is the ultimate price to pay for our faith. We would disagree on what types of actions constitute the advancement of God's kingdom, but we would definitely agree conceptually that giving one's life is admirable.

At this stage, the Islamic definition of jihad will be illuminating. Jihad essentially means, "to struggle, to strive." Muslims will be insistent to note there is the greater jihad, striving to perfect one's faith, and the lesser jihad, which is the holy war type of jihad. So wouldn't it be accurate to say that Jesus was engaged in greater jihad? Moreover, if Jesus died, wouldn't it be fair to say that he died while in jihad? So, when describing what Jesus did, you can actually say, Jesus paid the ultimate jihad for you. This may sound heretical, but it will frequently make sense to a Muslim. They likely will not commit their life to Christ right then and there, but the statement will carry meaning to them. Jesus was the ultimate jihad, giving his life for the cause of God.

If the discussion is moving toward the sacrifice of Jesus as an ignominious and humiliating event, hook into the Muslim mindset. Talk about Jesus as the ultimate jihad. Discuss how Jesus engaged in greater jihad to advance the cause of God by being fully obedient to His Father, even to His death.

Can God Die?

We ended our last section discussing the death of Jesus. Of course, Muslims will often tell the Christian how Christ did not die, but how He was rescued at the last minute and whisked away to heaven. We have already discussed some of the inversions relating to denying the death of Jesus. When dialoguing with Muslims, the subject of whether God can die tends to come up as a recurring theme. As such, we can again take this up a notch and consider how to unravel the following paradox. This may be a great way to start a conversation on deeper subjects. In this example, we will postulate three assumptions. By paradox, it will be shown that one of these assumptions must be wrong, and then we will ask which assumption is the incorrect one.

1. God has a greater ability to show love toward humans than humans do.
2. The ultimate way of showing love is by giving your life for someone or something else.
3. God cannot die.

Carefully consider the three suppositions above. If all of these statements are true, a paradox develops. If God has the supreme capacity for love, and the ultimate capacity to show love is through giving your life, then how can God be less capable of showing love than a human if He cannot die? To unravel this mystery, we will examine each point from logic itself, the Qur'an, and the Bible.

To start, examine the first proposition. God, by his very nature, loves us. After all, He created us, gives us the earth to live on, and seeks the best for us. He was the creator of love, and as such has the ultimate capacity for being able to love. From a logical point of view, it would follow that the creator of love would have the most capacity to love.

Both the Qur'an and the Bible support this proposition as well. In the Qur'an, this can be seen in the following verses.

Qur'an 2:222

...surely Allah loves those who turn much (to Him), and He loves those who purify themselves.

Qur'an 3:031

Say: If you love Allah, then follow me, Allah will love you and forgive you your faults, and Allah is Forgiving, Merciful.

The Qur'an makes many other references to Allah's love, such as 2:195, 3:134, 3:146, 3:148, 3:159, 5:13, 5:42, 5:93, 9:4, 9:7, 49:9, 60:8. Also, in Qur'an 11:90 and 85:14 Allah is referred to as Al-Wadûd, the loving one. He is not referred to as "a loving one," or "one who loves," but *the* loving one.

The Bible also speaks to this, so much so that it says God's love is so strong that nothing can separate us from it. No love could be stronger than one that cannot be severed under any circumstance. Romans 8:35:

> [35] Who will separate us from the love of Christ? Will tribulation, or distress, or persecution, or famine, or nakedness, or peril, or sword?

Other Biblical references regarding this surpassing love of God are found in John 3:16, John 14:21-23, Romans 5:5-6, Romans 8:38-39, Ephesians 2:4-5, Ephesians 3:19, Ephesians 5:2, Titus 3:4-5, 1 John 3:1, and 1 John 4:16.

So we see that no matter what the perspective, whether simple logic, the Qur'an, or the Bible, God is love, is the creator of love, and has the ability to love humans with a surpassing love that defies our understanding and capacity to love each other.

Next, we will examine proposition two, that the ultimate way to show love is through sacrificing to the point of death. Of course, when we talk about laying down one's life, we are not talking about a meaningless suicide, or worse yet, one made out of pity to leave surviving friends and family in misery. We are talking about the giving of one's life to accomplish a greater good for others. Anecdotally, I have heard Muslims say that they love their families so much that they would die for them. Self-sacrifice for the greater benefit of others is a virtue held in the highest esteem by many cultures. As people, we know love requires commitment and action. The greater the sacrifice made, the greater the love shown. The ultimate sacrifice of death thus corresponds to the ultimate act of love.

The Qur'an extols the virtue of this highest sacrifice. Allah makes reference to jihad, so all Muslims know about the ultimate price of dying in battle. According to the Qur'an, Allah honors such ultimate sacrifice so much that it is an instant ticket to paradise. No other act has such a promise from Allah. Allah holds this action in the highest esteem, to the point of its uniqueness with regard to the rewards promised.

Qur'an 2:154

> And say not of those who are slain in the way of Allah: "They are dead." Nay, they are living, though ye perceive (it) not.

Other Qur'anic references are 3:157-158, 4:74, 22:58, 47:4. The Bible also speaks about this ultimate display of love via sacrifice. Some verses are Romans 5:8, John 10:11, and 1 John 3:16. However, this next passage is as clear as it gets. John 15:12-13:

> [12]**This is My commandment, that you love one another, just as I have loved you. [13]Greater love has no one than this, that one lay down his life for his friends.**

So again we see from the perspective of logic, the Qur'an, or the Bible, self-sacrifice is the ultimate virtue. Dying for others is the highest price you can pay, and the willingness to do so is the highest form of showing love.

Finally, we come to proposition three: God cannot die. This also seems to be logically true. Of course, as the eternal God, God cannot *not* exist.

The Qur'an confirms that God cannot die. He is called Al-Qayyûm, the self-existent one.

Qur'an 2:255

> Allah! There is no god but He,-the Living, the Self-subsisting, Eternal. No slumber can seize Him nor sleep...

The Bible also states that God does not die. Psalm 102:27:

> ²⁷ But You are the same,
> And Your years will not come to an end.

The Bible confirms that God is everlasting and immortal in various other passages such as Genesis 21:33 Psalm 90:2, Isaiah 40:28, 1 Timothy 1:17, and 1 Timothy 6:16.

To recap, who can love better than any of us except God Himself? Yet how can God, who supposedly is capable of loving better than anyone, be incapable of showing the highest form of love by dying for another? If God cannot die, God apparently cannot show love to the extent that we humans can. It seems that we have a conundrum. How can God, who supposedly cannot die, show greater love for us if only we humans are qualified to show this ultimate act of love?

There is only way out. One of our initial propositions must be wrong. Either God does not have the highest capacity for love, giving your life is not the ultimate sacrifice, or God did exist in a form that experienced death. Herein lies the inversion. If God is restricted to being unable to exist in a form that can die, He becomes less able than humans to show supreme love. Again, it is time to elevate the conversation with our Muslim friend. Which part of the paradox is the problem? Of course, it is the third proposition that is incorrect.

It is hard to understand how an eternal being could die. In many ways, it does not make sense. To see this more clearly, consider our own existence. For any of us who hope in an afterlife, whether Muslim or Christian, death is not permanent. Even though we are eternal beings, the fact that we will all die someday stays true. So it is with God Himself. Even though Jesus knew that He would wake up in paradise after physical death, so too we as humans know that if we trust Christ, we will awake with Him after our death, too. The question is no different for us; do we truly die if we are granted paradise? Of course we do, just as God in human form can also experience human death before arising in heaven, His original home. From 2 Corinthians 5:8:

> [8] we are of good courage, I say, and prefer rather to be absent from the body and to be at home with the Lord.

The inversion is that by stating that God cannot die, the Muslim unwittingly limits God's ability to demonstrate His love for us. Yet the paradox reveals reality. God must be able to exist in a state where He can experience death to show greater love than humans can. This is a potential hook. By bringing up such a conversation, the gospel can come out in a thoughtful and unthreatening tone. A Muslim may claim that Christians are inconsistent when they say that Jesus was God, and yet simultaneously that He died on the cross. However, the true paradox is actually the reverse. If God is most capable of showing love, and the willingness to offer your life is the ultimate act of love, then God must be able to die. This can only be achieved if He existed in finite time and space in the form of the God-man, Jesus Christ. By following the logical clues, the Christian may be able to bring their Muslim friend the gospel without hitting them head-on with debate.

Hopefully, it is evident that recognition of the inversion can lead to a more in-depth dialogue that isn't confrontational. In the next chapter, some common topics such as revelation, miracles, and martyrdom will be considered. Again, in each case, it begins with an inverted argument and ends with the truth of Jesus.

Chapter 15

From Common Escapes to the Truth of Christ

In this chapter, we will continue discussing how to find hooks. A hook is a way to redirect a conversation back to the gospel of Christ. Once you recognize the inversion, you will discover that there are many such hooks available. Watch for them when delving into Islamic theology. Hopefully, these example hooks will help make them easier to spot when having each unique conversation with a Muslim friend.

Is the Qur'an Allah's Only Revelation?

One of the final places of retreat for a Muslim is the Qur'an. A Muslim will often fall back on this supposed sanctuary and discuss its sufficiency and beauty with regards to how it instructs the Muslim to lead their life. Many Christian apologists have been easily able to dismantle such an assertion through critical study and exposition, and I applaud such efforts. However, not everyone has studied the Qur'an extensively. When having a conversation with your Muslim friend, there might be a broader line of questioning. If the Qur'an is quoted to you as it often will be, stay alert to listen to its grammar, particularly subjects and verbs. By doing so, some fascinating claims about the word for word perfection of the Qur'an can be probed.

It has been previously noted that as a rule, Muslims have a wide variety of beliefs. However, every Muslim would agree that the Qur'an is the word of Allah. Given our focus on the grammar of the Qur'an, one interesting conversation that can help start a Muslim thinking is how to respond when examining excerpts from the Qur'an such as these:

Qur'an 1:5-7

> Thee do we worship, and Thine aid we seek. Show us the straight way, The way of those on whom Thou hast bestowed Thy Grace, those whose (portion) is not wrath, and who go not astray.

Remembering that the Muslim believes the entire Qur'an is the direct words of Allah, the question arises; "Who is doing the speaking here?"* If Allah is doing the speaking, then he is praying to himself. Any Muslim is quick to point out this seeming inconsistency when referring to Jesus, stating that if Jesus were God, He could not pray to Himself. Yet a Muslim does not quite see it the same way within the Qur'an. Alternatively, if Muhammad is doing the speaking, then the Qur'an is not written entirely by Allah as every Muslim would claim. The casual observer, which includes many Muslims, would respond that it is obvious that the verses cited are meant for prayer. In other words, Allah is telling Muslims what to say. Yet this argument does not hold up, because in other parts of the Qur'an, where Allah does give instructions for what Muslims are to speak, he specifically uses the word "say." (Qur'an 2:94, 2:97, 2:136 and many, many others) Therefore, one has to ask why the word "say" is missing here in Surah 1. Surely any all-knowing deity would not forgetfully create such confusion.

---

* There are other variations on this theme, such as Qur'an 9:30: "...Allah's curse be on them..." rather than "...Our curse be on them..." See also Qur'an 37:164-166.

So we are left with four alternatives. Are these the words of Allah praying to himself, are they additions by Muhammad, does Allah forget to use the word "say," or is the entire subject frivolous and irrelevant?

Certainly Allah would not pray to himself, as Allah is viewed as self-sufficient. If Muhammad is the author, then the Muslim would be admitting that the Qur'an is not entirely from Allah, which a Muslim would never do. Even suggesting that Allah would inadvertently leave out a word undermines the Muslim position that every word in the Qur'an is perfectly precise, beautiful, elegant, and beyond comparison.

That brings us to the final option, that the entire line of reasoning is a peripheral issue. This topic may seem a trivial one, but it opens up a huge Pandora's Box. The Muslim may flee to the issue of the sovereignty of Allah, saying that Allah deemed it necessary to use the word "say" in some places, and yet not in others. At this point, you have engaged someone in a thought experiment, and now you can begin to truly dialogue. Why does Allah choose to add the word "say" in some places, but not others? Islamic doctrine teaches that the Qur'an is so perfect it cannot even be translated, yet can it be that in some places the addition of a word makes no difference? Omitting a word that confuses the voice and person of the grammatical construct undermines the notion that the Qur'an is word for word perfect. That seems contradictory at best, and a complete undermining of the Islamic doctrine of the supremacy of Qur'anic poetry at worst. It raises the question: Why did Allah deem the extra word "say" necessary at some times and not at others, and what can a Muslim learn from this use versus lack of use? The point is that the omission of this word cannot be haphazard. Why might it be absent?

One response might be that the answer resides in the concept of poetic flow, which seems a fair enough guess. In other words, there is nothing specific for a Muslim to learn from the exact wording, because the poetic flow may take precedence to content.

That may be a bit harsh, but the eventuality of such a statement is disastrous to the Muslim. It would mean human limitations that impeded recitation of the Qur'an constrained Allah to make some shortcuts in his perfect revelation. No Muslim would ever question the sovereignty of Allah, but that is precisely what such a response does. Allah's sovereignty is undercut if he changed words or phrases of the Qur'an to make it more easily memorizable. As the creator of humankind, why would he create humans without the capacity to understand his perfect revelation? Why did he make humans capable of only understanding a constrained and limited revelation that required alteration for poetic flow?

If you get this far, you now have a hook into entering the subject of how a person can tell whether something is truly a revelation of God. It seems a massive dilemma is at hand. It is at times such as these that the relationship you have established with your Muslim friend can begin bearing fruit.

Did Muhammad Receive Other Revelations?

Another maneuver indicative of Muslims debating along these same topical lines is when Muslims stress the difference between the Qur'an and the Hadith. The Hadith are a collection of the life stories about Muhammad. These were collected by the companions of Muhammad, and differ slightly depending on the chain of narration. Turning back to whether the Qur'an is sufficient, a Muslim might argue that the Qur'an gives general information but the Hadith elaborates on it. For example, a Muslim might say something similar to this: "The Qur'an instructs the Muslim to keep up with prayer but never gives the specifics of how to perform it, and that is the role of the Hadith. The prophet Muhammad said to pray the way he had prayed."

Now that you are trained in listening, pay close attention to what was said. Ask the right questions. How did Muhammad know such specifics? Did he hear additional (*exoquranic*) revelations from Allah, or did he just make these things up? Ultimately, there are only three possibilities:

A. Muhammad received exoquranic revelations.
B. Muhammad just guessed.
C. Muhammad instinctively knew without being told.

Which way is a Muslim to turn? If he says "A," he admits the Qur'an is incomplete, and therefore not God's perfect word. If he says "B," he admits Muhammad was a charlatan. However, look closely at the last alternative. If he says "C," he has violated the Oneness of God. If Muhammad somehow knew divine instructions for rituals such as prayer, without ever being taught, Muhammad obtains some form of divinity. To know the mind of God without revelation is to be God. If God did not transmit the information to Muhammad (i.e., option A), then Muhammad contained divine information in his head not communicated by Allah. What other explanation could account for such unimparted knowledge? Muhammad must have either been given the revelations, or he must have always had them, equating his innate knowledge with that of Allah.

A Muslim may argue that Allah had blessed Muhammad with wisdom in methodologies of religion that were pleasing to Allah. However, such a statement only creates a layer of abstraction. If Muhammad were given peculiar divine wisdom besides that of the Qur'an, then the admission is option "A". This means that in the Muslim view, the Qur'an by itself is incomplete.

With all such discussions, a typical Muslim is not going to jump up and down at this point and scream for salvation, but some big questions have been posed that haven't been answered. Any thoughtful person is going to be spending some time in deep reflection. At this point, the clever Muslim will turn the tables on you, and ask you the same question. Since the Bible is the true Word of God, how is it that we as Christians know we hear from

Him? What else would God have to say to us since His Word is already complete? Doesn't the same line of reasoning apply to Christians? As a matter of fact, the question of how we hear from God is an excellent question indeed.

It is at this point that the door has been flung wide! You have just been granted carte blanche to elaborate on the Holy Spirit and His role. We know that God exists in multiple aspects, one of which is the Holy Spirit. Only by the Holy Spirit could such communication occur. Not only that, but such communication must always be in agreement with the Word of God, never adding to it. In such a conversation, you have been given the right to describe how God interacts with you, and how that interaction does not supersede the written Word of God, but pulls from it, agrees with it, and is timeless.

It's a Miracle!

One common escape for Muslims is to claim the Qur'an was of miraculous origin. Since Muhammad was said to be the unlettered prophet, one who could not read or write, the Muslim view is that the very existence of the Qur'an proves the prophetic nature of Muhammad's ministry. This assertion can lead into a discussion of miracles themselves, and what kind of message they provide. To fully understand how to make the transition from the Muslim view of the miraculous nature of the Qur'an to the truth of God giving us His only Son, one must first understand the nature of miracles within Islam.

When first learning about Islam, one thing that stands out is the lack of credible and recorded miracles performed by Muhammad. This seems plain enough since miracles are one logical way to identify an omnipotent God. Unfortunately, it is not that simple. Supernatural activity does not mandate the presence of God. In Exodus 7:8-12, when Moses threw down his staff, which turned into a serpent, what happened next? Pharaoh's sorcerers did the same. Nobody would claim that because the sorcerers recreated Moses' miracle that they were also messengers from God. Satan can act in the supernatural realm as well. Similarly, neither does the absence of miracles deny the existence of God. So while miracles can be a guide to identifying what God is doing, we must be careful not to give too much credence to supernatural activity. We also must be careful not to give too much credence to the lack of it as well.

Defining the nature of miracles from a Muslim perspective is even more unclear. While it seems logical that God would wish to communicate to us in a supernatural way, this assumes a personal God who wants to interact with us. Since Allah is distant and unknowable, it is consistent within Islam that he would not practice supernatural activity. So to a Muslim, it makes perfect sense that Muhammad did not engage in various sorts of supernatural activities either.

It gets even more convoluted than this. Many Muslims will tell you that the Qur'an itself is a miracle. In fact, when people asked Muhammad for a miracle, he told them to read the Qur'an (Qur'an 29-50-51, 17:88-94). From the Muslim perspective, the Qur'an is the miracle. In fact, the Arabic word for sign is ayah, the same word that refers to a verse of the Qur'an. These words are the same because, from a Muslim point of view, each ayah of the Qur'an is a sign from Allah. As Ahmed Deedat, a well-known recent Muslim apologist said:

> Again and again when miracles are demanded from the prophet of God by the cynical and frivolous few, he is made to point to the qur'an - message from high - as 'the miracle.' The miracle of miracles! And men of wisdom, people with literary and spiritual insight, who were honest enough to themselves, recognised and accepted al-qur'an as a genuine miracle.[44]

To better understand the Muslim mindset, imagine that instead of using the word verse, we referred to each passage of the Bible as miraculous. Each time a preacher took to a podium to begin reading a chapter, he would tell us to turn to book such-and-such, chapter so-and-so, miracle number 1. Therefore, in order to examine Muhammad's supposed miracle of bringing the Qur'an, we must view the Qur'an itself. Since the Qur'an itself is the miracle, we are forced to examine some of its passages to see what kind of miracle Muhammad was given. We will do so, at the same time comparing these to the miracles of Christ. As always, we will have our inversion detector toggled to the on position.

Looking back to Christ, consider the miracles He performed. As a few examples, He gave sight to a blind man (John 9), raised a man from the dead (John 11), healed a paralytic (Mark 2), and fed thousands of people starting with two fish and five loaves of bread (Matthew 14). Now contrast these to Muhammad's miracle, delivering the Qur'an. Close inspection reveals a very different type of miracle when turning the pages of the Qur'an. Muhammad's miracle states that Muslims should ask for permission before leaving Muhammad at a big event (Qur'an 24:62). Muhammad's wives would receive double punishment for indecency (Qur'an 33:30). Muhammad was able to take more wives than other Muslims (Qur'an 33:50). Muhammad was allowed to marry his adopted son's wife (Qur'an 33:37). Visitors to Muhammad's house were explicitly told to leave right after dinner so as not to be an annoyance (Qur'an 33:53). Private criticism of Muhammad is forbidden. (Qur'an 58:9). Finally, people speaking to Muhammad should do so in a soft voice (Qur'an 49:2).

A distinct pattern becomes evident. All of the miracles of Jesus were to help other people. Never once did He perform a miracle that aided his own earthly status as a human. He never once made food to feed Himself, used miracles to amuse Himself, or gave Himself special permission for something by supernatural means (Matthew 4:1-11). Even in the case where Jesus had Peter catch two fish to pay the two drachma tax, Jesus emphasized that this is not for His own benefit, but rather to keep others from being offended (Matthew 17:27).

On the other hand, in the case of Muhammad, many of his miraculous Qur'anic recitations were rather convenient to his earthly existence. Even one of Muhammad's wives noted this.

Bukhari Volume 7, Book 62, Number 48

> Khaula bint Hakim was one of those ladies who presented themselves to the Prophet for marriage. 'Aisha said, "Doesn't a lady feel ashamed for presenting herself to a man?" But when the Verse: "(O Muhammad) You may postpone (the turn of) any of them (your wives) that you please," (33.51) was revealed, 'Aisha said, "'O Allah's Apostle! I do not see, but, that your Lord hurries in pleasing you.'"[45]

1400 years later, it is hard to know how much sarcasm Muhammad's wife voiced in the above passage. What is not difficult to see is that Aisha recognized the quickness in which Muhammad's life was made more convenient and enjoyable at the revelation of this particular verse of the Qur'an. The miracle of the Qur'an made Muhammad's earthly life more pleasant, whereas the miracles of Jesus made other people's lives better. Indeed, we find the two historical figures in diametric opposition to each other. Jesus performed miracles to the benefit of others and never for Himself. In fact, often Jesus' miracles were done at a cost to Himself. Ultimately, the miracle of Jesus' resurrection was performed at the cost of a torturous death. Alternatively, Muhammad's miracle of the Qur'an made his own life more comfortable.

Remember that the whole point of this exercise is to lead Muslims to the beauty and truth of Christ. So here is the hook: Why is there this discrepancy? What does this say about these two miracle workers? Is one type of miracle more deserving of our respect than the other, and if so why? This can be a great segue into the sacrificial work of Jesus. Also, what is the point of miracles? Who are they for? What do they reveal? Why didn't Jesus ever do miracles to help Himself? These are questions where the contrast between Jesus and Muhammad can be discussed delicately to show their vast differences.

How Not to Be an Islamic Martyr

Another subject that seems to come up from time to time is the Muslim stance that Islam is unfairly misunderstood and persecuted in the West. Such statements can lead to political disputes, which have the tendency to drift off course from the truth of Christ. As always, it is much better to recognize the Islamic inversion, turn it around, and reveal the reality of Jesus. Of course, spotting how Islamic doctrine is inverted can often be tricky, and it takes practice. Yet the Spirit will guide the Christian when asked (James 1:5). If the inversions are not yet immediately apparent, don't worry. I had read this particular verse of the Qur'an a few times and didn't spot what now seems obvious. Just keep practicing on these and the pattern will continue becoming more evident.

Qur'an 16:106

> Any one who, after accepting faith in Allah, utters Unbelief,- except under compulsion, his heart remaining firm in Faith - but such as open their breast to Unbelief, on them is Wrath from Allah, and theirs will be a dreadful Penalty.

Here we see that uttering unbelief in Allah is worthy of receiving wrath. Interestingly, a special exemption is made for doing so under compulsion. In other words, as a Muslim, when your life is on the line, you are granted immunity from this rule. The Qur'an states that if you are being persecuted for your religious convictions to the point of death, you can wiggle your way out by saying what the persecutors want you to say. Of course, while the Muslim mouth is allowed to utter this feigned unbelief, his heart must still truly believe in Islam. To be clear, he can lie, but he must recognize he is doing so only to save his own skin. Now that we have thoroughly reviewed the meaning of this verse, let's take some time for dissection.

Even those who are not quite catching on to this inversion pattern will likely notice the deceptive nature of the command given in this verse. Deception is expressly allowed with regard to the Islamic belief system should your life be endangered for your religion. In Christianity, we are not given the choice to lie in order to save ourselves (Matthew 10:28, 32-33). When it is our own neck on the block, and it is faith alone that stands between life and death, only one choice is acceptable. That choice is following the example of our Lord and Savior, Jesus Christ, who gave his own life. Consequently, all of the apostles traveled this road and held fast to their faith, even though it meant martyrdom for all but one.

At this point, some people may notice the trend of Islam to be more focused on the immediate physical consequences rather than the eventual spiritual ramifications. It seems odd to deny god for material and earthly gain. Of course, our reaction should be exactly backward: deny material and earthly gain for heavenly rewards. We may not be spiritually mature enough to put the Spirit above the flesh, but nowhere does the Bible instruct us to put the temporal world over eternity when making decisions.

Such a completely antithetical approach when contrasted against Christianity exposes another aspect of Islam's bankruptcy. There is a big truth waiting here for those who want to grab it. The true religion needs not worry about the effects of persecution because God will ensure His children will continue proclaiming

His message, even if only a remnant (Matthew 16:18, Acts 14:17). On the flip side, any false religion cannot take the chance of the faithful dying in large numbers unless they are taking enemies with them.

All of the preceding points are valid, but what is most insidious about this passage is what it says about the god Muslims worship. When push comes to shove, when the Muslim is at the end of his rope, when there is no other hope, one is to rely on one's own self. When one's very life is endangered to the point of death, Allah is not there. The Muslim is forced to fall back on his own intelligence, charisma, street smarts, and ability to lie to maintain his life. As a Muslim, where is the all-knowing, all-powerful Allah when needed most? He is nowhere to be found. As Elijah said on Mt. Carmel regarding such a false god in 1 Kings 18:27, "either he is occupied or gone aside, or is on a journey, or perhaps he is asleep and needs to be awakened". The lack of Allah's presence at the most critical juncture of life and faith exposes the limited nature of Allah.

While life is important, God is in the business of proclaiming truth. That truth must be proclaimed regardless (Luke 21:15). A truly limitless God can tell His faithful to stand firm in declaring truth. Not only that, but a limitless God will be present for His followers. So much is God the Father there for us at this dire point, should the ultimate sacrifice be required, He tells us not even to prepare. He tells us His truth will shine through us. From Matthew 10:18-20:

> [18] and you will even be brought before governors and kings for My sake, as a testimony to them and to the Gentiles. [19] But when they hand you over, do not worry about how or what you are to say; for it will be given you in that hour what you are to say. [20] For it is not you who speak, but it is the Spirit of your Father who speaks in you.

Here we see a truly all-powerful God. We never need to rely on our own ability to escape. If our fate be death, God will use us. If He wants to save us, He will save us. Shadrach, Meshach, and Abed-nego knew this when they were sentenced to be thrown into the fiery furnace. Daniel 3:16-18:

> [16] Shadrach, Meshach and Abed-nego replied to the king, "O Nebuchadnezzar, we do not need to give you an answer concerning this matter. [17] If it be so, our God whom we serve is able to deliver us from the furnace of blazing fire; and He will deliver us out of your hand, O king. [18] But even if He does not, let it be known to you, O king, that we are not going to serve your gods or worship the golden image that you have set up."

They did not know whether God would save them or not. Nevertheless, they were confident that He could save them if that be His will. What we do know with absolute certainty is that we are never to rely upon our own instincts and attempt to duplicitously squirm our way out of persecution by denying God's name.

If that were not enough, the twisted logic does not even stop there. An inquisitive soul might sense the seeming paradox that in this circumstance Muslims are called to protect their earthly existence at the expense of truthfulness, while simultaneously other passages are interpreted by some to command and incite suicide bombings. With some insight, the common thread can be seen. In both cases, the common denominator is that the infidel is viewed as the enemy, and so it is acceptable to lie to them under persecution and yet kill them when it restores an Islamic advantage (Qur'an 47:35). Muslim thought dictates that choosing to die while harming infidels can be acceptable, yet allowing an infidel to choose the time of a Muslim's death is unconscionable.

Ultimately the goal of earthly Islamic domination is furthered in both cases, and this is consistent with other Islamic teachings (Qur'an 9:29).

Once again, we see the tremendous reversal between Islamic and Christian thought. The Christian is called to die for his belief, whereas the Muslim is called to deceive by any means necessary to achieve Islamic dominance. The cause for this discrepancy is clear. The Christian regards the life of the persecutor as more valuable than his own (Philippians 2:3-4), while the Muslim must value his survival as paramount. In other words, the persecutor is valued so highly that the Christian views the potential witness given by steadfast faith under ultimate duress as more precious than his own life. This is because Christ Himself values the enemy just as highly as the believer (Luke 6:32-36).

Steve Saint told how his father Nate relayed this concept so succinctly to him with reference to the Waodani tribe in Ecuador. The entire story comes from the book *Through Gates of Splendor*, upon which the movie *The End of the Spear* was based:

> I remember telling my dad, 'Please Dad, if the Waodani attack you, you will defend yourself! You will shoot them?' a 55-year-old Saint recalls in an interview. "My dad said, 'Son, we can't shoot the Waodani; they are not ready for heaven, but we are.'"[46]

Once again we see a marked contrast between Allah and YHWH. Allah has everything turned inside-out in ways that are disguised and therefore not immediately recognized. Once we move past the surface tenets of Islam and Christianity, we find everything is flipped and inverted into reverse modes of thought and practice. Don't miss the hooks that are exposed in these conversations. Why does Allah mandate Muslims protect their own self-interests, whereas Jesus teaches us to value others as more important than ourselves? Which is a better system of ethics, and why? Don't miss these questions. Islam is not just different. It is an exact anti-parallel, a complete reversal of the values Christ came to proclaim. When discussing these topics, compare the tenets of Islam to those of Christianity. Let Jesus' Word and deeds stand on their own merits. Often it is not even necessary to state that one is correct and the other is not. Rather, just note the differences and ask the Muslim his opinion.

In the final chapter, we will take a look at some of the most sinister inversions, and how to straighten them out and get the conversation headed back toward Jesus.

Chapter 16

From Diabolic Inversions to the Truth of Christ

In this last chapter, we will examine some of the most diabolical inversions Islam has to offer. These should be cited with caution, as they can have a volatile effect on Muslims. Hooking into these inversions to point back to Christ is powerful. As such, the inversions can have the power to draw Muslims to Christ, or the power to alienate. Proceed with caution.

Why Not Be a Mormon?

This may seem a strange topic, but it is worthwhile to review the beginnings of Islam. The following is a set of facts about Islam not under dispute.

- Muhammad came from humble beginnings and was not well educated.
- Muhammad claimed to receive the last revelation of God.
- Muhammad claimed to be visited by the angel Gabriel.
- There were no other eyewitnesses to the angelic visitations of Muhammad.
- The book given to Muhammad claimed to be from God.
- The book given to Muhammad offered a systematic way to lead life.

- Muhammad was told that all other previous religions had been corrupted.
- The book given to Muhammad offered correction to all that came before it.
- The book given to Muhammad says to worship the One True God.
- The book given claims to initially have been residing in paradise.
- The book allowed Muhammad and his followers to practice polygamy.

Now compare these facts to the beginnings of Mormonism.

- Joseph Smith came from humble beginnings and was not well educated.
- Joseph Smith claimed to receive the last revelation of God.
- Joseph Smith claimed to be visited by the angel Moroni.
- There were no other eyewitnesses to the angelic visitations of Joseph Smith.
- The book given to Joseph Smith claimed to be from God.
- The book given to Joseph Smith offered a systematic way to lead life.
- Joseph Smith was told that all other previous religions had been corrupted.
- The book given to Joseph Smith offered correction to all that came before it.
- The book given to Joseph Smith says to worship the One True God.
- The book given claims to have been residing in paradise.
- The book allowed Joseph Smith and his followers to practice polygamy.[47]

The similarities are nothing short of shocking. As we continue our efforts to analyze these facts on deeper levels, the real question comes forward. How does anyone know whether "The last prophet" is legitamtely the last prophet? In Islam and Mormonism, we find conflicting claims of exactly who is the final prophet. Muhammad claimed to be the final prophet; Joseph Smith claimed to be the final prophet. Each brought a book they claimed was dictated to them directly from God via an angel, and so on and so on. Yet no more than one of them could be right! Of course, logically they both could be charlatans, but the main point here is that they cannot both be prophets.

Just how does one distinguish between these two historical figures? Most Muslims will answer the question with a wave of the hand. They know that Muhammad is the last prophet and Joseph Smith is not because Muhammad brought the message of the one true God, while Joseph Smith furthered the polytheistic views of the Trinity. Of course, Mormons would say that they know Joseph Smith was the real last prophet, because he brought the true words of God, while Muhammad did not. To each group, the question has been asked and answered, never mind the circular logic.

Again we have to ask, "what went wrong here?" There are legitimate questions when comparing Islam and Mormonism. Depending upon the audience, this may allow the Christian to ask the Muslim to evaluate the differences to see the absurdity of the Islamic position. Since debating the status of Muhammad as a prophet directly is fruitless, it may be possible to come in via the back door by presenting this comparison. Remember that the goal is not to win the debate, but to get the Muslim to begin to ask the questions that cannot be answered without Jesus.

The real question is to define the difference between Muhammad and Joseph Smith. The smart Muslim may realize here that Muhammad must have been given the perfected religion because Allah would never deceive Muslims into believing a false religion. In other words, Muhammad must be a prophet because Allah would not be in the business of causing millions worldwide to be deceived by false claims. It would be unthinkable of Allah to falsely tell them Muhammad was the last prophet solely to get the pagan Arabs to stop their polytheism. It would not make sense for Allah knowingly to mislead so many people in such a way, and by this, they can be sure Muhammad was the last prophet. Muslims believe that since Muhammad says he is the last prophet first, he must be because Allah would not purposely deceive people into believing a false religion. In other words, Muslims are confident Allah told them to follow the last prophet because they are convinced he would not lead them astray. Hold that thought! In the next section, we will probe whether Allah ever practices deceit and what the implications of that will be.

We must dive into this issue more fully to see the big picture. Therefore, we must stop here at what seems an odd place. We have come to the conclusion that God is not in the business of purposely misleading people into following another god or a false religion. In the next section, we will run with this assertion and see where it leads. Therefore, we will follow this issue of who is the last prophet to its logical conclusion and take a look at it from the other direction. Not only can we ask the question with reference to a supposed prophet who came after Muhammad, but we can also follow the same line of reasoning for a prophet who came before Muhammad.

Was Allah Deceptive or Incompetent?

According to Islamic doctrine, Jesus was sent to preach Islam (Qur'an 3:52, 43:63-64). So what can be said regarding Jesus' track record from an Islamic standpoint? By necessity of logic, some of Jesus' followers rejected His message, thus rejecting one of Allah's greatest prophets. Others of Jesus' followers started a new supposed cult called Christianity based on His apparent death on the cross and subsequently misconstrued resurrection. Either way, nobody in the 1st century got the message of Islam, leaving Jesus with no Muslim converts, but rather leaving two highly divided groups. One group was destined for hell for denying the religion of Allah, the other destined for hell because they committed shirk, believing Jesus to be Allah's partner. So our first conclusion is that from the Islamic viewpoint Jesus must have been the most colossal failure in history. After all, if He was sent to preach Islam, where were all His followers? As a prophet of Islam, Jesus was utterly ineffective. This raises the question as to why Allah would allow one of the greatest prophets to have such the most dismal performance in history.

The Qur'an gets a little fuzzy as to how Jesus' ministry ended. A frequently quoted verse makes a feeble attempt to clear up the confusion.

Qur'an 4:157-158

> That they said (in boast), 'We killed Christ Jesus the son of Mary, the Messenger of Allah';- but they killed him not, nor crucified him, but so it was made to appear to them, and those who differ therein are full of doubts, with no (certain) knowledge, but only conjecture to follow, for of a surety they killed him not:- Nay, Allah raised him up unto Himself; and Allah is Exalted in Power, Wise;

The passage above quotes the renowned Qur'an translator Yusuf Ali. Other noted translators such as Pickthall and Shakir translate the key phrase here the same, that it was "made to appear" as if Jesus was crucified. Who made it appear that way? Was it not Allah himself who made Jesus appear to be crucified? There are a variety of theories within the Muslim community concerning these most pivotal events. However, the predominant Muslim position is one of substitution; that Allah made someone else to appear as Jesus.* Moreover, Muslims assert that it was Allah who then rescued the true Jesus and brought him to heaven.

Do not forget the previous section. Remember that it would be unthinkable of Allah to start a false religion by lying. Yet according to the Qur'an, this is exactly what Allah chose to do! Allah chose to cause confusion on the most massive scale ever by making it appear that Jesus was crucified, fooling billions throughout the ages! The Islamic position is that Allah took Jesus to heaven for protection, but Allah could have taken Him up to heaven without causing it to seem that He was first crucified. By preventing a fabricated crucifixion, Allah could have circumvented the biggest religious blunder of all time from the Islamic perspective. At a minimum, Allah could have given Jesus the message to warn His followers not to fall for the upcoming illusion. Yet Allah thought it best not to clue in the faithful to this fact, leaving billions stranded to commit shirk, the gravest sin possible, because of Allah's lack of forethought.

In the last section, it was shown that Muslims would typically say that Allah would not purposely create a false religion. So does the same logic now apply for the Muslim in reverse? Can we know that Allah is not God, because it would be uncharacteristic of God knowingly to deceive billions into a false religion? At this point, the Muslim will become quite uncomfortable looking for a way out. Therefore, the next step is to start closing the door on this inversion.

One dead end is that the whole Christian religion was accidental. Allah would never do this on purpose. David Wood, an apologist specializing on issues relating to Islam, addresses this point most effectively.

---

* The added irony here is that the Qur'an talks about how the Christians are "full of doubts," yet it is the Muslims who are in doubt, unable to explain what happened. While many Muslims assert a substitution theory, others assert a swoon theory, or that Christians created a crucifixion legend. The major Hadith are silent on the issue, and so a variety of competing alternative explanations are in vogue.

If Islam is correct, God started this idea when he decided to trick Jesus' enemies into thinking that they had killed Jesus. This leads to even more problems. If the deception of the disciples was *unintentional*, then we must conclude that God didn't realize that he was about to start the largest false religion in the world. If it was *intentional*, then God is in the business of starting false religions. Therefore, the God of Islam is either dreadfully ignorant or maliciously deceptive.[48]

The next attempted escape will be to put the whole blame on Paul or some other Christians. After all, Muslims will say that it was the early Christians who killed off the true Muslims, and then changed and corrupted the religion. Never mind the fact that according to the Qur'an it was Allah who tricked Paul into thinking Jesus was crucified. As always, Islam shoots itself in the foot as the Qur'an once again undermines the Muslim's position.

Qur'an 61:14

> O ye who believe! Be ye helpers of Allah: As said Jesus the son of Mary to the Disciples, 'Who will be my helpers to (the work of) Allah?' Said the disciples, 'We are Allah's helpers!' then a portion of the Children of Israel believed, and a portion disbelieved: But We gave power to those who believed, against their enemies, and they became the ones that prevailed."

According to the Qur'an, the ones that prevailed were the true believers! The Islamic view that Christians corrupted the scriptures and fabricated stories is again shown to be misguided. The Qur'an teaches that the true believers were given power. Therefore, correspondingly, if Paul's view of Jesus prevailed, he must have been a true believer. If the Qur'an asserts it was the true believers who prevailed, then we must look at the Nicene Creed, and other early church writings for true guidance. In them, we obviously find the incarnation, crucifixion, and resurrection staunchly upheld.

A typical Muslim will still try to wiggle out of this, but there isn't anywhere to go. Where are all these early Muslims who prevailed? Where are their writings and their records? Remember, the corrupting Christians could not have destroyed them because it was the true Muslims who prevailed according to the Qur'an, written 600 years later.

With that escape hatch closed, we return to the main point. It was Allah who started Christianity according to the Qur'an! This leaves the Muslim with only two choices. Choice one is that Allah was purposely deceptive on a scale never seen before by intentionally leading billions astray. Choice two is that Allah did not foresee the consequences of his actions, therefore proving he is not all-knowing, thus no god at all.

Yet this next passage goes even further:

Qur'an 2:253

> Those messengers We endowed with gifts, some above others: To one of them Allah spoke; others He raised to degrees (of honour); to Jesus the son of Mary We gave clear (Signs), and strengthened him with the holy spirit. If Allah had so willed, succeeding generations would not have fought among each other, after clear (Signs) had come to them, but they (chose) to wrangle, some believing and others rejecting. If Allah had so willed, they would not have fought each other; but Allah Fulfilleth His plan.

This verse is another mind-bender. According to the Qur'an, not only was Allah responsible for staging a fake crucifixion, but Allah was also responsible for the subsequent confusion! The people chose to wrangle, but if Allah had willed, they would not have. That means that Allah allowed this "false" teaching to prosper. What is the Muslim to do? Allah not only started Christianity but also then nurtured it to fulfill some master plan. The familiar Muslim creed "Allah knows best" rings a bit hollow here.

Many clever Muslims will counter by attempting to turn the tables. The question may be asked why the Christian God would allow Islam to prosper. Don't lose sight of the critical fact of this inversion. The Muslim viewpoint is that Allah started Christianity, but from the Christian standpoint, God did not start Islam. Yes, God allows the existence of all sorts of sinful actions because of the fallen nature of humanity, but God does not tempt anyone (Jeremiah. 14:13-14, James 1:13). Islam was started either from Muhammad's lustful desires, from demonic intervention, or perhaps some mixture of the two. In no way did God Himself start Islam, nor have a hand in nurturing it along.

If Muslims want to pin the start of Christianity on Satan, they may do so. Since the Qur'an says it was Allah who started the whole mess, the resulting conclusion speaks for itself. Following Islamic logic to its ultimate end winds up equating Allah and Satan. To be clear, the Qur'an teaches that it was Allah himself that caused the blunder and ensuing confusion of Christianity. If the Muslim wants to claim that Christianity was Satan's doing, he has inadvertently equated Allah and Satan. The shocking reality of Islamic reasoning imploding on itself never seems to stop.

The logic is unshakable. Being heard is the hard part. I truly pray that Christians can reach out to Muslims and be Christ to them so much so that such discussions can take place. Only through Christ's love will anyone be able to help Muslims through the maze that the deceitful entity Allah has laid before them.

Waiting for Al-Mahdi

An important arena of Islamic doctrine deals with its beliefs regarding the end times, and the signs of its approach. The subject of Islamic eschatology is one that deserves an entire book in and of itself. Such a treatise has already been written. So for those who want to experience this next shocking inversion in full force, grab a copy of *The Islamic Antichrist* by Joel Richardson. While Richardson's book goes into great detail on the subject, here we will focus on some major points that will tie in to exposing yet another inversion. As such, the topic as discussed here is only an introduction; there is much more to this particularly diabolical inversion. Nevertheless, we will cover the basics to expose this next inversion as well as pique some interest in understanding a very plausible end times scenario.

It would be helpful to quickly review what we know about Satan. First, we can agree that Satan exists. We also know that he is clever, and has methods of operation (Ephesians 6:11). Additionally, he masquerades as an angel of light (2 Corinthians 11:14). Given these facts, it is safe to say that Satan has not overlooked the 1.5 billion Muslims of the world, and his strategy will somehow make use of such a large number of possible followers. We also know that Satan is ready to hand over the reins to the antichrist (Revelation 13:2). With all this in mind, we are ready to look into the Islamic end time scenario.

Al–Mahdi is the name given to a prophetic figure within Islam. Sometimes referred to as the Hidden Imam or Twelfth Imam, Muslims believe he will return just before the end of days. By scouring the Hadith, Muslims have compiled a picture of Al-Mahdi that will allow them to recognize his coming. The following is a brief snapshot of the characteristics of Al-Mahdi. For a full reference of Islamic literature used to compile this snapshot, see the book mentioned above.[49]

- Al-Mahdi will lead a revolution, establishing a new world order founded on Islam.
- Al-Mahdi will institute Sharia law, part of which is the Islamic calendar.

- Al-Mahdi will rule from Jerusalem.
- Al-Mahdi will be the spiritual leader for Muslims.
- Al-Mahdi will either kill or convert the remaining Jews and Christians of the day.
- Al-Mahdi will make a peace treaty with the Jews for a period of either 7 or 9 years.
- Al-Mahdi will preside over a ten member council.

Does this character sound familiar? Does a possible 7-year peace treaty with the Jewish nation bring to mind any Scripture? Who is mentioned in the Bible matching this description? As always, using Scripture helps to spot the inversion. Who is being described in the following verses?

- He will establish a new world order founded on a false religion. (Daniel 7:23-24, Revelation 13:7)
- He will change the set times and laws (Daniel 7:25).
- He will declare himself God in the temple of Jerusalem (2 Thessalonians 2:4).
- He will be worshiped by all who dwell on the earth (Revelation 13:8).
- He goes to war with the remaining Jews and Christians (Revelation 12:17).
- He establishes a 7-year peace treaty with the Jews (Daniel 9:27).
- He will preside over a ten-nation coalition (Daniel 7:24).

The similarities seem way too numerous to be coincidental. Not only is the Antichrist coming, but one extremely plausible scenario is that Muslims worldwide are awaiting his advent and will herald it with excitement and optimism as never seen before. When Antichrist enters the scene, Islamic eschatology has been constructed to allow the group as a whole to welcome him with open arms as Imam Al-Mahdi, the awaited rightly guided one.

This small introduction to Islamic eschatology is just the tip of the iceberg. The correlation between other Islamic and Christian end-times figures multiply when learning about the Islamic view of Jesus' return.

We must take care neither to put words into the mouths of Muslims nor to teach Islamic doctrine. It is always frustrating to read a Muslim author incorrectly spouting Christian doctrine. Therefore, we must be cautious to avoid such a pitfall. Any good skeptic should be thinking along these lines. With this in mind, all of the characteristics of Al-Mahdi have been taken directly from Islamic literature. To give a specific example here, consider what a Muslim says about this topic. Muhammad Ibn 'Izzat and Muhammad 'Arif in their book "Al Mahdi and the End of Time," 'Izzat and Arif quote Ka'b al Ahbar as saying:

> I find the Mahdi recorded in the books of the Prophets...
> For instance, the Book of Revelation says: "And I saw
> and behold a white horse. He that sat on him...went
> forth conquering and to conquer."

The vast majority of Biblical scholars identify the rider of the white horse here in Revelation 6 as Antichrist, the imitation that comes to bring terror to the world before the true Savior comes in Revelation 19. Amazingly, not only do Muslims await the antichrist, they freely admit the character in Revelation 6:2 is Al-Mahdi! Now of course in the Muslim mind Scriptures have been corrupted and Christians have been tricked into missing Al-Mahdi for the true genius that he is. How many times must we see that Islam is the complete antithesis of Christianity? Even the person of the Antichrist is turned into a hero.

It is true that for this section, I have only glossed over the identification of Al-Mahdi. Those who have a healthy skepticism of this particular topic should keep three things in mind. First, the skeptic who has been paying attention should remember all the inversions cited so far and recognize that a pattern has been established. Second, Satan is not so stupid that he has failed to anticipate how to use 1,500,000,000 Muslims as end time events unfold. Finally, any skeptic worth his salt should want to see many more sources than I have provided and may do so by viewing the original source material.

Will the Real Satan Please Stand Up?

As our final example, we take direct aim at Satan. We do so only by Him who is in us, for we know that He who is in us is greater than he who is in the world (1 John 4:4). Of all the inversions cited so far, this next one most exposes the sinister nature of Islam. One of the many bizarre stories of the Qur'an is that of the casting out of Satan from paradise. For those not familiar, here is one of the Qur'anic references, which is repeated half a dozen times in other Surahs. The Qur'an gives the name Iblis to the great Satan, so let's read why he is accursed.

Qur'an 17:61-64

> Behold! We said to the angels: "Bow down unto Adam":
> They bowed down except Iblis: He said, "Shall I bow
> down to one whom Thou didst create from clay?" He
> said: "Seest Thou? this is the one whom Thou hast
> honoured above me! If Thou wilt but respite me to the
> Day of Judgment, I will surely bring his descendants
> under my sway - all but a few!" (Allah) said: "Go thy
> way; if any of them follow thee, verily Hell will be the
> recompense of you (all) - an ample recompense. "Lead
> to destruction those whom thou canst among them,
> with thy (seductive) voice; make assaults on them with
> thy cavalry and thy infantry; mutually share with them
> wealth and children; and make promises to them." But
> Satan promises them nothing but deceit.

Something is subtly wrong here, but what? Why was Satan cast out of heaven? The obvious answer is pride. Yet specifically, he was cast out because he did not obey Allah. However, in what way did he not obey Allah? Look closely at the command being disobeyed. What did Allah allegedly command him to do? Allah allegedly commanded him to bow down before Allah's creation rather than Allah himself! Doesn't Allah require Muslims not to bow down before idols or any of his other creations, but only to the creator? Isn't the creator to be worshiped, not His creations? The Qur'an claims Satan was cast out for refusing to do the very thing Allah strenuously teaches Muslims never to do! Upon close inspection, Satan is the unsung hero and not the villain of this story from the Qur'an.

Please do not miss this. The Qur'an claims Satan was cast out because he refused to commit idolatry! Obviously, idolatry is harshly condemned in the Qur'an (4:117, 6:74, 7:138, 14:35, 29:17, 39:17). It is denounced quite clearly, as exemplified in this sermon credited to Abraham:

Qur'an 9:25

> And he said: "For you, ye have taken (for worship) idols besides Allah, out of mutual love and regard between yourselves in this life; but on the Day of Judgment ye shall disown each other and curse each other: and your abode will be the Fire, and ye shall have none to help."

Bizarre as it is, while committing idolatry is clearly a major sin in Islam, the Qur'an claims Allah commanded Satan to do it. In other words, Satan was a good Muslim in that he refused to commit idolatry, a major sin. This is so dark, so sinister, that the realization should be shocking. By the testimony of the Qur'an, Satan was cast out for following Allah's law by not worshiping his creations. According to the Qur'an itself, Allah orders Satan to disobey previous orders. Either Satan disobeys a direct command to commit idolatry, or he obeys, thus committing idolatry and therefore disobeys the general command never to bow before God's creation. This twisted and perverted spiritual realization is so disturbing that even the term inverted reaches nowhere near far enough.

Before claiming I have made a leap from the language "bowing down" or "prostrating" as being the same as worship, it is true that I have. However, the Qur'an itself weaves the two inextricably together:

Qur'an 2:43

> And be steadfast in prayer; practise regular charity; and bow down your heads with those who bow down (in worship).

Qur'an 22:77

> O ye who believe! bow down, prostrate yourselves, and adore your Lord; and do good; that ye may prosper.

Muslim scholars also couple the act of bowing with worship. In the tafsir Al-Jalalayn, the noted Islamic commentator interprets the second passage just cited to mean that "O you who believe, bow down and prostrate yourselves in other words perform prayer and worship your Lord..."[50]

Satan has always desired for others to bow down while worshiping him (Matthew 4:9). There are many other such verses in the Qur'an as well, but the point is made. The Qur'an claims Satan was condemned for refusing to commit idolatry! The act of committing idolatry is clearly disallowed under any circumstance. Shadrach, Meshach, and Abednego knew it (Daniel 3:18). The Bible speaks clearly that worshiping the creation trades the truth of God for a lie. From Romans 1:25:

> [25] For they exchanged the truth of God for a lie,
> and worshiped and served the creature rather
> than the Creator, who is blessed forever. Amen.

The next question is, "If God told me to worship an idol, would I do it?" However, the real issue is whether God would ever require His subjects to commit idolatry, to put another God before Him, or to worship something else besides Him? God never commands the commission of sin, as it is not in His nature (James 1:13). Of course, any Christian knows God would never do this. Presented with such a paradox, the logical conclusion would be that such a command was not from God. Thus we get back to the issue at hand. Any order from God that goes against His Word or His character is not an order from God. Why would God ever order Satan to worship something other than God Himself? God telling Satan to worship humans is as ludicrous as God telling humans to worship Satan. Ultimately, Islam teaches Satan was cast out of paradise because Satan did a better job of interpreting Allah's rule than Allah did.

Can there be any doubt left as to the real identity of Allah?

Final Thoughts

So, dear friends, we reach the end of the analysis. It been shown that Satan is a master of concealing truth within lies, that this type of disguise is what counterfeiters must do, and that Islamic theology systematically follows this pattern. Islam may look good on the surface, but is completely opposite and inverted from what Jesus teaches. These inversions are so numerous that the pattern is no accident. They are often hard to spot, but by the Holy Spirit you can recognize them, since they are so pervasive. It is my sincere hope that in some small way God uses me to help others reach those dear ones currently lost in the hopelessness and mire of inverted Islamic doctrine.

Christ died for each of us, and time is running out. The situation looks discouraging at times, but God once shared something with me at a critical juncture in my life, and we all know this to be true: "Now to Him who is able to do far more abundantly beyond all that we ask or think, according to the power that works within us, to Him be the glory in the church and in Christ Jesus to all generations forever and ever."

Amen.

Appendix A

Equating Allah and Muhammad

List of Qur'an quotes comparing Muhammad to Allah

Explanation	Ayat	Quote from Qur'an
The preceding verse warns Muslims not to charge interest. If you do, either Allah or Muhammad may make war with you.	2:279	If ye do it not, Take notice of war from Allah and His Messenger: But if ye turn back, ye shall have your capital sums: Deal not unjustly, and ye shall not be dealt with unjustly.
Obedience to both Allah and Muhammad are required in order to be shown mercy	3:132	And obey Allah and the Apostle, that you may be shown mercy.

Explanation	Ayat	Quote from Qur'an
In this verse, if you seek forgiveness, Muhammad must also ask on your behalf as well before you can be forgiven.	4:64	And We did not send any apostle but that he should be obeyed by Allah's permission; and had they, when they were unjust to themselves, come to you and asked forgiveness of Allah and the Apostle had (also) asked forgiveness for them, they would have found Allah Oft-returning (to mercy), Merciful.
Obedience to Muhammad and to Allah are one in the same.	4:80	He who obeys the Messenger, obeys Allah.
Waging war against either Allah or Muhammad deserves both dismemberment and eternal punishment.	5:33	The punishment of those who wage war against Allah and His Messenger, and strive with might and main for mischief through the land is: execution, or crucifixion, or the cutting off of hands and feet from opposite sides, or exile from the land: that is their disgrace in this world, and a heavy punishment is theirs in the Hereafter;
Acting adversely toward either Allah or Muhammad deserves punishment.	8:13	This because they contended against Allah and His Messenger: If any contend against Allah and His Messenger, Allah is strict in punishment.
Obedience must be to both Allah and Muhammad	8:20	O ye who believe! Obey Allah and His Messenger, and turn not away from him when ye hear (him speak).

Explanation	Ayat	Quote from Qur'an
Again, obedience must be for both Allah and Muhammad.	8:46	And obey Allah and His Messenger; and fall into no disputes, lest ye lose heart and your power depart; and be patient and persevering: For Allah is with those who patiently persevere:
Allah and Muhammad have special dispensation to break treaties.	9:3	And an announcement from Allah and His Messenger, to the people (assembled) on the day of the Great Pilgrimage,- that Allah and His Messenger dissolve (treaty) obligations with the Pagans. If then, ye repent, it were best for you; but if ye turn away, know ye that ye cannot frustrate Allah. And proclaim a grievous penalty to those who reject Faith.
If you don't love both Allah and Muhammad more than loved ones, you just wait and see what you will get.	9:24	Say: If it be that your fathers, your sons, your brothers, your mates, or your kindred; the wealth that ye have gained; the commerce in which ye fear a decline: or the dwellings in which ye delight - are dearer to you than Allah, or His Messenger, or the striving in His cause;- then wait until Allah brings about His decision: and Allah guides not the rebellious.
If you don't forbid what either Allah or Muhammad has forbidden, you deserve to be warred against, even if you are Christian.	9:29	Fight those who believe not in Allah nor the Last Day, nor hold that forbidden which hath been forbidden by Allah and His Messenger, nor acknowledge the religion of Truth, (even if they are) of the People of the Book, until they pay the Jizya with willing submission, and feel themselves subdued.

Explanation	Ayat	Quote from Qur'an
Opposition to Allah or Muhammad is punishable by hell.	9:63	Know they not that for those who oppose Allah and His Messenger, is the Fire of Hell?- wherein they shall dwell. That is the supreme disgrace.
It was both Allah and Muhammad that enriched the people.	9:74	They swear by Allah that they said nothing (evil), but indeed they uttered blasphemy, and they did it after accepting Islam; and they meditated a plot which they were unable to carry out: this revenge of theirs was (their) only return for the bounty with which Allah and His Messenger had enriched them!
Both Allah and Muhammad will observe actions.	9:94	They will present their excuses to you when ye return to them. Say thou: "Present no excuses: we shall not believe you: Allah hath already informed us of the true state of matters concerning you: It is your actions that Allah and His Messenger will observe:
The implication here is that Muhammad is equally as just as Allah.	24:50	Is it that there is a disease in their hearts? or do they doubt, or are they in fear, that Allah and His Messenger will deal unjustly with them? Nay, it is they themselves who do wrong.
Truth came both from Allah and Muhammad.	33:22	When the Believers saw the Confederate forces, they said: "This is what Allah and his Messenger had promised us, and Allah and His Messenger told us what was true." And it only added to their faith and their zeal in obedience.

Explanation	Ayat	Quote from Qur'an
A Muslim is to seek both Allah and Muhammad.	33.29	But if ye seek Allah and His Messenger, and the Home of the Hereafter, verily Allah has prepared for the well-doers amongst you a great reward.
Muhammad gets to help Allah decide how people should live their lives.	33:36	It is not fitting for a Believer, man or woman, when a matter has been decided by Allah and His Messenger to have any option about their decision: if any one disobeys Allah and His Messenger, he is indeed on a clearly wrong Path.
Annoying either Allah or Muhammad deserves punishment.	33:57	"Those who annoy Allah and His Messenger - Allah has cursed them in this World and in the Hereafter, and has prepared for them a humiliating Punishment."
Plighting fealty (swearing allegiance) to Muhammad is the same as doing so to Allah.	48:10	Verily those who plight their fealty to thee do no less than plight their fealty to Allah:
Don't be forward when in the presence of Allah or Muhammad.	49:1	O Ye who believe! Put not yourselves forward before Allah and His Messenger; but fear Allah: for Allah is He Who hears and knows all things.

Explanation	Ayat	Quote from Qur'an
Is showing faith in Allah enough? Here is how to show faith in Allah and Muhammad.	58:4	And if any has not (the wherewithal), he should fast for two months consecutively before they touch each other. But if any is unable to do so, he should feed sixty indigent ones, this, that ye may show your faith in Allah and His Messenger. Those are limits (set by) Allah.
As a Muslim, you are required not to love anyone who resists either Allah or Muhammad.	58:22	Thou wilt not find any people who believe in Allah and the Last Day, loving those who resist Allah and His Messenger, even though they were their fathers or their sons, or their brothers, or their kindred.
Hellfire is guaranteed for those who disobey Allah and His messenger.	72:23	Unless I proclaim what I receive from Allah and His Messages: for any that disobey Allah and His Messenger,- for them is Hell: they shall dwell therein for ever.
According to Hadith, Muhammad claimed to be an associate of Allah, and the Earth was somehow his property.	Al-Bukhari	Muhammad, the Apostle, said " . . . you should know that the Earth belongs to Allah and His Apostle." (Sahih Bukhari, Volume 9, Book 85, Number 77, and also Volume 4, Book 53, Number 392, both narrated by Abu Huraira)

Bibliography

Abuzola. *'jesus And Islam' According To The Bible- Be The Judge*. July 23, 2009. http://www.nairaland.com/300566/jesus-islam-according-bible-judge.

Al-Jalalayn, "10 - Yunus (Jonah)." *QuranX.com*. February 22, 2018. http://quranx.com/Tafsirs/10.94.

Ali, Achmed. *Is Atonement Necessary for Salvation*. March 31, 2018. issuu.com.

Al-Tabari, Abu Ja'far Muhammad B. Jarir. *The Commentary on the Qur'an*. Oxford: Oxford University Press, 1987.

Bramsen, Paul D. *Communicating the Message to Muslims*. GreenVille, SC, 2005.

Caner, Dr. Ergun. "Why former muslim Dr. Ergun Caner became a Christian part 1 of 2." October 20, 2010. https://www.youtube.com/watch?v=c7AjWO_-Ei4.

Caraballo, Simon Alfredo. *My Great Love For Jesus Led Me to Islam*. Gharb Alnasseem. 2009.

Caraballo, Simon Alfredo. "My Great Love For Jesus Led me to Islaam." *Isalmic Board*. February 09 2017. https://www.islamicboard.com/comparative-religion/1770-love-jesus-led-islaam.html.

Deedat, Ahmed. *AL-QUR'AN, The Miracle of Miracles*. February 20, 2017. http://www.jannah.org/articles/qurdeed.html.

Dictionary.com. February 11, 2017. http://www.dictionary.com/browse/exegesis?s=t.

Fischer, John. "Alleluia." *The New Covenant (A Musical)*. Cond. Clark Gassman. 1975.

Fultcher of Chartres. "Urban II: Speech at Council of Clermont, 1095, Five Versions of the Speech," *Medieval Sourcebook*. December 10, 2014. http://www.fordham.edu/halsall/source/urban2-5vers.html.

Ghattas, Raouf Ghattas and Carol B. *A Christian Guide to the Qur'an*. Grand Rapids, MI: Kregel Publications. 2009.

Hadith of Law laak. March 7, 2017. http://www.sunnah.org/msaec/articles/hadith_of_lawlaak.htm.

Hooper, Ibrahim. "Jesus and Muhammad are Brothers." *CAIR: Council on American-Islamic Relations*. March 11, 2015. https://www.cair.com/press-center/op-eds/11676-jesus-and-muhammad-are-brothers.html.

Hoskins, Edward J. *A Muslims' Heart: What Every Christian Needs To Know To Share Christ With Muslims*. Colorado Springs, CO. Dawwsonmedia. 2003.

Jordan, Anna. *A Comparison of the Book of James and Quran*. 2013. http://submission.org/Book_of_James.html.

Joseph Smith - History. September 1, 2016. https://www.lds.org/scriptures/pgp/js-h/1?lang=eng.

Kareem, Abdullah. *The Crucifixion of Judas*. February 12, 2017. http://www.answering-christianity.com/abdullah_smith/crucifixion_of_judas.htm.

Kennedy, Dr. D. James. *The Fingerprints of God*. February 09, 2017. http://www.oldsite.eagles-lair.org/robl/trinity.html.

King, Martin Luther. "Martin Luther King Jr. Quotes." *Xavier University Center for Mission and Identity*. September 9, 2017. https://www.xavier.edu/jesuitresource/online-resources/martin-luther-king-quotes.cfm.

Küçük, Rasit. *The Importance of Prophet Muhammad and His Status as a Role Model*. September 25, 2013. http://www.lastprophet.info/the-importance-of-prophet-muhammad-and-his-status-as-a-role-model.

Lone, Ibrahim. *Shaming the Shameless Apologists of Islam (I): Apostasy in Islam*. December 24, 2008. http://www.true-islam.org/Ibrahim.Lone/Shaming-Shameless-Apostasy-in-Islam.htm.

Luther, Martin. "The Table Talk of Martin Luther." Translated by Esq. William Hazlitt. Philidelphia. *The Lutheran Publication Society*. 1957.

McTernan, John. *Muhammad or Jesus the Prophet Like Unto Moses*. 2011. http://www.defendproclaimthefaith.org/muhammad_or_jesus_unto_moses.html.

Quran Tafsir ibn Kathi. February 11, 2017. http://www.qtafsir.com/index. php?option=com_content&task=view&id=564&Itemid=46#2.

Richardson, Joel. *Anitchrist, Islam's Awaited Messiah*. Enumclaw, WA: Pleasent Word. 2006.

Robertson, A.T. *Robertson's Word Pictures in the New Testament*. February 9, 2017. https://www.studylight.org/commentaries/rwp/john-5. html.

Shamoun, Sam. *The Jewish Messiah And The Prophet of Islam*. Febrary 20, 2017. http://www.answering-islam.org/Shamoun/messiah.htm.

Shoebat, Walid with Richardson, Joel. *God's War On Terror*. Executive Media. 2008.

Siddiqi, Dr. Muzammil H. *Prophet Muhammad: Exalted Example of Character*. July 14, 2016. http://aboutislam.net/counseling/ask-the-scholar/muslim-creed/prophet-muhammad-exalted-example-of-character/.

Siddiqi, Shamim A. *The Importance of Hijrah*. April 5, 2000. http://www. dawahinamericas.com/hijra.htm.

Syed, Ibrahim B. *The Significance of the Hijrah*. April 15, 2017. http://www. irfi.org/articles/articles_451_500/significance_of_the_hijrah.htm.

Tafsir al-Jalalayn. 2016. http://www.altafsir.com/Tafsir.asp?tMadhNo= 0&tTafsirNo=74&tSoraNo=22&tAyahNo=77&tDisplay= yes&UserProfile=0&LanguageId=2 (accessed February 27, 2017).

Taymiyyah, Shaikh ul-Islaam Ibn. *The Correct Reply To the One Who Changed the Religion of the Messiah*. February 9, 2017. http://www. salafipublications.com/sps/downloads/pdf/MSS050003.pdf.

"The Hijra (Migration)." *A Restatement of the History of Islam and Muslims*. April 15, 2017. https://www.al-islam.org/restatement-history-islam-and-muslims-sayyid-ali-ashgar-razwy/hijra-migration.

The Two Testimonies. June 19, 2014. http://dawahnigeria.com/articles/ faith-and-creed/two-testimonies-ash-shahadatayn-0.

Usman, Huja. "Shirk The Ultimate Crime." *Ummah The Online Muslim Community*. December 13, 2003. http://www.ummah.com/forum/ showthread.php?28577-Shirk-the-ultimate-crime.

Wartian, James. *End of the Spear*. January 18, 2006. http://ncbcmissions. blogspot.com/2006_01_01_archive.html.

Wierenga, Emily T. *BetterNot Bitter*. 2006. https://www.christianity.ca/ sslpage.aspx?pid=9637.

Wood, David. *Deceptive God, Incompetent Messiah*. Febrary 27, 2017. http://www.answering-islam.org/Authors/Wood/deceptive_god.htm.

Zacharias, Ravi. *How do you know that Christianity is the one true worldview?* April 2, 2012. https://www.youtube.com/watch?v=nWY-6xBA0Pk

Endnotes

1   Edward J. Hoskins, A Muslim's Heart: What Every Christian Needs To Know To Share Christ With Muslims, (Colorado Springs, CO. Dawsonmedia, 2003), 27.

2   Martin Luther King, "Martin Luther King Jr. Quotes," Jesuitsource. org, last Google crawl March 20, 2018, accessed March 31, 2018, https://www.xavier.edu/jesuitresource/online-resources/martin-luther-king-quotes.cfm.

3   Dr. Ergun Caner, Why former muslim Dr. Ergun Caner became a Christian part 1 of 2, October 20, 2010, accessed March 31, 2018, https://www.youtube.com/watch?v=c7AjWO_-Ei4.

4   Paul D. Bramsen, Communicating the Message to Muslims, (Greenville, SC, 2005), 5.

5   Ibrahim Hooper, "Jesus and Muhammad are Brothers," CAIR: Council on American-Islamic Relations, last updated March 11, 2015, accessed February 08, 2017, https://www.cair.com/ press-center/op-eds/11676-jesus-and-muhammad-are-brothers.html.

6   Martin Luther, The Table Talk of Martin Luther, Translated by William Hazlitt, Philidelphia: The Lutheran Publication Society, 1957, Section DCCCXXIX.

7   A.T. Robertson, Robertson's Word Pictures in the New Testament, last Google crawl March 21, 2018, accessed March 25, 2018, https://www.studylight.org/commentaries/rwp/john-5.html.

8   Shaikh ul-Islaam Ibn Taymiyyah, The Correct Reply To the One Who Changed the Religion of the Messiah, last modified September 16, 2017, accessed January 11, 2017, http://www.salafipublications.com/sps/downloads/pdf/MSS050003.pdf, 7.

9   Dr. D. James Kennedy, The Fingerprints of God, last modified November 7, 2009, accessed February 9 2017, http://www.oldsite. eagles-lair.org/robl/trinity.html.

10   Simon Alfredo Caraballo, "Great Love For Jesus Led me to Islaam," Islamic Board, April 24, 2005, accessed February 17, 2018, https:// www.islamicboard.com/comparative-religion/1770-love-jesus-led-islaam.html.

11   Abuzola, "'jesus And Islam' According To The Bible- Be The Judge," last modifeid July 23, 2009, accessed February 17, 2018, http://www. nairaland.com/300566/jesus-islam-according-bible-judge.

12   Simon Alfredo Caraballo, My Great Love for Jesus Led Me To Islaam, (Gharb Alnasseem, n.d.), 107.

13   Al-Jalalayn, "10 - Yunus (Jonah)," QuranX.com, accessed February 22, 2018, http://quranx.com/Tafsirs/10.94.

14   Quran Tafsir ibn Kathir, accessed February 11, 2017, http://www. qtafsir.com/index.php?option=com_content&task=view&id=564& Itemid=46#2.

15   Abu Ja'far Muhammad B. Jarir Al-Tabari, The Commentary on the Qur'an, Oxford: Oxford University Press, 1987, page 474.

16   Ravi Zacharias, How do you know that Christianity is the one true worldview?, last modified April 2, 2012, accessed February 24, 2018, https://www.youtube.com/watch?v=nWY-6xBA0Pk.

17   Ibrahim B Syed, The Significance of the Hijrah, last mdofied Febarruy 16, 2017, accessed April 15, 2017, http://www.irfi.org/articles/ articles_451_500/significance_of_the_hijrah.htm.

18   Shamim A Siddiqi, The Importance of Hijrah, last modiffied May 9, 2008, accessed March 31, 2018, http://www.dawahinamericas.com/ hijra.htm.

19   "The Hijra (Migration)," A Restatement of the History of Islam and Muslims, last Google crawl March 28, 2018, accessed March 31, 2018, https://www.al-islam.org/restatement-history-islam-and-muslims-sayyid-ali-ashgar-razwy/hijra-migration.

20   Raouf Ghattas and Carol B. Ghattas, A Christian Guide to the Qur'an, (Grand Rapids, MI: Kregel Publications, 2009), 25.

21   "Exegesis," Dictionary.com, last Google crawl March 13, 2018, accessed March 16, 2018, http://www.dictionary.com/browse/ exegesis?s=t.

22 Abdullah Kareem, The Crucifixion of Judas, last modified August 26, 2011, accessed March 16, 2018, http://www.answering-christianity. com/abdullah_smith/crucifixion_of_judas.htm.

23 Achmed Ali, Is Atonement Necessary for Salvation?, last Google crawl January 22, 2018, accessed March 31, 2018, https://issuu.com/ tmcpeace/docs/atonment, 101.

24 John McTernan, Muhammad or Jesus the Prophet Like Unto Moses, last modifeid December 12, 2017, accessed March 17, 2018, http:// www.defendproclaimthefaith.org/muhammad_or_jesus_unto_ moses.html.

25 Simon Alfredo Caraballo, My Great Love for Jesus Led Me To Islaam, (Gharb Alnasseem, n.d.), 106.

26 Fultcher of Chartres, "Urban II: Speech at Council of Clermont, 1095, Five Versions of the Speech," Medieval Sourcebook, last modified December 10, 2014, accessed March 20, 2018, http://www.fordham. edu/halsall/source/urban2-5vers.html.

27 Al Shaikh Muhammad Al Harira Al Bayyumi, The Jewish Messiah And The Prophet of Islam, last modified August 9, 2012, accessed March 20, 2018, http://www.answering-islam.org/Shamoun/ messiah.htm.

28 Huja Usman, "Shirk The Ultimate Crime," Ummah The Online Muslim Community, December 13, 2003, accessed March 31, 2018, http://www.ummah.com/forum/showthread.php?28577-Shirk- the-ultimate-crime.

29 Walid Shoebat with Joel Richardson, God's War On Terror, (New York City: Top Executive Media, 2008), 44.

30 Rasit Küçük, Ph. D., "The Importance of Prophet Muhammad and His Status as a Role Model," last prophet.info, last Google crawl March 29, 2018, accessed March 31, 2018, http://www.lastprophet.info/the- importance-of-prophet-muhammad-and-his-status-as-a-role-model.

31 John Fischer, "Alleluia", The New Covenant (A Musical), Arranged by Clark Gassman, 1975, accessed May 14, 2018, https://www. reverbnation.com/johnfischermusic/song/21309037-alleluia.

32 "The Two Testimonies," DN ARTICLES, last Google crawl February 20, 2018, accessed March 31, 2018, http://dawahnigeria.com/articles/ faith-and-creed/two-testimonies-ash-shahadatayn.

33 Anna Jordan, "A Comparison of the Book of James and Quran," submission.org: Your best source for submission (Islam), last modified

283

February 10, 2018, accessed March 31, 2018, http://submission.org/Book_of_James.html.

34 Ibn 'Umar (narrator), "The Book of Clothes and Adornment," Sahih Muslim, last Google crawl February 9, 2018, accessed March 23, 2018, https://sunnah.com/muslim/37.

35 Al-Bara' (narrator), "The Book of Virtues," Sahih Muslim, last Google crawl February 9, 2018, accessed March 23, 2018, https://sunnah.com/muslim/43.

36 Ibn Sirrn (narrator), Volume I, Book 4, Number 171, Sahih Bukhari, accessed March 24, 2018, http://www.sahih-bukhari.com/Pages/results.php.

37 Jabir bin 'Abdullah (narrator), Volume I, Book 7, Number 331, Sahih Bukhari, accessed March 24, 2018, http://www.sahih-bukhari.com/Pages/results.php.

38 Abu Huraira (narrator), "The Book of Virtues," Sahih Muslim, last Google crawl March 10, 2018, accessed March 24, 2018, https://sunnah.com/muslim/43.

39 Hadith of Law laak, last modified December 2, 2012, accessed March 24, 2018, http://www.sunnah.org/msaec/articles/hadith_of_lawlaak.htm.

40 ibid.

41 ibid.

42 Dr. Muzammil H Siddiqi, "Muhamad: A Unique Character," Prophet Muhammad: Exalted Example of Character, last Google crawl March 15, 2018, accessed March 24, 2018, http://aboutislam.net/counseling/ask-the-scholar/muslim-creed/prophet-muhammad-exalted-example-of-character/.

43 Ibrahim Lone, "Shaming the Shameless Apologists of Islam (I): Apostasy in Islam," The True Islam: Presenting Islam in Its True Color, last modified November 14, 2015, accessed March 24, 2018, http://www.true-islam.org/Ibrahim.Lone/Shaming-Shameless-Apostasy-in-Islam.htm.

44 Ahmed Deedat, "AL-QUR'AN, The Miracle of Miracles," Islam: some articles, last modifed November 10, 2006, accessed March 25, 2018, http://www.jannah.org/articles/qurdeed.html.

45 Hisham's father (narrator), Volume 7, Book 62, Number 48, Sahih Bukhari, accessed March 25, 2018. http://www.sahih-bukhari.com/Pages/Bukhari_7_62.php.

46 Emily T. Wierenga. BetterNot Bitter. 2006, accessed February 20, 2017, https://www.christianity.ca/sslpage.aspx?pid=9637.

47 "Joseph Smith – History," The Perl of Great Price, last updated September 1, 2016, accessed March 25, 2018, https://www.lds.org/scriptures/pgp/js-h/1?lang=eng.

48. David Wood, "Allah Starts Christianity…By Accident," Deceptive God, Incompetent Messiah, last modified May 14, 2010, accessed March 25, 2018, http://www.answering-islam.org/Authors/Wood/deceptive_god.htm.

49 Joel Richardson, Antichrist: Islam's Awaited Messiah, (Enumclaw, WA: Pleasent Word, 2006), 40-70.

50 Trans. Feras Hamza "Tafsir al-Jalalayn," The Tafsirs, last Google crawl March 21, 2018, accessed March 21, 2018, http://www.altafsir.com/Tafasir.asp?tMadhNo=0&tTafsirNo=74&tSoraNo=22&tAyahNo=77&tDisplay=yes&UserProfile=0&LanguageId=2.

Scripture Index

About the Author

Robert has spent the last 15 years studying Islamic theology and interacting with Muslims from his home town and around the world. He has spoken in numerous church settings and at the southeast Regional International Students Incorporated retreat to help equip Christians to understand the Islamic thought process. He currently runs a blog comparing and contrasting Islamic and Christian theology at www.unravelingislam.com.

Robert graduated from the University of Illinois with a Bachelor's degree in Teaching of Mathematics and Physics. He possesses a Masters in Religion with an emphasis in Islamic-Christian interaction from Urbana Theological Seminary. Robert has been married to his wife Mary for over 12 years.

Robert currently works as a contractor for the Army Corps of Engineers as an Application Data Base Analyst.